Educational Governance Research

Volume 3

Educational Governance Research

Aims and Scope

This series presents recent insights in educational governance gained from research that focuses on the interplay between educational institutions and societies and markets. Education is not an isolated sector. Educational institutions at all levels are embedded in and connected to international, national and local societies and markets. One needs to understand governance relations and the changes that occur if one is to understand the frameworks, expectations, practice, room for manoeuvre, and the relations between professionals, public, policy makers and market place actors.

The aim of this series is to address issues related to structures and discourses by which authority is exercised in an accessible manner. It will present findings on a variety of types of educational governance: public, political and administrative, as well as private, market place and self-governance. International and multidisciplinary in scope, the series will cover the subject area from both a worldwide and local perspective and will describe educational governance as it is practised in all parts of the world and in all sectors: state, market, and NGOs.

The series:
- Covers a broad range of topics and power domains
- Positions itself in a field between politics and management/leadership
- Provides a platform for the vivid field of educational governance research
- Looks into ways in which authority is transformed within chains of educational governance
- Uncovers relations between state, private sector and market place influences on education, professionals and students.

More information about this series at http://www.springer.com/series/13077

Romuald Normand

The Changing Epistemic Governance of European Education

The Fabrication of the Homo Academicus Europeanus?

 Springer

Romuald Normand
Research Unit CNRS SAGE
University of Strasbourg
Strasbourg, France

ISSN 2365-9548   ISSN 2365-9556   (electronic)
Educational Governance Research
ISBN 978-3-319-31774-8   ISBN 978-3-319-31776-2   (eBook)
DOI 10.1007/978-3-319-31776-2

Library of Congress Control Number: 2016943477

Printed on acid-free paper

This Springer imprint is published by Springer Nature
The registered company is Springer International Publishing AG Switzerland

Foreword: Martin Lawn

Since 2000, there has been a small and heterogeneous movement of scholars, now growing in number, who have been researching national education policies and practices and their relation to European and international influences. They have drawn upon analyses in political science, in globalisation studies and increasingly on comparative reports from other country studies. A recognition that the boundaries of the European nation–state were not impervious to cross-border policies was followed by attempts to conceptualise an emerging common area or space in which policies and practices appeared to be linked and constructed. The idea of the European Policy Space in Education illuminated and enabled the efforts of many new researchers in European education. However, it still left many issues about the ways in which a common space could be understood and how it was constructed.

In this very interesting and comprehensive book, Romuald Normand explains this problem. He provides a major synthesis of the relation between governance and knowledge in European education systems and advances an ambitious argument about how new knowledge instruments, working through networks, experts, data and standards, are shaping and restructuring education in Europe. Using this approach, the old borders seem weakened although not replaced. In particular, he shows how knowledge-based technologies have become an effective way of governing Europe, especially in European education, a field in which there are no direct centre–local political levers.

It is Normand's stress on the importance of knowledge-based governance which reveals how shifts in knowledge production, the use of advanced technologies, a redesigned public management and hybrid forms of science/policy and academic/experts have generated the European policy space in education. It is not intergovernmental or centre–periphery relations, the old approach to this problem, which is crucial but the new metrics and standards of cross-border governance in Europe and its education systems.

Romuald Normand has produced an admirable guide for the educational researcher in the new sociopolitics of education across Europe.

School of Education   Martin Lawn
University of Edinburgh
Edinburgh, Scotland, UK

Foreword: Thomas S. Popkewitz

In the introduction, Romuald Normand immediately highlights the significance of this book in placing the knowledge of social science in the problematic of the politics of education. 'In the analysis of educational policies, knowledge production in the relationship between science, expertise and politics are often discarded by researchers.' This seemingly simple statement makes a profound observation about the optics and myopia of the field of education. If I can reference the edited volume by Solodny and Craven's *Cold War Social Science* (2012), the social sciences are social actors. They create objects of thought and practice for social planning and are intricately embodied in the complex set of social changes that constitute modernity and the (re)visioning of the welfare state. The new theoretical, methodological and technological changes in the conduct of the social sciences, whether those of the post-war sciences or today's 'big data' are never merely descriptions about what exists or, to use a current phrase, 'scientific evidence' about what works. The distinctions and classifications in the expertise embody cultural theses and principles about the moral order. Desires of the future in the present were articulated, for example, in the American post-war years about the democratic personality that would never allow authoritarianism and fascism to rear their heads again. Today the desires articulated different social values and kinds of people that circulate through the technologies of the measurements performed at the intersection of international agencies, national policies and local research communities.

Focusing on Europe and the European Union, Normand makes a powerful argument for the study of science through exploring its expertise in governing educational institutional practices and the visions generated about people, society and the normal and the pathological. Normand continually explores how the education sciences are deeply embedded in social projects that they theorise and assess. The projects of social change are always given in the beneficial languages about 'national health', prosperity and social welfare, such as the Knowledge or Innovative Society. The historical analyses, for example, make visible how the new theories and technologies of social science were key in the creation of international agencies to develop comparative expertise to represent economic development, measures of human happiness, educational attainments and national futures, such as in post-war years by UNESCO (1945) and OECD (1948). The new international agencies, however, were more than descriptions about assessing and interpreting national school system results and finding pathways for national educational improvement. The measures of educational outcomes and national development, Normand argues persuasively, function as knowledge systems to shape and fashion judgements about nations, schools and societies that inscribe principles about the present as the desire of some unspoken future. Moving through the chapters are explorations of how the seemingly descriptive measurements and magnitudes of student achievement visualise schooling through particular values. These values order and constitute social and moral 'health' of the nation and cultural theses about people universalised, for example, in discourses of lifelong learning.

The historical sociology of the book enables us to think about the education sciences as produced in uneven historical processes that are reassembled and connected to current practices. The analysis moves through multiple and different layers of analysis to connect what otherwise would be disparate literatures. Norman brings together Anglo-American concerns with institutional structures, science and technology studies, concerns with disciplinary cultures and its modes of producing knowledge and French scholarship that is about the expertise of knowledge production and the making of social facts. Bringing the different literatures together enables Normand to explore the assumptions, implications and consequences of current practices as simultaneously institutional and epistemological questions that require historical, sociological and comparative analyses. The book enables us to understand of how particular kinds of science emerge, the complexity of those processes and how particular ways of telling the truth and falsehood are established that have resonance (and limits) for today's research and academic community concerned with education.

Let me focus more on an important aspect of the argument that Normand develops. The international agencies explored in the book operate in the *grey zone*, spaces where actors contribute and mediate how the international assessments are to be interpreted, change models produced, and recommendations made to nations about educational improvement.[1] Today, international agencies are pushing governing beyond the institutional and spatial boundaries of the 'modern nation–state/society constellation'. The significance of the 'grey zone' is, at one level, how it forms a space that operates below the formal radar normally examined when looking at research outputs or policy arenas. The *grey zone* does not operate by the canons of research communities or do directly bear the same responsibility as policymakers

---

[1] Sverker Lindblad of Gothenburg University suggested this term as we worked on a Swedish Science Foundation project to review peer journal articles that drew on research about international student performances. These agencies included OECD but also the consulting firm of McKinsey & Company that produce international educational reports about how to improve national school systems and to address educational issues, such as youth unemployment. Lindblad, S., Petersson, D., & Popkewitz, T. (2015). International comparisons of school results: A systematic review of research on large-scale assessments in education, from https://publikationer.vr.se/produkt/international-comparisons-of-school-results-a-systematic-review-of-research-on-large-scale-assessments-in-education/

and elected officials. Intersecting with its institutional norms, the agencies and their knowledge production are processes of governing through the principles generated to delineate the problems of education through its 'needs' – statements about educational systems and the targets of its change.

The creation of international grey zones has become more important in the past few decades. At one level, the comparisons are taken into national deliberations as ways of telling the 'truth' about nations' educational system performance and its points of strength/weakness for educational policy. The numbers of comparing nations in science, mathematics and literacy, for example, translate the complex phenomena of school practices into standardised features. The codifications are then given as the logical order and stages for modernisations. But the measuring procedures do more. The numbers are embedded in models of school systems that locate the stages of educational performance with the development of teachers' competence which in turn is related to the child's psychological and sociological well-being, including family and community characteristics.

The models of assessing school efficiency, perfection and equality, however, do not merely perform as a mechanical indicator of the quality of schools. The international comparative measures of student performance discussed in the book give visibility to how the new institutions and its expertise function as 'actors' that embody moral and political philosophical principles. Norman draws on actor–network theory to consider how the epistemological principles enacted to order and classify schools are never merely descriptions of phenomena but in fact function to create the problem arena for the enactment of higher education and schooling. This is done through analyses of policy and the measurement practices in the international assessments and in comparative studies of the USA, Britain and France.

The book gives focus to the intersection of knowledge and power in which these international performance assessments operate. This issue of power and knowledge brings into view two elements of contemporary science studies that Normand productively uses in the analysis of educational practices. One is how knowledge has a materiality. The theories about school systems and assessment are actors in what is constituted as the problems of education and the categories and classifications that represent its social functions and outcomes, as well as the modes of rectification. The locating of the field of relations that connect policy, research and educational spaces of the grey zone is, I believe, important for understanding how theories and abstractions of the social (and education) sciences 'act' to mobilise an order to social problems and methods of change.

Normand argues that the implications of the new accounting features and its arenas of expertise influence the ways in which we think about academic freedom. The 'acting' of knowledge is the creation of the European Area of Higher Education. The book moves between historical analyses of the problem of measurement to contemporary international assessment and their inscription within different European countries. The argument considers how ranking and performance indicators have consequences not only in coordinating activities but also in functioning to form relationships among academics. Norman rightly asks will the academic model that he traces to the Middle Ages be eradicated, maintained or restructured?

This leads me to a second element of science studies that the book engages, that is, numbers as an actor in constituting how truth is told about schools, people and societies. The seemingly technical appearances of the numbers enter into cultural realms that are never merely numbers but codifications and standardisations of what are to constitute reality and planning. Numbers, then, are never merely about the mathematics and numerical symbol. Mathematics is a product of human activity, as Hacking (1983) argues, that 'alienates itself' from human activities which has produced it. In doing so, it moves into social life and 'lives'/acquires a certain autonomy from the activity which has produced it.

Yet that autonomy is a chimera when examined in relation to the more general phenomena of the grey zone. Governing is more and more premised on numbers for solving problems that in one way or another address transborder issues that are not only about education but climate change, financial crises, pandemics and terrorism. The numbers, magnitudes and comparative statistics in the international assessment of schools are cultural practices about how to make judgements, to recognise types of objects and to draw conclusions in making manageable fields of existence. The algorithms reflect choices and aspirations of relevance and prediction that travel from one specific location or context. This travelling entails immense particularities and characteristics expressed through numbers and magnitudes about teachers, students, families and communities. Their principles differentiate and classify work into policy and educational practices in which the models nicely condense complexities to act and exercise power. If I take OECD, these choices entail defining context as it relates to the measureable elements of its management models of change, removing social class, among other social categories, as statistic 'noise'; 'that is a characteristic experimental way of getting rid of unwanted phenomena' (Hacking 1983, P. 257).

The numbers act in this global context as not merely correlations. They perform as justifications for pre-emptive interventions. Consider, for example, the use of big data in the generation of social media and Internet companies (Hansen 2015, p.214) and today in arguments for their use in the learning sciences to identify children and families that pose future risks. Numbers are inscribed as road maps and 'highways' to the desired future – not only of school but also of the family and society. One can read the nation reports and the comparative studies in Normand's book to consider how the expertise of science embodies problem creation and government actions that are pre-emptive interventions. International performance models are used as national studies to develop programmes that are anticipatory in their qualities.

These correlational and pre-emptive qualities of international assessments and intervention are odd in relation to what I think of empirical facts. The international assessment talk about the future through a science that is correlative and has no significance as general laws about what bodes well for the future of economic development or political 'health' of a nation's populations. And the knowledge that is purported to talk about the future knowledge that children need to know for participation in society does not come from any direct experiences but as objects and social processes mobilised about desires that the mathematics and numerical practices are to measure and produce. It is a data behaviourism that profiles nations and people that is to prepare for action about what to do next.

Normand's analysis directs attention to how knowledge has a materiality. The book obligates us to rethink the dichotomies of realism and idealism and even what some people might call the new realism, which tends to treat knowledge as an epiphenomenon to some structural forces. Normand focuses on the actors as institutional and social actors but also knowledge as an actor that forms boundaries around what is possible as decision-making and what constitutes practice. The careful, detailed and thoughtful arguments throughout this book continually engage the historical complexity of the changes in expertise to govern social planning and policy. The new epistemic forms given through the algorisms and 'big data' of international measures of performances are actors in their social arenas, generating principles that construct the objects known in the institutional forms in which they operate. The technologies of mass algorism that make possible the measurements and their constant comparative qualities of people, what I think of as 'the Google effect', are important elements in the principles of governing spoken about in the book. The complexity of knowledge and power often gets lost in analyses of educational phenomena and its expertise.

University of Wisconsin-Madison   Thomas S. Popkewitz
Madison, WI, USA

References

Hacking, I. (1983). *Representing and intervening: Introductory topics in the philosophy of natural science* (Vol. 5, No. 1). Cambridge: Cambridge University Press.

Hansen, H. K. (2015). Numerical operations, transparency illusions and the datafication of governance. *European Journal of Social Theory, 18*(2), 203–220.

Contents

Part II   Expertise, Entrepreneurship and Management: The New Spirit of Academic Capitalism

Introduction

In the analysis of education policies, knowledge production and the relationship between science, expertise and politics are often disregarded by researchers. They prefer to focus on discourse analysis, while some of them participate in legitimising positivist and experimental approaches inspired by the natural science model which strengthens the normative and prescriptive features of knowledge in educational sciences. This book is going to explore the transformations of epistemic governance in education and the way in which some actors are shaping new knowledge which is in turn impacting on other actors in charge of implementing this knowledge in the context of the decision-making process and practice.

We are inspired by the works of Michel Foucault who demonstrated that the institutionalisation of forms of power related to a body of knowledge contributes to the conception, conceptualisation and representation of certain forms of government. The French philosopher defines governmentality as 'the ensemble formed by the institutions, procedures, analyses and reflections, the calculations and tactics that allow the exercise of this very specific albeit complex form of power, which has as its target population, as its principal form of knowledge political economy, and as its essential technical means apparatuses of security' (Foucault et al. 1991, 102). In his opinion, when studying governmentality you need to take into account not only the technical dimension of power but also its cognitive and ethical features when analysing devices and technologies of control but also the regimes of truth by which new subjectivities and identities are shaped.

As Rose and Miller (1992) demonstrated, when extending Foucault's theory, there has not been a retreat from the state but an extension of governing at distance in which social technologies attribute individual responsibilities to autonomous entities: companies, communities, professional organisations and individuals themselves. Contracts, targets and performance measurements are linked to local and individual autonomy in order to make people accountable for their actions. Individuals are required to become experts of themselves; to master their body, psyche and behaviour; and to become 'entrepreneurs' of their life. This entrepreneurship is expressed through the choices they make, the risks they face and the

© Springer International Publishing Switzerland 2016

R. Normand, *The Changing Epistemic Governance of European Education*, Educational Governance Research 3, DOI 10.1007/978-3-319-31776-2_1

responsibilities they have to assume. The citizen as a consumer becomes an active agent in the regulation of professional expertise from consumption to work. The analysis of governmentality is relevant to analysing the instruments of political regulation which characterise the transformations of the state. The type of instruments, their choice by policymakers, allows observation and calculation justifying rationality beyond discourses while inscribing political action in spaces of visibility and representation that give a legitimacy to governmental decision-making. Since Foucault, we have known that the mechanisms of power can be based on laws and rules and disciplinary techniques, in securing programmes against risk. But governmentality is also supported by knowledge facilitating the control of the population, while the observation and calculation elements are provided by statistical instrumentation.

As Thomas Popkewitz also wrote, knowledge policy in social and educational sciences is related to a certain type of social epistemology, the inscription of a rationalising project in the knowledge and government of individuals (Popkewitz 1997; Popkewitz and Brennan 1997). The use of data was a breakthrough in the links between education and politics. It allowed for the implementation of technologies objectifying the self, particularly through the first developments of psychology, and it also defined proper strategies of groups and institutions pursuing objectives of change. Instrumental knowledge is therefore essential for the social construction of reflexivity and modern life and the historicity of the knowledge issue, as a social epistemology, helping to enlighten the relationship between power, knowledge and change (Popkewitz 1999). Social epistemology specifies a context in which rules and standards frame certain categories of perception and some conceptions of the self. It helps to localise objects built by knowledge and the modern reason in historical and situated practices regarding some groups and institutions as being different types of distinction and with a classification which is considered as legitimate.

In studying epistemic governance of education, we shall not only interest ourselves in the forms of language as different modalities of persuasion and negotiation between actors, even if they are essential in the quest for legitimacy and in the implementation of institutional and political arrangements around knowledge. We shall also explore knowledge-based technologies and the number-crunching methods which produce modes of representation, cognitive categories and value-based judgements determining and guiding actions and interactions between actors. Our approach is related to the cognitive turn in public policies, particularly research regarding instruments of public action, while at the same time, some concepts have been borrowed from pragmatic sociology studying the practical effects of knowledge on the definition and solving of public problems.

Our work shall develop some insights from the Sociology of Science and Technology (SST). STT has demonstrated that scientific knowledge production implies cultural, political and social factors but also competitive and collective interests with regard to access to resources and recognition (Latour and Woolgar 2013). From the laboratory to society, alliances are composed between human and non-human beings to set up interconnected spaces which ally the interests of scientists, professionals and policymakers across power relationships and compromise.

The politics of science gives birth to empowering and translating processes in addition to sociotechnical assemblages in accordance with certain intermediary steps between invention and policymaking. As argued by Karin Knorr-Cetina, the study of the social conditions of knowledge challenges explanations of a natural scientific knowledge by characterising the social and symbolic dimensions of science beyond technical ones (Knorr-Cetina 2007). Science is made up of epistemic cultures and machineries in the building of knowledge, and it is the result of the fragmentation of knowledge and expertise but also of different meanings and ontologies. More than a representation or a technological product, knowledge is a practice related to engagements and rituals in a complex scientific life and setting. It defines an agency from different cultures in personhood, subjectivity and identity but also through the mediation of objects as instruments, laboratories, centres, networks or infrastructures that produce science. We will later see how this issue of agency is central in understanding the transformations of academic work.

As different studies demonstrate, knowledge is not only a matter of interpretation and scientific controversies, it is an instrument of power aiming to persuade some groups and to exclude others and to give a legitimate authority to decision-making. It attributes a qualified and objective value to a certain social reality, and it problematises situations subjected to politicisation (or depoliticisation), thus making it (or not) a public problem. These solutions are far from being neutral because, even if they rely on scientific and technical knowledge, they are social constructions in which actors give meanings, values, interests, convictions and ideals. We will illustrate this statement throughout this book by investigating the governance of knowledge (or epistemic governance) in education at the European level and its implications in the building of norms, decisions and actions emerging from a multitude of actors and institutions.

Our use of the actor–network theory concerns the mechanics of power (Law 1992). But it does not take power for granted as a macrosocial system of exploitation as it is often assumed by post-Marxist theory. We are interested in interactions and how some kinds of interactions are more or less successful in stabilising and reproducing themselves. The concept of heterogeneous networks is essential in suggesting that organisations, agents and instruments are generated by patterned networks of human and non-human beings and that knowledge and power can be considered as a product of this heterogeneity. It appears in the form of the skills embodied in scientists and experts but also in a variety of material forms. Power and knowledge are a matter of organising and ordering those materials and interactions so that they fit together in a set of scientific products. These networks are composed of people, machines, tools, texts, money and architectures, and our task as sociologists is to characterise their heterogeneity and their effects on organisation, social relationships, knowledge and power. As symbolic interactionism demonstrates, social agents are never located in bodies alone but in a network of heterogeneous relations produced by such networks. It means that organisation or agents are not completely autonomous with a single centre and a set of stable relations. They belong to a network of relationships translated into devices, agents and institutions, not only as a mechanism of surveillance but to perform the relations, communications, mobility, representations and strategies embodied in a range of sustainable materials.

Our work has also been inspired by Boltanski and Thévenot's sociology of critical capacity which enables us to understand social order as a plural way of engaging people with the world and justifying their actions. Such a pluralistic approach emphasises the sense of justice among agents and their view of the common good in public disputes and democratic polity. They argue that there is a social distribution of the common good in society and that human beings try to articulate reality and uncertainty through the different 'hardships' or 'trials' they face in the course of their action. Ordinary actors are equipped with critical and moral capacities, and they use them to judge and to participate in different forms of sociality beyond a search for interest and power. These activities of justification are processual and empirical according to changing circumstances while people are capable of establishing different orders of worth with different conceptions of the common good whose validity can be confirmed or undermined by means of different trials (or hardships). So, when they are engaged in disputes, protests or contestation, people demonstrate a competence to assess what is possible or not realistically by making their judgements and decision through a changing set of interactions. In a democratic way of searching for agreements, because people cannot remain permanently in a situation of conflict and civil war, they are obliged to make compromises between different orders of justification.

On the basis of this social theory, Luc Boltanski provides a comprehensive account of capitalist modes or organisation in Western Europe by studying the mechanisms of legitimisation of discourses that celebrate a neo-managerial vision of the economic and social order. He demonstrates, along with Eve Chiapello (1999), that this discourse is powerful and based on different principles of justification. It cannot be simplistically reduced to the post-Marxist idea of domination, alienation and exploitation because it is constitutive of public spheres, orders of worth and trials which produce a diversity of normative arrangements and practices. By emphasising 'flexibility', 'adaptability', 'creativity' and 'mobility' beyond market-driven principles, this 'new spirit of capitalism' implements a neo-managerialism that subverts the traditional modes of opposition and resistance while using some social and artistic critiques expressed in the relegation of bureaucratic, planning and hierarchical organisations. By celebrating networks and the 'networked man', this new spirit is able to incorporate normative processes based on critical discourse into new modes of relationships and devices. Consequently, it has shifted the analysis of domination and exploitation, and it has required sociology to reinvent their analytical tools and critique to reflect on these important transformations.

Consequently, our conception of epistemic governance concerns transformations of academic capitalism and the ways in which academics, engaged in heterogeneous networks, are capable of developing new interactions as well as facing new trials imposed by the changing conditions of producing knowledge in their scientific community and within their institutions. Knowledge is not only an instrument of power but a process of legitimisation that expresses the diversity of the common good.

As Carol Weiss has written, different meanings characterise the utilisation of research (Weiss 1979). The knowledge-driven model which has been borrowed from natural sciences assumes that research pre-exists its development and use, but that is not well adjusted to social sciences because of its non-replicability and the politicisation of societal issues. However, this model continues to fascinate researchers and policymakers, and, as we will see further on, nowadays, it has, to a certain extent, reconquered a certain legitimacy in education. The problem-solving model provides empirical evidence to solve a political problem, while the decision-making process commands the application of research according to a consensus on common objectives. Evidence can be quantitative or qualitative. Research anticipates political claims, or the issue can be perceived by researchers as a problem of society or policymakers can themselves order researchers to carry out some research programmes. This model, which is broader in its scope than the previous one, has in the end had little effect on policy. It explains why there has been some criticism about it, notably in the USA and in the UK in debates on the finalities of educational research. The interactive model characterises cases in which social sciences enter in the political arena along with stakeholders. It is largely emphasised by international organisations and particularly the European Commission. According to this model, the use of research is a small cog in a complex political process among a diversity of opinions and interests. The political model corresponds to the use of knowledge in serving partisan aims against political adversaries. It presents important risks of misinterpretations and distortion of data because they are manipulated to conform to an ideological vision. This model has been extended in the past few decades, particularly in the development of think tanks, and it has been used by the New Right to advance certain ideological beliefs. The tactical model is a strategic approach used by some agencies and institutions to empower social scientists, thus preventing criticism and previously taken legitimate decisions. In the end, the model of Enlightenment fosters the representation that theoretical concepts and perspectives in social sciences inform the public through numerous channels, particularly the media, and enable policymakers to give meaning to a complex world. This model is at the root of the traditional conception of academic work. But, in fact, generalisation and conceptualisation in social and educational sciences are often perceived in simplistic, partial and biased ways, with significant distortions, while the model of Enlightenment is not very effective in reaching political audiences.

As we have seen above, public policy in education is far from being objective and rational: it combines heterogeneous elements as objectives, values, instruments and consequences (Majone 1989). According to Majone, the hard scientific evidence standard cannot be used to develop a perfect solution for complicated social problems. The scientific method would require an impossibly high level of resources including time, money, relevant data, tested subjects and applicable theory. There are no perfect scientific measures, statistics, tools or mathematic equations that can make sense of most policy issues. Furthermore, social concerns or ethical issues do not in themselves lead to empirical, scientific experimentation on human subjects. According to Majone, a dialectic discussion between a wide variety of stakeholders sharing viewpoints, assumptions, values, interpretations and experiences is imperative for the adoption and implementation of a successful policy: this policy does not need more objectivity but rather more deliberation, criticism and advocacy. However, instead, public policy analysis in education has become trapped in decisionism and has become the process of making rational calculated choices between clear alternatives. Decisionism focuses on short-term outcomes with little concerns for long-term processes and effects.

Peter Weingart has arrived at the same conclusions. He shows that the 'decisionist model' in the relationship between power and scientific knowledge, which assumes a clear distinction between 'objective knowledge' and 'subjective values', has to be questioned while an increasing scientification of policy is being observed (Weingart 1999). It reduces the choices of options to the best objective decision according to a fully biased instrumental rationality. In this technocratic model, the policymaker is dependent on the expert, and policy becomes a scientifically rationalised administration assuming a quasi-natural scientific and technical development. In fact, the growing interaction between science and policy has led to the scientification of policy and the politicisation of science. Scientification privileges expertise in the definition of public problems and in the search for solutions that facilitate decision-making through the elaboration of compromises. But it also dissimulates the political features of choices. The politicisation of science uses scientific programmes and results to build a legitimacy in the political space. This dominant model of 'independent' and 'neutral' expertise does not stand up to scrutiny. Indeed, science is increasingly participating in the definition of public problems and the setting of political agendas. Scientific knowledge is also used to lend legitimacy to different political stances and decisions in the way problems are defined, the degree of consensus being obtained and the social values and interests being mobilised. Scientists themselves protect their interests, are in competition with each other and are engaged in defending a particular cause.

Diane Stone (1997) also underlines the multiple interactions and paradoxes between knowledge production and decision-making resulting from narrowly intertwined stories. From a conceptual toolbox, she analyses political texts as stories and includes different rhetorical devices such as metaphors, languages of interest, causal stories and numbers. In these texts, metaphors are used to make a problem similar to another problem and to adopt a similar strategic solution without taking into account variations of context. The language of interests also serves to present problems as if they were competing interests which need to be overcome in the building of the common good. Causal stories are employed to determine the cause of a problem, to link it to an effect and to attribute responsibility to some actors while excluding others and other stories. Facts and numbers are used to directly access negotiations and to take a stance during political debates. Through the study of various policy documents, Diane Stone has demonstrated that knowledge is narrowly intertwined with the politics of facts but also with the politics of interests and values. She argues that these hegemonic discourses exclude other discourses in society while reducing discording voices to silence.

In this book, we shall also demonstrate that political solutions in education are invented through a strong interaction between expertise and politics instead of using scientific knowledge per se or only some aspects of it. The technical knowledge of experts spills over into scientific knowledge because it can better manage uncertainty and risk, as short-term decision-making. This importance of expertise in education policies is nothing new. If we take the example of the USA, the emphasis on positivism and technocratic methods within government was recurrent at the turn of the twentieth century. In education, this technocratic conception has its roots in the 'Progressive Era' which introduced the principles of Taylor's scientific management into education systems (Tyack and Hansot 1982). Educative reforms were based on a 'behaviourist approach' promoted by experimental psychology. So, rational problem-solving and fixed objectives had to replace the irrationality of local administrators and elite by the experts of efficiency (Callahan 1962). This new science of government promised to eliminate wastage and to implement efficiency in methods and practices of school management. Experts were themselves organised into powerful networks and institutions to spread this new way of building education reform.

According to this context, it is interesting to return to the intellectual debate generated by the development of expertise during this period. It opposed Walter Lippmann and John Dewey. Lippmann considered that modern society does not have any institutions in which there is a large participation by the public in the political process (Goodwin 1995). He preferred a small educated and well-informed elite capable of delivering expertise, who could be trusted and take responsibility in the production of knowledge. Social sciences, which had not yet developed the experimental method, were incapable of providing reliable evidence and interesting policymakers and businessmen. The solution was to make research findings more useful in the decision-making process by delegating the translation of knowledge to experts capable of assembling, translating, simplifying, generalising and showcasing it. Lippmann proposed that experts would have the same working conditions as academics but their actions would be coordinated by bureaus and agencies close to government. The missions of these bureaus would be to improve policymakers' decision-making and to accumulate data to be generalised and disseminated into a body of political doctrines to be used by the press.

On the contrary, John Dewey has questioned the role of experts and the ethical uses of scientific knowledge in public policies (Westhoff 1995). He was concerned with the threat caused by the dependency on experts in a democratic society. He believes that social sciences, through their professionalisation and specialisation in a permanent quest for objectivity, could risk becoming isolated from the community and the general public. In order to avoid this shift, it is necessary to popularise knowledge and to implement democratic and participative decision-making. Having observed the failure of the standard methodology as proposed by positivist approaches, he suggested developing a method of social inquiry and not just science based on quantified and impersonal data. According to Dewey, experts have narrowly defined specialities and privileged knowledge giving them an overwhelming influence in the arena of public discourse. This privileging of the voice of the expert, the development and use of technical language and the erosion of communication across publics have widened the gap between government and citizens (Evans

2000). The ordinary citizen's voice is being drowned out, and participation in decision-making and policymaking affecting the common good has been reduced to a meaningless ritual. Dewey argued that a well-educated democratic community has both the capability to control technology and to use it to enhance the life of all, rather than the life of the few, as well as an ethical or moral imperative to do so.

More recently, the debate on the democratisation of expertise led to a major and famous controversy in the field of Sociology of Science and Technology (SST). The issue was defined as follows: 'Should the political legitimacy of technical decisions in the public domain be maximised by referring them to the widest democratic process, or should such decisions be based on the best expert advice?' The controversy opposed two camps. The first one, represented by Harry Collins and Robert Evans, proposed a 'third wave' in SST including more issues related to decision-making but one in which experts remain at a distance from populism (Collins and Evans 2002, 2008). The other camp, represented by Sheila Jasanoff (1996, 2003a) and Brian Wynne (2003), argued that the participation of non-experts in the production of knowledge and public deliberation was a necessity.

Collins and Evans (2002) explained that SST has been successful in demonstrating the importance of technical issues and the implication of many actors in policymaking but they provide an unsatisfactory response to delimitate the participation of the public and expertise. They see expertise as being divided into three types: 'interactional' (sufficient to converse with experts in a given field), 'contributory' (sufficient to contribute to the field itself) and 'referred' (sufficient to understand what it means to contribute to a field). Experts should have two additional faculties: 'translation' (ability to move between different social worlds) and 'discrimination' (ability to make distinctions between different kinds of claims and sources of credibility). Finally, Collin and Evans divided science itself into four types: normal, Golem (science which has the potential to become normal science, but has not yet reached closure to the satisfaction of the core-set), historical and reflexive historical, each requiring a different approach to decision-making. These categories of expertise, expert faculties and science are intended to help people draw the line between appropriate and inappropriate inclusiveness in technical debates conducted in public domains. Considering that this is needed to set these boundaries, they have propose a normative theory of expertise based on the distinction between different types of knowledge and different forms of capacities. Taking the example of sociology, they have distinguished different levels of expertise (2008):

1. No expertise: that is the degree of expertise with which a fieldworker sets out; it is insufficient to conduct a sociological analysis or do quasi-participatory fieldwork.
2. Interactional expertise: this means enough expertise to interact intelligently with participants and to carry out a sociological analysis.
3. Contributory expertise: this means enough expertise to contribute to the science of the field being analysed.

These categories have to define the contribution of different groups to policymaking and the implication of experts, but also the different types of science, some of them oriented towards problem-solving by predesignated experts and others requiring more relationships between policy and public debate.

Against this analysis, we share some critics addressed by Jasanoff and Wynne. Firstly, they contested the fact that it is possible to demarcate technical issues from political ones via authentic knowledge which is not accessible to lay people and which is institutionally legitimate. This demarcation project appears naive and misguided when putting forwards the notion that the participation of citizens guarantees that the power of experts will be circumscribed. Thus, the definition of what is 'political' or 'scientific' comes from intimate negotiations between science and society, while science can seize emergent political issues through linear and independent ways. It is more a process of hybridisation of science and policy, and there is no fix point from which it would be possible to distinguish what is related, or not, to expertise. The public engagement of citizens is necessary to test and contest the framing of issues by experts (Jasanoff 2003b, c). Without this critical supervision, the latter produces nonrelevant advice and asks the wrong questions. Indeed, institutions using expertise have to be controlled by lay people. With participation comes the possibility of disseminating knowledge and increasing civic capacities to offer reflexive responses to modernity.

In fact, since the mythical controversy between Walter Lippmann and John Dewey, the landscape of knowledge production and expertise has shifted. The democratisation which Dewey hoped for has been achieved via social movements acting outside of institutions and searching for more participation in the political process (Maassen and Weingart 2006). But scientists have been increasingly engaged in the process of politicisation and instrumentalisation as experts according to Walter Lippmann's vision. However, experts, like scientists, have progressively lost their legitimacy as political advisers. The relative democratisation of expertise has paradoxically demystified scientific knowledge, while researchers have been strongly incited to provide useful results and become accountable. As we shall see in this book, the democratisation of expertise in education does not really profit national states but rather international or transnational organisations (the World Bank, OECD, European Commission, etc.) which have the capacity to create new stakeholders and expert networks distant from national interests.

These developments have been accompanied by a claim for more robust knowledge, while knowledge production has been diversified beyond the academic field within institutions like agencies or think tanks (Weingart 2008). Therefore, the quality and reliability of educational research is at the centre of debates, while a new epistemic governance is attempting to define new relationships between science and policy on behalf of the knowledge economy. This new environment has created a proliferation of experts and modes of expertise at different governing scales. Expertise (re)covers a multitude of specialised knowledge beyond established disciplines. Sometimes, this expertise is no longer searching to achieve its objectives because it serves partisan causes and aims to influence public opinion beyond politicians. The problem evoked by Dewey remains, and expert knowledge has taken so much importance that his warning is still topical: expertise has been captured by the political sphere and the media in an increasing competition to defend short-term interests. It marks the end of the monopoly of academic science in the establishment of truth but also its distance from a large majority of citizens.

In this new interaction between science, expertise and politics, the positivist argument is highly 'persuasive' (Alexander 1982). It is based on two postulates: firstly, there is a radical difference between empirical observation and nonempirical statements, and, secondly, 'philosophical' or 'metaphysical' issues have no place in the practice of an academic discipline based on empiricism. The arguments assimilate social and educational sciences to natural sciences in order to escape from subjectivism. We can once again return to history to reveal the strong inscription of the positivist argument within social sciences as proven by the developments of quantification and experimentation during the modern era. According to Theodore Porter, the spread of administration increased the demand for objectivity from social sciences (Porter 1992). Knowledge, by becoming instrumental and standardised, had to finish with arbitrary judgements particularly in using mathematics and statistics. Technicians could replace enlightened 'amateurs' in the building of population measurement instruments by using correlation and regression calculations (Porter 1995; Hacking 1990; Desrosières 2002). Economists, psychologists, political scientists and sociologists were concerned with the definition of methodological rules putting 'subjectivity' at a distance to serve the needs of the bureaucratic administration (Bannister 1991; Ross 1992).

If many social scientists considered experimentation on human subjects as not very practicable, psychology already had a long-standing tradition in this area (Danziger 1994). So it came naturally during the first experiments comparing experimental and control groups (Dehue 2000). For example, in 1923, William A. McCall, an educational psychologist at Columbia University, published a manual entitled *How to Experiment in Education* (McCall 1923). The book estimated that an increase of efficiency and experimentation in education would save billions of dollars for the US administration. This was not the first time that randomisation was used for experimental purposes. As early as the 1870s, psychophysical experimenters used randomised trials to thwart the expectations of experimental subjects on the stimuli to come. Even Charles Merriam, an eminent political scientist and head of the department of political sciences at the University of Chicago, launched along with Harold Gosnell experimentations for his research on voting during elections (*Non-Voting* 1924; *Getting out the Vote*, 1927). Merriam and Gosnell wanted to deal with the problem posed by the abstention of a large proportion of migrants who were not registered on electoral lists. They used experimental devices to promote a 'scientific' development of studies in political sciences.

Several decades later, Donald Campbell, a psychologist and pioneer of 'quasi-experimental' research methods in policy evaluation, resumed these arguments. In 1969, for a review of social experiments, he published a paper which became a reference for specialists in evaluation (Campbell 1969). He argued that 'true' experiments imply that groups of individuals are subjected to a treatment and compared to a control group. Consequently, the evaluation of a public policy had to overcome humanitarian and practical objections to randomly expose individuals to treatments during the period of the experiment. *Reforms as experiments* was not the first publication in which Campbell extended the 'logic of the laboratory' to all of society. Along with the statistician Julian C. Stanley, he published a book entitled *Experimental and Quasi-Experimental Designs for Research* (Campbell and Stanley 1966). This bestseller was considered as a new standard for research as it defended the idea that the researcher has to be the 'methodological servitor of the experimental society'.

This experimentalism is today re-emerging in social and educational sciences as it is in politics. There has been a huge surge of interest, particularly in the 1990s, in arguments for evidence-based policy (Smith et al. 2000; Davies et al. 2007). As we shall see in this book, technologies of evidence have had an impact on governments and allocation of public expenditure. If we take the example of the UK, the evidence-based policy, using experimental approaches and randomised controlled trials (RCTs), first penetrated medicine and then other social sectors such as education. In 1997, the Labour government was elected using the slogan 'What counts is what works'. Some similar movements were noticeable both in Europe and the USA. As recently as 2013, the UK Department for Education announced it was running two RCTs to research the impact of a child protection assessment tool on school attainment in mathematics and science. This and other UK government papers advocating increased usage of RCTs across public policy (Haynes et al. 2012), and particularly in the education sector, have prompted extensive debate among teachers, education researchers and other commentators (Hargreaves 1997; Hammersley 1997, 2002, 2005; Whitty 2006).

For the advocates of experimentalism, academic knowledge is depicted as part of the problem and is accused of being opaque and beyond scrutiny. Over-reliance on such knowledge is considered to be harmful, and the case for RCTs has helped to raise powerful critiques against academic judgement while sustaining claims for accountability and transparency. The idea that everything is observable as factual events and has discernible causes has been largely disseminated by the promoters of this methodology. As well as responding to the limitations of expertise, RCTs appear to be an effective response to criticism that the UK government's policymaking is purely ideological and unfettered by evidence. So RCTs seem to offer a an improvement in decision-making in which politicians dominate as well as technocratic models which, as Peter Weingart wrote, are in turn dominated by experts. RCTs bring the promise of a rich data set which can be analysed and interpreted in multiple ways by multiple actors through the creation of public policy 'information architectures' supported by 'big data'. In education, this experimental approach, through the development of evidence-based education (EBE), has become increasingly popular with policymakers who consider it is a means to improve the quality and impact of research. Taking its references from medicine, this new positivism has developed technologies of evidence, such as RCTs, aiming to transform the relationships between educational research, policy and practice. It often leads to the erroneous assumption that what works in one educational system will inevitably work well in another.

As Gita Steiner-Khamsi argues, evidence-based policy planning is often justified through three facades: the facade of rationality, the facade of precision and the facade of universality. The facade of rationality has been thoroughly dismantled in policy studies, including by critics who have shed doubt on whether 'governance by numbers' is less political or more rational than other modes of regulation (see chapter "The Politics of Standards and Quality"). A second group of researchers has demystified statistics by illuminating the 'facade of precision' and problematising the uncontested authority attached to numbers. As Gita Steiner-Khamsi (2013) herself noticed in her study, there are vast discrepancies in reports on dropout statistics, even among departments within the same ministry. The facade of universality has been seriously under examined. Dealing with comparisons over time and across spaces or contexts, she explains that there is a risk of decontextualised interpretation in research designs characterised by simple comparison. This concern applies to quasi-experimental designs that rest upon on two cases (the control group and the treatment group) and draw on a time-series analysis (typically before and after the treatment/intervention/reform). As with simple impact evaluations, there is a risk that the difference in context may be reduced to a difference in the degree of external intervention, whereby other cultural, contextual or systemic factors are downplayed or neglected. Furthermore, standardised comparisons through indicators, benchmarks or league tables as used by international organisations legitimise a what-went-right analysis focusing narrowly on how the system failed or performed better.

A parallel criticism has been addressed to a certain vision of education policy research, divided between a more academically oriented research of policy and research for policy akin to commissioned research (Lingard 2013). As Bob Lingard wrote, beyond the definition of education research, its impact relates to a certain complexity which cannot only be measured through journal impacts or other measurements of academic quality. Otherwise, it diminishes curiosity-driven research which is essential to creativity. Indeed, the research–policy relationship is subjected to some clinical and objective operations which are closely linked to ideology and politics. It is framed by governments, policymakers and ministers but also mediated by professional rules and heterogeneous professional discourses. This is the case for policy research which considers the relationship between policy and research as a form of problem-solving engineering. It gives the opportunity for 'political entrepreneurs' such as the McKinsey group, to penetrate the political agendas of current governments and international organisations or to serve the ideological aims of political parties and think tanks. Gert Biesta (2007) similarly stated that educational research has taken a technocratic turn by focusing on issues and means of effectiveness and limiting opportunities for practitioners to produce judgements related to context and settings. He criticises the fact that a professional model of action, as highlighted by evidence-based research and practice, reduces education to a treatment or an intervention based on a causal and external model borrowed from natural sciences. Judgements in education are not only factual but also founded on values.

This return of experimentalism and the development of evidence- or informed-based policy, coupled with the powerful emergence of expertise to orientate policymaking, have called into question the permanence of the 'model of Enlightenment' conveyed by the academic tradition and social and educational sciences. Faced with transformations of their epistemological and political settings, academics in education are being forced to adapt themselves to these new rules of knowledge production. The creation of a European space of higher education and research, along with the academic regime entering the knowledge economy and society, has challenged the principles of academic autonomy and regulation by peers. At the European level, the university model, based on neutral knowledge and independence among peers, is increasingly in competition with knowledge production outside of the academic sphere. European research policy in education tends to legitimate a new mode of knowledge production giving a greater focus on decision-making and the representation of different interest groups or stakeholders not only by the definition of the criteria and content of research but also in dissemination and valorisation activities. New academics have also been subjected to norms of assessment and quality assurance mechanisms shaping the orientation of works as well as relationships between researchers, funders and sponsors. Some academics are benefitting from this new policy–research relationship to invest their expertise in European or international educational programmes. Most of them have to develop interdisciplinary activities, and though their public funding is decreasing, they are required to be efficient and accountable and to compete for access to resources. Will the *Homo Academicus* model which began in the Middle Ages with the first universities, and then morphed into a certain scientific rationality through a division of labour in educational disciplines, be eradicated, maintained or restructured? What are the new emerging relationships between science and policy in the field of education? What are the new forms and tensions being experienced by academic work?

In this book, we shall provide an analytical framework regarding the transformations of higher education which overlap with research objects and findings from several areas: the conduct of public policies and decision-making, the social theory of standards and science studies, the pragmatic sociology of justice and the regimes of engagement, as well as studies on globalisation and Europeanisation in education and on New Public Management and professionalism. Firstly, there is a difference with regard to a constituted field of research privileging neo-institutionalist readings or international comparisons based on large statistical surveys. The former tends to underestimate indeterminacy and uncertainty when building relationships between actors and during the institutionalising processes. The latter displays homogeneous statistical categories on a social reality embedded in local contexts and adjusted to circumstances. We shall also critique and make comparisons with some theories of globalisation which focus their analyses on class conflicts, reproduction and domination. Moreover, the ideas of a capitalist state or a cultural political economy tend to overemphasise the imaginary of the capitalist crises and contradictions subsumed under a super-global neo-liberal project which masks the variety of neocapitalist regimes within countries and continents.

By considering expertise as a central object, we are also distancing ourselves from discourses claiming that experts can be the objective allies of power and domination. On the contrary, we show the multiple paths and principles of justice by which knowledge is legitimated and validated into policymaking. At the same time, we argue that spheres of academia and expertise are narrowly linked and that they maintain many relationships through the creation of networks and tools supporting the production, mediation and dissemination of scientific knowledge. However, we have not underestimated the hierarchies and asymmetries established between regimes of evidence and discourses of truth, as well as the supremacy of statistical instruments, particularly international surveys, in the guidance of problems and the search for political solutions. Instead of holding a dualist view, rehabilitating a hypothetical golden age of the academic profession, we show that expertise is linked to deep and ineluctable transformations of the regime of knowledge production. It leads us to reflect on the project of social and educational sciences in a world in which competition and new spaces of legitimisation of knowledge are emerging. This reconfiguration, for which the new experimentalism and big data are the most visible constituents, invites us to question the resilience of the academic profession in maintaining an autonomous space but also of its capacity to break free from a disciplinary and mono-statist vision.

Our double openness to the sociology of sciences and the sociology of justification has shed new light on the place of networks in the global architecture which is currently outlined at the boundaries of science, expertise and politics. By avoiding a structuralist bias, and without being trapped in a narrow social constructivism, for which only the local and bottom-up processes have to be investigated, we have attempted to describe a new global academic space between hierarchies and the market, the local and the global and proximity and distance, by echoing certain theories explaining the new spatial and temporal scales of globalisation. We show how a multiplicity of actors participate in the reconfiguration of European higher education by resisting the idea that there exists a unique centre or meta-reflexive agents who or which decide everything, even if we know that international organisations have a real framing and influencing power. However, in using the actor–network theory, we obviously consider that operations of translation, shifts and inscriptions by which ideas, discourses and representations are delegated to artefacts as grids, classifications, indicators or other objects and devices give a certain degree of immutability and irreversibility to implemented mechanisms and technologies. Therefore, a historical perspective and a long-term reflexion are central in providing evidence regarding continuities and ruptures in the upcoming new order.

Far from reifying this order, we have given an important significance to the human agency which corresponds to the new definition of the academic. We argue against the idea that he or she will lose his or her autonomy in favour of a dependency on standards; we argue that his or her new academic environment offers a new space for potentialities and manoeuvres by shifting the stakes of professionalism as well as the modalities of recognition and assessment. Obviously, tradition has lost its place, but other figures of commitment are valued and invested by academics who are quite dissatisfied with the previous order. The social theory of justice highlights orders of worth and visions of the common good which relativise criticism or prevent its deployment. A sense of justice finds its expression through the extension of human capacities into more recognised areas such as creativity, innovation, entrepreneurship or leadership. Changes do not always lead to the reinforcement of the domination and exploitation of people even if some of them do suffer from humiliation, contempt or exclusion because they have not been included in this new academic order.

It is therefore through this interplay between 'networks' and 'agency' that this book chose its two-part formalisation. The first part seeks to understand the progressive structuration of epistemic governance of knowledge at the European scale by the cognitive and instrumental mediation of networks, institutions, agencies and centres. International surveys, indicators, standards, rankings and benchmarks are the material forms by which a European policy has been implemented in order to redefine the relationships between science and decision-making. This governance has no hierarchical and commanding lines imposed by Brussels. Even if it is partially structured by the European Commission through incentives and recommendations, it is not statutory for the states. It corresponds to a heterogeneous assemblage of interactions, discourses, initiatives and ideas translated and stabilised into concrete devices and programmes progressively institutionalising a new discourse of truth and a normative order which is preparing the coming of another academic world. The second part of the book narrates how the human agency is being confronted by this new academic order at the European scale. It shows that epistemic governance of knowledge is being supported by the extension of the new spirit of capitalism into academic spheres and institutions. The global and the local are articulated through the institutionalisation of diverse neo-managerial devices and arrangements which challenge academic professionalism. In addition to an epistemic dimension which profoundly restructures the production of knowledge, as illustrated in the first part of the book, the new spirit of capitalism is based on a moral dimension transforming conceptions of the common good to which the academic tradition was previously linked. The academic is required to reinvent himself or herself, by liberating his or her mind in order to become an expert or an entrepreneur and to fit within new trials structuring his or her existence and relationships with others. But it is also an ontological conversion which has generated an unfortunate experience among some academics which in turn fuels the critique and can lead to opposition and new forms of resistance.

This book is also the first theoretical part of a research project funded by the French National Research Agency and entitled *The new academic condition in the European Higher and Education Research Area*. Some interviews are currently being conducted with European academics in France, Norway, Denmark, Italy, Spain and Portugal. The data is being progressively analysed, and this will provide empirical evidence of some of the views and concepts expressed in the following chapters. To formulate this theoretical approach, we have mainly used the work of sociology of education and political sciences as devolved to higher education. We also read some reports from international organisations such as the OECD and the European Commission. The aim was to build an analytic framework which includes, but without denying the constructivist approach, some reflections regarding the long-term transformations of the academic condition, by restoring historicity and rehabilitating a sociology of knowledge in education focusing on new forms of objectivity and epistemology. We have put on the back burner for the moment statistical data and studies on the academic work as well as a lot of research on the

Bologna process. We have not sought to establish a dialogue with the sociology of work and professions even if Julia Evetts' work was particularly useful for our analyses in the second part. Rather, in the first part of the book, we have focused our outlook on debates and studies on the development of the knowledge-based economy and society. The second part privileges empirical, qualitative and situated research findings on the transformations of the academic work subjected to New Public Management. We have not taken into account changes related to the institutional governance of universities or the penetration of insurance quality mechanisms within organisations. We have also mapped critiques regarding the new spirit of academic capitalism by researchers and activists close to professional associations and trade unions, from students to global activists, but this would have diverted us from our research priorities. Furthermore, the issue of collective and protesting commitments in the European space of education has not been well developed in research, contrary to the literature on institutional actors, and thus there are not many contextualised findings.

We shall now provide a brief outline of the book's chapters.

The first part of the book 'European Politics: Governing Knowledge, Standards and Evidence' describes the restructuring of higher education policies in the area of European education and the manner a new epistemic governance is implemented. Three major changes are particularly highlighted: the transformation in the relationships between educational sciences and policy, the legitimisation of mode 2 in the knowledge production and the transnationalisation of governance technologies, the developments of standards and metrics which impose a certain definition of quality in education and impact on academic activities and the international circulation of evidence-based policy and its instruments which redefine modes of evidence in educational research.

Chapter titled "An Epistemic Governance of European Education" explores the specification of knowledge regimes in different countries under the impact of globalisation as well as the circulation of knowledge-based technologies and their consequences on the emergence of a new epistemic governance in European education. While each country maintains specific organisational and institutional properties, the chapter demonstrates the importance of international networks and travelling policies, mediated by numbers and measurement tools, in the genesis of the European knowledge-based economy which legitimises the power of expertise and a new conception of the relationships between science and policy. This technocratic and neo-liberal turn serves as a political project promoting entrepreneurial university and utilitarian research findings.

In focusing on standardisation and its consequences, chapter "The Politics of Standards and Quality" describes the developments of quality politics narrowly linked to the Europeanisation process which articulate flows, tools and networks through a new mediation between different actors. The building of big data and indicators, as well as standards, serves to enhance the knowledge-based economy and lifelong learning area in Europe. It also reconfigures education systems despite national or local hybridisations and adaptations. The chapter studies the manner those standards and metrics shape new technologies in quality governance which impact on higher education as well as on other European strategy's areas. It questioned the type of human agency created by these standardisation and normalisation processes as well as its limitations or shortcomings.

Chapter "'What Works?' The Shaping of the European Politics of Evidence" explores the way evidence-based policy progressively transform assessment modes in educational research. It focuses on the genesis of this policy at global level, its technologies' dissemination and circulation and also its transfer mechanisms from health to education. This regime of evidence is related to the mode 2 of knowledge production while it legitimises a new experimentalism in welfare policies. In studying this policy's main international actors, and its takeover by the European Commission, it is possible to demonstrate that evidence-based political technologies, despite debates and controversies they have created, are imposed as the gold standard for assessment in public policies. Evidently, it has consequences for the conception for educational research required to produce 'objective', 'useful' and 'rigorous' knowledge for policymakers and practitioners.

The second part of the book titled 'Expertise, Entrepreneurship and Management: The New Spirit of Academic Capitalism' is devoted to transformations induced by European epistemic governance into the academic work as tasks and responsibilities done by academics. Transformations of knowledge production have entailed the development of expertise which influence education policies. Indeed, globalisation effects and the creation of the European area of higher education have some consequences on the regulation of higher education institutions, the coordination of academic activities and relationships between academics. By following up the implementation of management and its impact on the academic work, as well as shifts generated by the new spirit of capitalism, the chapter analyses the gradual shaping of a new *Homo Academicus*.

Chapter, "The Multiple Worlds of Expertise", described different modalities of expertise the academic work is required to produce through a utilitarian and short-term knowledge for decision-making. From a position of insider-researcher, different modes of policy learning linking experts and policymakers have been studied. Far from being a direct and linear process, expertise provided by academics in different European networks is defined through multiple interactions, while knowledge production is related to different socialising experiences. Types of encounters between expertise and policy have different features while expert content itself influences more or less decision-making. However, while the worlds of expertise are plural, they produce and legitimise sciences of government which compete with knowledge produced by the academic world, while other institutions like think tanks and agencies become more influent.

Chapter "The New Spirit of Managerialism" focuses on the effects of European governance technologies on the academic profession. These technologies, whether they concern knowledge production, quality standards or evidence, support the development of a new spirit of academic capitalism which penetrates the academic world through New Public Management. This new managerial regime shifts the trials instituted by the academic tradition by drawing the figures of a new professionalism and promoting two ideal types, the expert and the entrepreneur. These new academic work conventions, elaborated from the criticism addressed to the profession, give rise to trends which undermine the collegial and corporatist model considered as unadjusted to a global world.

These different trials are analysed in chapter "The Making of a New Homo Academicus?". Firstly, the defences of the academic community have been weakened by the development of capitalism and the implementation of governmental and managerial technologies. Secondly, the foundations of the community have been challenged while academic work conditions were deteriorated. The academic institution itself has produced discourses of truth claiming for other legitimised regulations and representations of academic activities. The dismantlement/restructuration of academic community and work has generated a diversity of trials fostered by New Public Management. However, academics have been differently committed in accordance with different principles of justice in which they believe. Far from being univocal, the response of academics to managerialism reveals various arrangements and compromises. Consequently, the criticism addressed to the new spirit of academic capitalism is used to claim new reformist proposals considered as necessary or radical transformations to rebalance power between academics and managers. In any case, these changes question the sense of common good and the conception of agency related to this reformist ideology which reduces *Homo Academicus* to a liberal, calculative and instrumental self and often ignores the diversity of academics' moral commitments and virtues.

References

Alexander, J. C. (1982). *Theoretical logic in sociology, vol.1 positivism presuppositions and current controversies*. London: Routledge.

Bannister, R. C. (1991). *Sociology and scientism: The American quest for objectivity, 1880–1940*. Chapel Hill: UNC Press Books.

Biesta, G. (2007). Why "what works" won't work: Evidence-based practice and the democratic deficit in educational research. *Educational Theory, 57*(1), 1–22.

Boltanski, L., & Chiapello, E. (1999), Le nouvel esprit du capitalisme, Paris, Gallimard.

Callahan, R. E. (1962). *Education and the cult of efficiency: Study of the social forces that have shaped the administration of the public schools*. Chicago: University of Chicago Press.

Campbell, D. T. (1969). Reforms as experiments. *American Psychologist, 24*, 409–429.

Campbell, D. T., & Stanley, J. (1966). *Experimental and quasi-experimental designs for research*. Boston: Houghton Mifflin Company.

Collins, H., & Evans, R. (2002). The third wave of science studies. Studies of expertise and experience. *Social Studies of Science, 32*(2), 235–296.

Collins, H., & Evans, R. (2008). *Rethinking expertise*. Chicago: University of Chicago Press.

Danziger, K. (1994). *Constructing the subject: Historical origins of psychological research*. Cambridge: Cambridge University Press.

Davies, H. T. O., Nutley, S. M., & Smith, P. C. (2007). *What works? Evidence-based policy and practice in public services*. Bristol: The Policy Press.

Dehue, T. (2000). Establishing the experimenting society: The historical origin of social experimentation according to the randomized controlled design. *The American Journal of Psychology, 114*(2), 283–302.

Desrosières, A. (2002). *The politics of large numbers: A history of statistical reasoning*. Cambridge, MA: Harvard University Press.

Evans, K. G. (2000). Reclaiming John Dewey democracy, inquiry, pragmatism, and public management. *Administration & Society, 32*(3), 308–328.

Foucault, M., Burchell, G., Gordon, C., & Miller, P. (Eds.). (1991). *The Foucault effect: Studies in governmentality*. Chicago: University of Chicago Press.

Goodwin, C. D. (1995). The promise of expertise: Walter Lippmann and the policy sciences. *Policy Sciences, 28*(4), 317–345.

Hacking, I. (1990). *The taming of chance* (Vol. 17). Cambridge: Cambridge University Press.

Hammersley, M. (1997). Educational research and teaching: A response to David Hargreaves' TTA lecture. *British Educational Research Journal, 23*(2), 141–161.

Hammersley, M. (Ed.). (2002). *Educational research, policymaking and practice*. London: Sage, Paul Chapman.

Hammersley, M. (2005). Is the evidence-based practice movement doing more good than harm? Reflections on Iain Chalmers' case for research-based policy making and practice. *Evidence & Policy: A Journal of Research, Debate and Practice, 1*(1), 85–100.

Hargreaves, D. H. (1997). In defence of research for evidence-based teaching: A rejoinder to. *British Educational Research Journal, 23*(4), 405–419.

Haynes, L., Service, D., Goldacre, B., & Torgerson, D. (2012). *Test, learn, adapt: Developing public policy with randomised controlled trials*. London: Cabinet Office.

Jasanoff, S. (1996). Beyond epistemology: Relativism and engagement in the politics of science. *Social Studies of Science, 26*(2), 393–418.

Jasanoff, S. (2003a). Breaking the waves in science studies. Comment on Collins & Evans: "The third wave of science studies". *Social Studies of Science, 33*, 389–400.

Jasanoff, S. (2003b). (No?) Accounting for expertise. *Science and Public Policy, 30*(3), 157–162.

Jasanoff, S. (2003c). Technologies of humility: Citizen participation in governing science. *Minerva, 41*(3), 223–244.

Knorr-Cetina, K. K. (2007). Culture in global knowledge societies: Knowledge cultures and epistemic cultures. *Interdisciplinary Science Reviews, 32*(4), 361–375.

Latour, B., & Woolgar, S. (2013). *Laboratory life: The construction of scientific facts*. Princeton: Princeton University Press.

Law, J. (1992). Notes on the theory of the actor-network: Ordering, strategy and heterogeneity. *Systems Practice, 5*(1992), 379–393.

Lingard, B. (2013). The impact of research on education policy in an era of evidence-based policy. *Critical Studies in Education, 54*(2), 113–131.

Maassen, S., & Weingart, P. (Eds.). (2006). *Democratization of expertise?: Exploring novel forms of scientific advice in political decision-making* (Vol. 24). Dordrecht: Springer Science & Business Media.

Majone, G. (1989). *Evidence, argument, and persuasion in the policy process*. New Haven: Yale University Press.

McCall, W. A. (1923). *How to experiment in education*. New York: Macmillan.

Popkewitz, T. S. (1997). A changing terrain of knowledge and power: A social epistemology of educational research. *Educational Researcher, 26*(9), 18–29.

Popkewitz, T. S. (1999). A social epistemology of educational research. In *Critical theories in education: Changing terrains of knowledge and politics* (pp. 17–42). New York/London: Routledge.

Popkewitz, T. S., & Brennan, M. (1997). Restructuring of social and political theory in education: Foucault and a social epistemology of school practices. *Educational Theory, 47*(3), 287–313.

Porter, T. M. (1992). Objectivity as standardization: The rhetoric of impersonality in measurement, statistics, and cost-benefit analysis. *Annals of Scholarship, 9*(1/2), 19–59.

Porter, T. M. (1995). *Trust in numbers. The pursuit of objectivity in science and public life*. Princeton: Princeton University Press.

Rose, N., & Miller, P. (1992). Political power beyond the state: Problematics of government. *British Journal of Sociology, 43*, 173–205.

Ross, D. (Ed.). (1992). *The origins of American social science* (Vol. 19). Cambridge: Cambridge University Press.

Smith, P. C., Davies, H. T., & Nutley, S. M. (2000). *What works?: Evidence-based policy and practice in public services*. Bristol: Policy.

Steiner-Khamsi, G. (2013). What is wrong with the 'What-Went-Right' approach in educational policy? *European Educational Research Journal, 12*(1), 20–33.

Stone, D. (1997). *Policy paradox: The art of political decision making* (p. 138). New York: WW Norton.

Tyack, D., & Hansot, H. (1982). *Managers of virtue: Public school leadership in America, 1820–1980*. New York: Basic Books.

Weingart, P. (1999). Scientific expertise and political accountability: Paradoxes of science in politics. *Science and Public Policy, 26*(3), 151–161.

Weingart, P. (2008). How robust is "socially robust knowledge"? In M. Carrier, D. Howard, & J. Kourany (Eds.), *The challenge of the social and the pressure of practice: Science and values revisited* (pp. 131–145). Pittsburgh: University of Pittsburgh Press.

Weiss, C. (1979). The many meanings of research utilization. *Public Administration Review, 39*(5), 426–431.

Westhoff, L. M. (1995). The popularization of knowledge: John Dewey on experts and American democracy. *History of Education Quarterly, 35*, 27–47.

Whitty, G. (2006). Education (al) research and education policy making: Is conflict inevitable? *British Educational Research Journal, 32*(2), 159–176.

Wynne, B. (2003). Seasick on the third wave? Subverting the hegemony of propositionalism: Response to Collins & Evans (2002). *Social Studies of Science, 33*, 401–417.

Part I
European Politics: Governing Knowledge, Standards and Evidence

An Epistemic Governance of European Education

Introduction

In this chapter, we intend to characterise a new epistemic governance redefining the relationships between science and policy in the field of education. It is supported by a new approach in the production of knowledge distancing itself from the academic tradition and shifting the boundaries between research and expertise, scholars and laypersons, public and private, universities and business. This new regime of knowledge is being disseminated worldwide under the action of international organisations, via their programmes and reports, which regularly address recommendations for countries to transform their modes of intervention towards the scientific community.

Without ignoring the specificity of national regimes of knowledge, according to some path dependency and hybridisation revealed by certain researchers, we will demonstrate in this book, by focusing our analysis mainly on the European Higher Education and Research Area, that national models of knowledge production are influenced by the internationalisation of expertise and its dissemination among policymakers. The research produced on both global expert networks and knowledge transfer and policy borrowing has relativised the idea of the autonomy and self-determination of states in their guidance of knowledge policies. But the maintenance of the state as a central player in many European countries undermines the idea that knowledge will be progressively challenged by marketisation and privatisation.

While international organisations are taking a technocratic turn, it is also important to study new standards framing and regulating knowledge according to a variety of new principles. This modernising reformism outlines a new architecture having progressively effects on the way educational research is viewed in its relations to economy and society. Beyond the globalisation movement, it is defining a policy of quality and evidence that is likely to have an impact as much on research types and contents as on academic work.

© Springer International Publishing Switzerland 2016   23
R. Normand, *The Changing Epistemic Governance of European Education*,
Educational Governance Research 3, DOI 10.1007/978-3-319-31776-2_2

We shall begin by discussing the relevance of institutionalism in its approach of knowledge regimes by showing that this kind of analysis ignores the epistemic conditions of knowledge-based policy but also the role of instruments and institutional isomorphism. Then, we shall take the example of PISA, which is largely disputed at the European level, to characterise the international circulation of knowledge at the crossroads of expertise and politics, by focusing on the link between national and international levels but also by underlying the processes of neutralisation and depoliticisation/repoliticisation of this instrument in the public debate. We shall then show how this transnationalisation of an international regime of knowledge is perceptible in the standards and recommendations addressed to educational research by international organisations particularly the OECD. It shall lead to the analysis of a particular configuration: the institutionalisation of mode 2 of knowledge production in the European strategy for lifelong learning. Some assumptions shall be formulated in relation to the introduction and impact of this new regime on the valuing of the entrepreneurial model of the European university. In conclusion, we shall present the conceptual framework enabling us to specify the features of an epistemic governance.

Globalisation and Regimes of Knowledge

To characterise different knowledge regimes, as data, research, theories and political recommendations, influencing policymaking, it is possible to resume the typology of Campbell and Pederson who describe different modes or organisations and actors in countries (Campbell and Pederson 2011). It is useful to define knowledge regimes in education policies and to specify the types and scales of governance in the perspective of globalisation. If the authors recognise that knowledge regimes are historically transformed to share common analytical practices, particularly databanks, econometric methodologies and forecasting models, via dissemination and increased use of the Internet, with some effects on the recommendations addressed to policymakers, they rescue the idea that there is a convergence of national regimes of knowledge according to a neo-liberal logic. For them, each regime maintains some specific institutional and organisational proprieties which distinguish each country from another.

It seems that this way of defining the debate between the convergence and hybridisation of national models, as often found in the sociology of education, is based on hypotheses which tend to underestimate the position of epistemic knowledge and the role of instruments and technologies in governance while it fixes knowledge regimes in a national framework in the assumption that the state is the central actor of these policies. In the following pages, we will propose an alternative way of thinking even though we are aware that in social sciences this debate is far for being closed. Before that, we would like to specify the interest and limitations of Campbell and Pederson's typology from three specific cases we have studied in our previous research (the USA, the UK and France). We are discarding the case of

Germany, which we also studied, because we do not have sufficient knowledge and background information.

Knowledge Regimes in Three Countries

In terms of education policy, it is possible to make the distinction, as the authors suggest, between liberal market economies, as in the USA and the UK, in which the market has an influence on education systems according to a principle of competition, and coordination market economies such as Germany and France, where education policies break free from the market logic to be defined by informal networks (interest groups), formal and corporatist negotiations (trade unions), associations (parents) and different forms of state interventions and regulations (curriculum, assessment, training, etc.) according to a logic of institutional cooperation. Centralised and closed states, as it is the case for France, make their decisions from a relative isolation with regard to the external influence of civil society. These states, in which the central government has an important role, are supported by an extensive civil service and professional bureaucracy. At the opposite end, decentralised and open states, such as the USA, are more open to an external influence, while the political authority is shared or delegated at low levels of governance (decentralisation) and the civil service has a less of a presence.

As explained by the typology, this type of organisation, particularly the position of the state and the market, has an impact on the type of policymaking which structures research and expertise activities. We agree with Campbell and Pederson when they relativise the assumptions that there is a marketisation of knowledge and research which is valuable for English-speaking countries but less relevant for a number of West European countries. Indeed we are of the same opinion as the authors when they make the distinction between the public and private interests which shape research entities and their aims.[1] There are academic-style scholarly research entities, linked to universities, including researchers, which depend on public funds and publish books and articles for the academic world. Secondly, there are advocacy research entities which are funded on a private basis while adopting a political and partisan stance. They disseminate the research findings and expertise of others through policy briefs or in the media in order to influence the ideological climate and the political debate. Thirdly, some political party-focused research entities provide expert advice to members of parties and sometimes belong to the party's apparatus. The last category corresponds to state research entities which are directly affiliated to a ministry or a ministerial department or which are an ad hoc creation by the government.

---

[1] Contrary to them, we use the word "research entities" instead of "research units" to avoid any confusion about the tasks achieved in some of these institutions outside of academia, which are often more expertise than research.

When the position of both the state and the market in education policies is combined with the type of organisations which govern research and expertise in the production of knowledge, it is possible to distinguish different configurations among countries. The USA is characterised by a liberal market economy with decentralised and open states. In education as in other sectors, business is organised and influent, while trade unions are weak at national and federal levels compared to European countries. The decentralisation of political power, combined with the separation between legislative and executive branches, along with a less-developed civil service, reflects a particular knowledge regime. If research entities are numerous, particularly in the city of Washington, the presence of such philanthropy organisations as the Carnegie Foundation, the Hoover Institution or the Brookings Institution is strong. Their aims were originally to rationalise policymaking but not to influence the political agenda. But after the Second World War, a second generation of scholarly research entities such as the RAND Corporation or other university-based research institutes was set up and contracted by the federal government to develop or participate in major programmes, particularly in compensatory education and the fight against poverty (Stone et al. 1998). During the 1970s, a generation of advocacy research entities was developed by conservatives such as the Heritage Foundation, the Cato Institute and the Manhattan Institute and enters into competition against liberal organisations such as the Institute for Policy Studies. This led to an ideological war and a spirit of revenge from the conservatives in the field of education (Apple 2006). These institutions were active as interest groups putting pressure on policymakers to implement policies compatible with their religious and ideological beliefs.

In the USA, there are no political party-focused research entities but state research units such as the General Accounting Office, the Congressional Budget Office (CBO), the Congressional Research Service (CRS) and the Office of Management and Budget (OMB) which play an important role in the promotion of accountability policies. Some agencies, such as the National Science Foundation and the Office of Educational Research and Improvement, have influence with regard to the direction of research programmes and the development of evidence-based policies. On the one hand, the regime of knowledge in US education is dominated by the scholarly and advocacy research entities, in a competitive market in which ideas compete to attract the attention of policymakers and the media and to influence public opinion. On the other hand, it is supported by the development of evidence-based policy with the creation of the Institute of Educational Sciences, linked to the federal government, which develops experimental approaches and randomised controlled trials (RCTs) and gives recommendations to research and policymaking (see chapter "'What works?' The Shaping of the European Politics of Evidence").

The UK is a liberal market economy with a centralised and closed state. The party in power controls the two executive and legislative branches, and it is supported by an extensive, professional and permanent civil service. Contrary to US federalism, the power of the state is centralised, and policymaking is ensured by the prime minister's cabinet and the civil service. Scholarly research entities are smaller and funded with public funds. Historically, advocacy research entities such as the

Fabian Society are close to the Labour Party or, in the case of the society of the Mont Pélerin, are close to conservatives (Mirowski and Plehwe 2009). From the 1970s onwards, more advocacy research entities emerged under the influence of the latter such as the Centre for Policy Studies and the Adam Smith Institute which was founded in 1974 by Sir Keith Joseph and Margaret Thatcher to support, in particular, their claims regarding education reforms (Denham and Garnett 1998, 2004; Stone 1996; Chitty 1989). At the end of the 1980s, the Left reacted by creating the Institute for Public Policy Research (IPPR) and Demos to reverse the intellectual domination of the Right while advancing reformist educative proposals.

Advocacy research entities now represent a large proportion of research entities in the UK, but, compared to the USA, they have less staff and funding even if they have extended their influence (Ball 2012). The UK also has a lot of state research entities because of less private funding and the weight of the state and the civil service in public policies. The culture of public service, present among the elite of high-rank civil servants, and the principle of neutrality within Whitehall maintain a certain distance from the expertise provided by external policy institutes. The centralisation of policymaking provides only some opportunity windows to advocacy research entities, while the possibilities of direct access to the state are limited, even if the UK, like the USA, has become a competitive market for ideas. The creation of agencies, think tanks and other research institutes has deeply restructured the landscape of academic knowledge production, while academics have been strongly subjected to a narrow regime of quality assessment. In education, some programmes like the Teaching and Learning Research Programme (TLRP) or the creation of the Evidence-Based Policy and Practice Initiative Centre at the London Institute of Education had a significant impact on the definition of criteria for the quality of research and evidence.

Between 1999 and 2009, the TLRP ensured the coordination of more than 700 researchers and 70 project teams through an important thematic programme covering the main areas of teaching and learning (Pollard 2010). Based on the creation of new research centres and the National Educational Research Forum (NERF), while it had a major public funding, it irrigated much of the UK educational research for one decade. The objective was to increase the role of users, policymakers and practitioners, but also to make theoretical and innovative advancements for a 'comprehensive pedagogy'. This programme was at the core of an important dispute among the educational research community while it proposed to generate independent evidence for the public debate and decision-making processes. By claiming the raise of research quality and by meeting the objectives set up by the Economic Social and Research Council and the Higher Education Funding Council, this policy was a new orientation for the relationships between research and policy, and it sought to promote mixed methods, cross-sectorial analyses and also interdisciplinary devices and evidence-based technologies. The programme aimed to develop research involving users, more 'interactive, iterative, constructive, distributed and transformative'. If all types of research were encouraged, we focus primarily on those informing policy and practice and enabling the delivery of material and cognitive resources to practitioners in terms of 'capacity building' while expertise in quantitative methods was strengthened. The creation of the Strategic Forum for Research in Education, replacing NERF, was a means to gather practitioners, policymakers and researchers during several days in accordance with a 'knowledge management system' model which has been taken over and adopted by the OECD Centre for Research and Innovation (CERI) to work on the assessments of national systems.

Compared to the USA and the UK, France is an example of a coordinated market economy with a centralised and closed state. As an heir to the planning system, the state is involved in formal consultations with the representatives of the worlds of labour and business. Governance is relatively statist and built upon a corporatist compromise. This is true in education where trade unions occupy a major position but the whole education system itself maintains a strong mistrust against business. Policymaking is dependent on the national government which seeks to maintain interest groups at a distance while it is supported by a bureaucratic, permanent and extensive public service (Derouet and Normand 2010). A lot of research programs and political analyses are led by state research entities: some national institutes like National Institute of Statistics and Economic Studies (INSEE) or National Institute of Demographic Studies (INED) or National Institute of Health and Medical Research (INSERM) play an important role in the production of social, economic and political quantitative data. In education, the Directorate of Evaluation, Forecasting and Performance (DEPP) regularly produces data on the education system while it contributes to policymaking and to the attachment of policymakers to quantitative data. However, each ministry has it owns cabinet and expert team including high-ranking civil servants and academics. These cabinets have a great influence on the elaboration of policymaking and agenda setting even if the techno structure of ministries is an important filter. Future policymakers are often recruited from the general inspectorate. The knowledge regime is supported by a network of scholarly research entities which belong to the National Centre for Scientific Research (CNRS). However, educational sciences have no recognition and legitimacy within the CNRS. Political party-focused research units correspond to clubs gathering expert groups, researchers and political advisers. Affiliated to political parties, they tend to be in competition with think tanks like Terra Nova for the Left and the Foundation for Political Innovation for the Right.

During the 2000s, several reports and initiatives sought to develop a coherent programme for educational research, but these attempts failed. Published in 2001, the report of Antoine Prost, a famous historian in education close to the Socialist Party circles, proposed a 15-year national strategic programme for educational research from his own review of the existing situation. The aim was to 'propose measures which, in strengthening the scientific coherence of educational research, bring them to better answer to the both expectations of the institution and its actors'. The report drew a state of the educational research and current surveys. It showed that research findings were less used because research projects were insufficiently coordinated and assessed. The second part of the report, titled 'Required Efforts', underlined the areas of educational research which were not much investigated as learning at the primary school, violence and its management in schools and in teaching practices, effects of decentralisation and positive discrimination policies as well as teacher training and professionalism. Antoine Prost suggested to design a 'strategic programme' for 15 years with a consequent budget and the creation of a steering committee.

This steering committee appeared with the creation of the Programme Incitatif de Recherche en Education et Formation (PIREF – Incentive Programme for Research in Education and Training). The PIREF was created by the minister of education in 2001 to develop and renew interdisciplinary research perspectives in education and training. It had to translate strategic stakes in education and training systems into research issues and to elaborate long-term work programmes. The aim was also to mobilise disciplines treating education, training and learning issues and to create a scientific and public space of debate open to international exchanges. The PIREF had to ensure a mission of coordination of public research in education, to facilitate partnerships with the state and public authorities, to participate in the definition of calls for tender and to contribute to the restructuring of educational research by facilitating its inclusion globally. It had to support the young researchers' training and to develop networking research teams leading studies on precise topics and to disseminate research findings. But after few calls were launched and a few conferences of consensus organised, this programme was deleted by the succeeding minister.

This extension of advocacy research entities which are close to political parties has developed since the middle of 1990s, even if is less important than in the USA and the UK, and has been increasingly influential in public debate and policymaking in education as well as other sectors. However, the culture of public service shared by policymakers and the internal expertise of the state limits the use of research entities in civil society. The parliament itself, contrary to the USA, is not really on the lookout for independent expertise. There is therefore not much link between educational research and policymaking. However, for the past few decades, the French Institute of Education has maintained strong links with the Ministry of Education though its capacity of action has diminished during the last years due to the progressive withdrawal of state funding. The INSEE, the Paris School of Economics (a similar institution to the LSE) and Sciences Po are the preferred institutions for the assessment of education policies, particularly for randomised controlled trials. Even if the development of agencies such as the Agency for the Evaluation of Higher Education and Research (AERES) and the National Research Agency (ANR) can be observed in the evaluation and funding of research, the government prefers more often than not to rely on High Councils or High Authorities who are more dependent on the State (High Council of Evaluation of the School System, High Council of Education, National Council for the Evaluation of the School System, etc.). The absence of private philanthropy and the hostility of policymakers to market forces, and also business' lack of interest in humanities and social sciences, explain why the knowledge regime is dominated by state research entities and scholarly research entities strongly linked to the state. This regime is not only statist and technocratic but strongly elitist and concentrated in Paris where experts, researchers and intellectuals provide most of the advice to policymakers, sometimes via personal connections related to their belonging to political parties and free masonry.

So, in terms of governance of knowledge, the USA, the UK and France have some specific features. The USA is characterised by an important private funding of their research activities, particularly through foundations, and public funding is ensured partly by agencies which represent the federal government. However, some contracts are also passed with local and state authorities, or some stakeholders in districts and national states. In the UK, the state continues to be the main funder of public research, but its action is increasingly shared with private funders (charity organisations, foundations, think tanks, business, etc.). In France, funding mainly comes from the state and private funding is marginal. This distinction between the three countries is also true for the sources of research and expert knowledge: it comes from a great variety of actors and institutions in the USA, and the UK is more monopolistic, while it comes mainly from state organisations in the French case.

Comparing Knowledge Regimes: Historical Isomorphism

Does this specificity of national knowledge regimes flows against the idea that these regimes are interdependent in the context of globalisation, as it is assumed by Campbell and Pederson? Is it possible to conclude that each country has its own path dependency and that there is no convergence? While his work is criticised by the authors because they accuse him of a lack of evidence, the research of John Meyer, one of the leaders of institutionalism theory, sheds light on some aspects not taken into account by Campbell and Pederson. As Meyer and his colleagues wrote, the enactment of global models creates considerable institutional similarity among different situated states. They shape nation–state identities, structures and behaviour via worldwide cultural and associational processes (Meyer et al. 1997). States are not only responsive to local, cultural, functional or power processes but structured by the world-cultural order consisting of model-defining agents (e.g. nation–states, individuals), purposes (e.g. development, progress) and principles (e.g. human rights, justice). These cultural elements are not sufficiently described by Campbell and Pederson. For Meyer, four main elements contribute to implementing the tenets of this order: international government organisations, particularly those in the UN system; nation–states which copy them, thus leading to their diffusion; voluntary associations in many different fields, some operating as social movements; and scientists and professionals, as experts whose own authority derives from world-cultural principles. And Meyer adds that, because of the highly rationalised and universalistic world culture, nation–states invariably present themselves as rationalised actors and claim the key features of rational state actors – territory, sovereign authority and so on. World culture exerts pressure towards isomorphism and its institutionalisation leads to structural similarity. Thus, nation–states adopt similar constitutional forms, public education systems, policies on women's rights and the environment, etc.

Developing his ideas about education, Meyer writes that much modern comparative research in the sociology of education has noted the striking tendency of the world's educational systems to reflect common models of enrolment, curriculum and organisation. He sees education an excellent instance of the globalising processes. Curricular changes occur around the world and rapidly are copied by others as demonstrated by the reforms in science and mathematics education. The expanded enrolment of women in all parts of the world is another example. Organisational structures parallel each other (university reforms or decentralisation). Primary education is almost universal, and secondary education (even in poor countries) moves in the same direction as each individual in the world is to be taught the general principles of global society.

We shall now take some historical and current examples from our own research on international measurement policies and shall carry out comparisons between the three countries to illustrate and confirm Meyer's statements. The Societies for the Child Study created by Stanley Hall in the USA at the end of the nineteenth century, which inspired the development of the psychological studies of childhood, inspired the creation of the French Société Libre pour l'Etude Expérimentale de l'Enfance [Free Society for the Experimental Study of Childhood] (or SLEPE) in which Ferdinand Buisson (founder of the republican school system), Emile Durkheim (founder of the French educational sciences and sociology of education) and Alfred Binet (inventor of the intelligence tests) all had an important role while the French society was multiplying studies on young students (Normand 2013). SLEPE research interested characters who belonged to three social movements: the first one in favour of the development of hygiene in public schools, the second one concerned with the protection of childhood in 'moral danger' and the third one gathering alienists and physicians specialised in abnormal childhood.

The first works in the SLEPE were to establish a state of the children moral sense and to draw a typology of his qualities and defaults in order to reach a scientific knowledge of children behaviours and aptitudes. Surveys were divided in the study of defaults (anger, lie and indiscipline), qualities (the best action, probity) and social sanctions (blames and rewards). While the SLEPE members avoided ideological conflicts, they did not agree about methods and experimentation used by Binet. The society was split in two camps: those, close to Buisson, who were pedagogues eager to provide a good moral teaching to pupils and others, more psychologists, concerned about the objective knowledge on the child. A tension remained between the moralising inclination of the former and the scientific concerns of the latter. During the first years of the society, the moralising tendency predominates. It was supported by Buisson and Durkheim who sought ways to improve pupil behaviour in schools. This group was also eager to review the results obtained by teaching morals in the primary school system. It explains why Buisson had asked Binet to study three child defaults (anger, lie and indiscipline). But Binet was reluctant to draw general conclusions on children morality. For him, moral qualities could not meet the requirements of scientific objectivisation because of the impossibility to implement experimentation. His election at the presidency of the society helped him to move towards this experimental approach. He created working commissions on topics compatible with the experimental approach: abnormal children, individual aptitudes, physical education, memory, moral feelings and graphology. Then, he found the metric scale of intelligence which ensured his fame and served to develop intelligent tests in the USA.

In the field of social sciences, the Rockefeller Foundation had a significant role in the creation of the London School of Economics and Political Science which led English research in the 1930s and resumed US hereditarianism, while the Ford Foundation funded the creation of the French House of Social Sciences (Maison des Sciences de l'Homme) in Paris, the most prestigious institution in this field of research, with the effect of challenging Marxism on its own ground (Darhendorf 1995; Mazon 1988). The Memorial Laura Spelman Fund at the foundation of the London School of Economics and Political Science wanted to subsidise other research centres in Europe and to develop a new generation of young researchers in France. According to the Rockefeller Foundation, which had studied the French context, the intellectual production was rich but relatively scattered: the whole social sciences lacked of resources and coordination. The leaders of the foundation accepted to engage two projects they judged promising: those of Charles Rist, economist, and Marcel Mauss, anthropologist. Charles Rist, who had addressed a report on the state of social sciences, had suggested the creation of an institute of social and economic sciences. The foundation helped him to achieve this project by giving him financial and juridical autonomy from the French University with the support of business funds. The project proposed by Mauss appeared too undefined for the American leaders (Mazon 1988, pp. 45–50). Furthermore, they were very suspicious of Mauss' academic value and socialist commitment, a suspicion maintained by Charles Rist. In 1931, in face of the relative wait-and-see attitudes of the US foundation, the anthropologist proposed the creation of a new thematic section in the area of sociology, political sciences, law and social history at the Ecole Pratique des Hautes Etudes. Because of a change in the majority at the French parliament, Mauss expected that his leftist political supports would help him to concretise this ambitious project. But his insistence reinforced the scepticism of the US leaders towards him. At the end, the Rockefeller Foundation decided to grant the Institute of Comparative Law at the Paris Faculty of Law, the Institute of Ethnology where Lucien Levy-Bruhl and Marcel Mauss were working, and the Documentation Centre managed by Celestin Bouglé, a sociologist also close to Durkheim who had already got in touch with Charles Merriam (the representative of the Foundation) in Paris. The topics and methodologies privileged by the foundation progressively influence French research in social sciences. Granted studies became more methodical and they established new traditions and empirical methods, particularly experimental ones. French academics unreservedly welcome US grants while for the first time money was available to achieve surveys, missions on the field and collective research programmes. Celestin Bouglé was pleased of the orientation of different works enabling to develop and organise social sciences in the trend wished by his 'US friends'. Then, sociological studies were more and more marked by the priority given to the experimental study of facts in accordance with a conception of 'inductive' sociology.

At the beginning of the 1980s, because of a lot of criticisms and the economic crisis, the planning system slowly designed by the OECD has appeared less adjusted. Then, the USA has exercised a strong pressure to obtain that quality becomes the priority objective in the programmes devolved by the international organisation to education (Henry et al. 2001, pp. 61–82). The definition of quality became the subject of virulent debates between the Member States' representatives. The camp of conservatives, including the UK and USA, wished to strengthen assessments of students and teachers in accordance with the accountability policies they had already implemented in their education systems. Opponents, Scandinavians at the exception of Sweden, defended the idea that educational objectives could not be all quantifiable and that tests could not have an excessive role at the detriment of other learning aspects. Despite these divergences, while France stood in full solidarity with US claims, ministers of education ended up with an agreement stipulating that the quality would be one of the priorities in the OECD agenda. Since, the organisation has sought to clarify this notion of quality while it has developed a reflexion on indicators. An ambitious project for designing international indicators in education has pursued existing international comparisons but also guided the Member States' education policies (Henry et al. 2001, pp. 83–105). However, the US National Centre for Education Statistics has played an action role beside the international organisation to implement this project aiming to improve education systems' effectiveness and equity (Bottani and Tuijnman 1994).

The INES project has developed a system of international comparative indicators, to facilitate the cooperation and exchanges of information between policymakers and to promote the methodologies for assessing effectiveness and equity (Hutmacher et al. 2001). It has been implemented through three main networks:

The first network (network A), led by the USA, had the mission of developing measurement indicators in learning to feed OECD publications and to adapt them to new international comparative data (shift from the TIMSS survey to the PISA survey). It also has participated in the PISA programme. The network gathered experts in the area of educational sociology and psychology. It aimed at creating measurement of student self-learning, developing assessment framework for the 'analytical problem-solving', exploring assessment possibilities in the area of ICTs and improving the presentation and dissemination of indicators in the context of PISA.

The second network (network B) led by Sweden had to design social and economic indicators of results: gathering Eurostat and Cedefop representatives, this network had already built many indicators for the publication Education at a Glance. It was focused on further training, transition from school to employment, social and human capital and equity. It had also to reflect on measurements for the participation of adults in education and further training and dropouts, and it was involved with Eurostat in the development of a system of collecting statistical data at European level.

The last one (network C), led by the Netherlands, was devolved to indicators of structures and processes: it had conceived indicators and the features and processes of schooling by mobilising 35 Member States and UNESCO representatives. He has focused on indicators related to teachers (work time, instruction time, salaries, sex, age, etc.), while it has collected data on learning and school organisations. It has been also in charge of examining means to improve indicators on teachers and teaching practices. The leading team of the network C, beginning its activities in 1989, has worked firstly within the French ministry of education before joining (in 1992) the Centre for Applied Research in Education at the University of Twente (Netherlands). Since 1992, the OECD has published several series of Education at a Glance to guide education policies in Member States and to provide a basis for international comparisons of the education systems' effectiveness and quality. After this project has been launched, France was at the initiative in 1995 of the creation of the European network of educational policymakers for the assessment of education systems with the aim to discuss methodologies and content of international comparisons as well as national evaluations conducted in each country. But this project has failed because of the lack of recognition by the European authorities.

The INES project launched in France, at Poitiers, with the support of the French Ministry of Education, the US Federal Department of Education and the OECD Centre for Research and Innovation, structured for several years the building of international indicators guiding education policies at the international level. The value-added indicators for schools and Education Priority Areas in France were copied from the British example (Henry et al. 2001; Normand 2011). The US theory of human capital was largely disseminated by nearby researchers and policymakers in France and in the UK before structuring the European Expert Network on Economics of Education (EENEE) which presented itself as a think tank advising the European Commission which had created it for this purpose. The policy of basic skills adopted in the USA after the *A Nation at Risk* (1983) report was adopted at the same time in England but only in 2005 in France entailing the development of educational research on literacy and numeracy.

From these few examples, it is easy to understand that the production of knowledge related to endogenous but also exogenous factors overthrows the role of the state and corresponds to an international circulation which itself is the result of scientific, political and social movements guiding the fabrication of sciences and their relationships to the state. It is therefore important to reflect on the limitations caused by the comparison and juxtaposition of national case studies, particularly when they ignore this epistemic background in their study of the relationship between science and policy/politics. Moreover, the analysis of relations between the knowledge economy and education at the global level requires the recognition of different scales of governance (Dale 1999; Rizvi and Lingard 2010). But often, nation–states and their boundaries are considered as natural containers of societies and the adjusted unit for analysis in social sciences. It is particularly true for comparative education which develops case studies focused on a national education system while the comparison is implicitly built from within its own system.

As Roger Dale explains, these features of methodological nationalism are important in understanding and overcoming this form of comparativism. The study of comparative 'national' 'education' 'systems' has many consequences for the area of study, both methodological and 'political'. The risk is to ossify, restrict and even obstruct opportunities to analyse globalisation and the ways in which institutional and everyday life has been transformed (Dale and Robertson 2009). Researchers are confronted not just with methodological nationalism but with methodological statism and educationism. Then, objects of comparison become fixed, abstract and absolute in a nominal continuity provided by the same concepts as if globalisation could be refracted through the lenses of unproblematic conceptions of nation–states and education systems. The most widely recognised of the 'isms' is methodological nationalism because the nation–state has been for long at the core of comparative education. Methodological nationalism sees the nation–state as the container of 'society' and based comparison on the national level from which statistics have been gathered. It considers also that the national is affected by or mediated the global and provides a particular imaginary of the rules related to 'sovereignty', 'territoriality' and 'authority'. Methodological statism refers to the tendency to assume that there is a particular form intrinsic to all states. All polities would be ruled, organised and administered in essentially the same way, with the same set of problems and responsibilities and through the same set of institutions. The model of the state becomes taken for granted in academic discourse while it shows extreme variations in developing countries. The state is considered vertically above civil society, community and family or to the contrary fused with the nation. Finally, 'educationism' refers to the tendency to regard 'education' as a single category for purposes of analysis, with an assumed common scope, and a set of implicitly shared knowledge, practices and assumptions. It occurs when education is treated as abstract, fixed, absolute, ahistorical and universal, when no distinctions are made between its use to describe purpose, process, practice and outcomes.

The 'transnational' (across nations) and 'international' (between nations) conceptions are often used in comparative education in assuming the national level as the basis of social, political and economic activities. Comparatively, the concept of 'supranational' (beyond nations) characterises a separated non-reducible level to the national scale. This non-reduction of education policies to the activities of the nation–state establishes an essential qualitative difference as illustrated by Europe. Indeed, the European Union represents a distinct scale of political activities irreducible to the interests of Member States. However, methodological nationalism, as it is the case in France, considers that the national scale is predominant by using statistical descriptions and theories of development which refer to the building of the national as an entity and by assuming that the state is the mediator of globalisation. In fact, it impedes the analysis of other activities; structures and processes which operate at different subnational, international, transnational and global scales. The homogenisation of nation–states and the levelling out of divisions and distinctions are particularly noticeable in comparative studies when they compare education policies by linguistic blocs (with regard to the French-speaking world) or when they consider each country as a homogeneous entity while at the same time forgetting internal institutional, cultural and linguistic divides (e.g. in Canada, Belgium and Switzerland).

National statism, strongly present in France, assumes that the state is the main source of governmental activities and ignores the games and relations of power exercised at other levels. An alternative approach is to focus on governance instead of the state, e.g. the division of labour decomposed into a series of activities which do not all belong to the state but correspond to different scales of governance. The main question then becomes: what are the new forms of implemented governance (the coordination of coordination) and what is the specific role of the state in this coordination? To illustrate this conception, it is interesting to consider the travelling politics of PISA and the international survey designed by the OECD and broadly disseminated worldwide.

Policy Networks and Travelling Politics of PISA

Studies led by such international organisations as the PISA programme and the building of the corresponding European indicators and benchmarks clearly illustrate the new relationship between knowledge and policy (Novoa 2014). They contribute strongly in determining the conclusions and recommendations addressed to states and in restructuring political debates and national agendas while producing a normative vision of education systems by disseminating the ideas of effectiveness, quality and accountability and making the discourse about performance a global assumption. The internationalisation of education policies leads to the dissemination of international knowledge with the same standards applied in different places and placing countries in a narrow system of surveillance and mutual adjustment (see chapter "The Politics of Standards and Quality"). According to Antonio Novoa, the conception of governance promoted by the European Union attempts to compensate the disenchantment created by the democratic deficit by the implementation of benchmarks, standards and guidelines in the assumption of sharing best practices between Member States. Benchmarking has become the main tool of this governance, while the search for data becomes an objective per se as if indicators and targets alone can assess best practices and the progress of states confronted with objectives which are difficult to achieve and constantly postponed in the European agenda.

Comparative Knowledge from PISA

In this European and global governance of education, data have taken a considerable place. PISA is one of the best examples of this international circulation and of the creation of a common calculation space between states (Meyer and Benavot 2013; Waldow 2013). We will look at it in more depth in chapter "The Politics of

Standards and Quality". We are going to take PISA as the guiding thread of our analysis of this international circulation of knowledge and the global political networks which support it. As Luis Miguel Carvalho (2014) wrote, PISA is part of a long-term movement towards the institutionalisation of a form of comparative knowledge and in building a scenario for knowledge–policy relationships. It reshapes the knowledge tradition of comparative education by building indicators for decision-making. In processing its own data, the OECD has acquired capacities in transnational governance in education and can claim to be the provider of an expert-based independent framework for the monitoring and steering of school systems. The programme incorporates and disseminates ways of thinking–doing that are intended to enable policymakers to naturally take part in monitoring and mutual surveillance exercises. PISA is also a complex of activities involving multiple social worlds (public and private centres, experts, OECD professionals, policymakers, civil servants and technicians from multiple countries) as well as those which are indirectly involved: the media and national politicians. In bringing together those actors through an organised flow of activities and in producing inquiry-related activities, it develops effective associations in support of the production, dissemination and use of its own knowledge-related materials.

At the country level, PISA is also supported by accountability systems which develop assessment tests and have transformed inspection regimes in Europe (Ozga et al. 2011). These assessment and calculative methods are strongly linked to the production of this international data by executives and policymakers. The role of experts and expertise is central while they are mobile and employed by different political and research institutions (Grek 2012). Relatively invisible, even if they are present at different stages of the process, they guarantee evidence for policy and legitimise the production of knowledge. Through 'technicisation' and 'depoliticisation' of educative problems, knowledge becomes a policy in which expertise markets a series of options in terms of governance. The OECD has become the boundary organisation in the field of transnational education governance. With its work on the construction of performance indicators and more recently with its success in international comparative testing, it has emerged as the central producer of policy-oriented knowledge in the developed world; and it offers not only measureable and comparable data but also – what is considered as – reliable guidance for policymaking.

This global expert network dates back to the creation of the Network A in the INES project which designed international indicators in education (see below). The network was subsequently extended to structure an international epistemic community including psychometricians and economists from different institutions: OECD, Australian Council for Educational Research, US Educational Testing Service (ETS), Cito (a Dutch testing and assessment company) and the European Centre for Research on Education and Lifelong Learning (CRELL). At the beginning of international surveys, the International Association for the Evaluation of Educational Achievement (IEA) joined forces with the ETS through its IEA Data Processing and Research Center and set up a joint venture, the IEA-ETS Research Institute, with the aim of developing and implementing large-scale assessments, training experts and policymakers in the field, collecting data and disseminating the outcomes of international surveys like TIMSS (mathematics and science), the Progress in International Reading Literacy Study (PIRLS), the International Adult Literacy Survey (IALS) and PISA (reading, mathematics and science).

How can we evaluate this knowledge regime at the scale of nation–states? There are conflicting theories and arguments. Some researchers consider that the PISA survey has little effect on the guidance of education policies and that policy learning is only one element among others in the public debate (Pons 2011). However, these assumptions ignore the place of statistical instruments as technologies of governance, their genealogy and inscription into tools of comparison and benchmarking at national and international levels (Tröhler 2013). Other researchers use PISA to valorise best governance and pedagogical practices at the country scale: it minimises the historical, linguistic and cultural contexts explaining performance gaps between countries and generating numerous biases in international comparison (Simola 2005; Zhao and Meyer 2013). Some researchers consider PISA as a Trojan horse, while states such as France, for example, are exposed to unexpected consequences regarding their participation in the survey and its effects on their national education policies (Martens and Wolf 2009). It is true that they were dissensions among countries when the INES project was launched, but France supported it at the beginning, and later it organised conferences and ordered reports to justify the development of international indicators and surveys. It was affirmed by French policymakers and the High Council of Evaluation of the School System (Haut Conseil de l'Evaluation de l'Ecole) that France had to contribute to the work of the OECD and the European Commission; a proposal was concretised by its participation in the Standing Group on Indicators and Benchmarks. There is a last argument made regarding the neutralisation or depoliticisation of the PISA survey in order to make it acceptable to the national community. It would be also interesting to consider the movement of politicising the issues at stake while these indicators are included as tools of governance, as was the case in France after PISA measurements were embedded into accountability indicators.

PISA as a Boundary Object

In our opinion, the PISA survey is an inextricable mix of global and national influences that structures the education policy in different dimensions. It appears as a boundary object, constructed, stabilised and interpreted according to interactions and interlocutions between individuals or groups. It elicits narratives and interpretations from multiple social agents (experts, policymakers, scholars, stakeholders, trade unionists, etc.) seeking to solve a particular problem. They are engaged in the production of knowledge and the confrontation of more or less subjective arguments related to some cognitive and normative challenges. PISA's narrative begins with people who act as representatives and who orientate their claims and interpretations towards society. This narrative configuration is also a dramatic one in the sense that the arguments are laid out on the public stage to make them tangible and visible.

This process of making the object visible is essential, as are the framing operations which allow the object made public to be reshaped. Categorisations and classifications are also decisive (Bowker and Star 1999). On the basis of interactions and interlocution and through these intersecting representations, the object is constructed in reality, and it becomes legitimate. For example, in France, PISA has become the cause of a collective action in which some actors attribute causes and responsibilities in the production of inequalities, identify those who are to blame, propose solutions and share experiences, resources, knowledge and skills through the building of a narrative (Normand 2015). In order to do so, global experts and policymakers have mastered a set of rhetorical rules enabling their arguments to be acceptable, relevant and legitimate from a moral or scientific viewpoint.

Generally, then, a boundary object is contextualised. Its building and reception conditions entail a spatial and temporal dynamic in relation to controversies and oppositions from different stakeholders in public arenas (Callon et al. 2009). It can be invested by 'moral entrepreneurs' who make it public, for example, by using the media and eliciting a reaction from institutional actors (Becker 1973). Narratives and configurations of actors involved in the public debate include different regimes of discursive practices and public arenas where some typical arguments are performed. The first one is the scientific arena, where researchers confront their arguments and methods to categorise, discuss and interpret the international survey and its data within their research community (Callon 1986; Latour 1987). They try to formalise a new state of knowledge based on evidence produced by statistical reasoning. The confrontation of their statements can result in scientific controversy. Arguments against or in favour of PISA may also trigger ethical, moral or philosophical controversies, sometimes showcased in the media and involving journalists and intellectuals. This is a polemical arena. Sometimes the scientific and the polemical arenas overlap.

A third arena is policymaking. Policymakers use the international survey to make comments regarding the situation of the education system, to justify reforms and to address recommendations and the instructions to implement them. They maintain some links with other policymakers and international organisations through peer learning activities and exchanges of best practices (Lange and Alexiadou 2010). A fourth, less public, arena is the world of experts. Even if it includes some scientists, expertise is characterised by its cult of discretion and secrecy in the design of PISA-related tools, reports and recommendations. Experts are positioned in the shadow of policymaking, and they work in closed circuits and networks which have close links to international organisations in preparing their decision-making (Radaelli 1999). The fifth arena is occupied by activists. They interpret the international survey according to their ideological vision and in defence of their members' interests (political parties, trade unions, professional associations, cultural groups, etc.).

Before a public debate emerges at the national level, a coalition of actors can impose a definition of the object, via formulations, statistics and tools but also institutional routines which create a sort of irreversibility. The framing of a boundary object can take place in a confined space in which experts, policymakers and activists decide to elaborate a compromise that prevents the emergence of competing claims in the public space (Cobb and Ross 1997). The framing can be political but also technical or scientific (Snow et al. 1986). The categorisation of the object gives legitimacy to areas of expertise by delegating skills to specialised agents who try to impose a certain definition. The definition of a boundary object is therefore not only cognitive: it depends on influence and power, as each actor seeks to own it and to get legitimacy from it (Rochefort and Cobb 1994). It is a political issue in the sense that it sets up relative positions and a hierarchy among competing actors. Furthermore, not everything is publicly debated: before a boundary object is placed on the public agenda, it is also discussed in more confidential and confined arenas involving only a few select actors.

Therefore, to some extent, the PISA survey, despite its imperfections and the criticism it has come under, has been reaffirmed as a common good on the political agenda, while it was worked out beforehand by international experts so that it can be showcased as a good measure of the effectiveness, equity and quality of education systems. It was then included into mechanisms of governance and New Public Management on the basis of non-challenged evidence and subjected to a successive process of depoliticisation and repoliticisation at national level making less visible the global expert network that had influenced its conception. PISA remains however a good example of the institutional and political isomorphism which produces a certain standardisation and rationalisation of education policies.

Transnationalisation of Knowledge and Evidence-Based Research Policy

As we have seen with PISA, in the context of globalisation, knowledge plays a particular role in the development of the economy. Most policymakers consider it as the driver of competitiveness, and it is also promoted by international organisations as a mean of social and cultural development. However, the direction given to PISA and the indicators of the Open Method of Coordination are influenced by the idea promoted by economists of human capital. This conception, as we shall see in the next chapter, resumed in the Lisbon Declaration and European political discourses, is shared by numerous reports demanding more innovation in education systems, the improvement of skills for the workforce and the fight against social exclusion.

During the last decades, it has structured a common agenda embedded in travelling policies and exchanges between transnational agencies and networks of experts finding their resources in national, regional and local spaces while preconising recommendations which challenge traditions and ideologies but also contesting social movements (Jones 2001). Of course, the conditions of reception vary according to their appropriation by elites and the degree of resistance by trade unions and other types of associations. But standards carried by international organisations remain a main mark for national policies even if their implementation is controversial (Dale 2000; Lingard 2010). Supranational agencies and organisations put real pressure on national policies. Held together by the principles of management and accountability, reports and recommendations succeed each other to justify a restructuring of educational professions and a focus on PISA results while some measurement technologies (indicators, benchmarks, rankings) are used to compare countries. Furthermore, these recommendations aim to reform higher education systems and research to ensure a better contribution to the knowledge economy. As we will observe later in this chapter, research in education is particularly targeted and called to develop knowledge, thus legitimising some practices and policies according to an instrumental and technical approach, while evidence, considered reliable and relevant, is required to inform and support practitioners and policymakers.

The Emergence of Knowledge Economy

However, the idea of the knowledge economy and society is not new (Husén 1968). The role of knowledge in economic and social development had been underlined by Daniel Bell during the 1960s (Bell 1973). He explained that post-industrial society funds its sources of innovation and growth in research and development and the production of knowledge defined by its intellectual ownership and commercial value. Manuel Castells (1996) in his analysis of network society also showed that the new economy was transformed by communication technologies and flexible modes of connection generating information and knowledge flows. The ideas of the knowledge economy, the knowledge society or the learning society developed by Thorsten Husén (1974) have since invaded the international organisations' reports.

In 2001, the OECD published the report *Knowledge Management in the Learning Society* (OECD 2001) following forums funded by the US National Science Foundation (Robertson 2005). It defended the idea that schools had to serve the knowledge society and improve their performances in the production of knowledge. Students had to manage their lifelong learning, while teachers had to adapt their skills and better invest in human capital. Later, the World Bank's report *Lifelong Learning in the Global Knowledge Economy* (2003) argued that the knowledge economy depended on the creation of new knowledge and innovation, and thus education systems had to be transformed, and different types of learning beyond formal education had to be implemented in order to focus on skills and problem-solving. Digital technologies are considered to be key in changing the role of teachers.

For the World Bank, the advancement towards a knowledge economy was based on four main pillars (Dale and Robertson 2009): information and infrastructures (the OECD and the World Bank have implemented numerous programmes to develop ICT), economic and institutional regimes (the change to systems of governance which are more open to the market and the private sector), knowledge and innovation systems (the idea is that the production, dissemination and usage of knowledge define the structure of knowledge production in each country) and the development of lifelong learning skills (as an investment in human capital capable of sustaining growth and economic competitiveness). UNESCO also wrote a report on knowledge societies (2005).

The OECD's interest in the production of knowledge also dates (Henry et al. 2001, pp. 127–155; Husén and Kogan 1984). In its different reports, the international organisation has highlighted that the shift from an industrial society to a post-industrial society based on knowledge was determinant for economic growth and technical progress (OECD 1996, 2000). Inspired by the reflections of economists in human capital and innovation theories, the reports emphasised the intensive role of knowledge in guaranteeing high employment and a qualified workforce. Governments had to develop innovation and infrastructures to encourage investment in research and training. The objective was to better disseminate knowledge and to bring closer together universities, industry and government, to promote new information technologies, to update the human capital by extending skills and to change modes of organisation by developing flexibility and networking. Calling for the abolition of differences between science and technology, the international organisation invited the production of knowledge to be expanded to other actors and to use private funding. It also emphasised the modalities of knowledge transfer in the economy and society beyond traditional networks and research institutions which had to contribute to socio-economic problem-solving. The mediation of knowledge was also evoked, along with business and consultancy firms having to play a role in the provision of knowledge directed to a larger spectrum of users and in the development of interactive learning processes to better work collectively in problem-solving.

Education, Research and the Quest for Evidence

It was only between 1990 and 2000 that the OECD, under the influence of the USA, developed an interest in the quality of research in education. In 1994, the OECD Centre for Research and Innovation (CERI), with the US Federal Department of Education, organised an international meeting on this issue. This first seminar proposed to draw up a state of the art and to reflect on the means to improve educational research. Discussions focused on the needs of practitioners and policymakers, on a better organisation of public-funded programmes and on improving pedagogical practices. The following year, a more official document was published by the OECD – *Educational Research and Development: Trends, Issues and Challenges* (1995) – which formulated recommendations from research via the 'Olympus model' or from the 'researcher prisoner in his ivory tower' principle to adopt the 'model of the agora'. According to the report, educational research needed to better take into account deciders and interest groups, to better disseminate research findings and to monitor them better. The steering of scientific projects had to be reinforced and centres of excellence developed. The same year, another meeting on the same issue was organised in Europe with the cooperation of the Netherlands Ministry of Education. The discussions were about how the CERI could continue to work on improving educational research: a programme of activities was discussed between experts as well as the possible role of the CERI in disseminating knowledge useful for decision-making. The experts also talked about the development of tools for decentralised systems, the promotion of new 'entrepreneurs' in a role of mediation and use of knowledge and the extension of international activities (such as the INES project which was mentioned several times).

Progressively the idea of evidence-based research and policy came to the fore. We will detail the full story further in chapter "The Multiple Worlds of Expertise". Before we do so, we would like just to describe how the CERI seized this new issue to strengthen its influence at the global level and legitimised a new mode of knowledge production that will be analysed further in this chapter (Schuller 2006). In 2004, an initial workshop was organised in Washington DC with the Institute of Educational Sciences (US Federal Department of Education) and some representatives of the New Zealand Ministry who had already experienced evidence-based research in their country. The CERI considered that policymakers had to be supported by good, rigorous and extended educational research and the seminar's aim was to reflect upon the requirements and constraints of evidence-based policy, to explore sources and motives of resistance to experiments and to study the practical results obtained in various countries. The discussion focused on randomised controlled trials taken from a file given to the participants who had to answer the following questions: What is evidence-based policy? What are the available methods for producing evidence in social and educational sciences? What does 'scientific rigour' mean in these fields? What are the conditions for conducting randomised controlled trials and what are their limitations? What is the value and what are the adjusted circumstances for combining different methods of research?

In September, during a round table at the European Conference on Educational Research, Tom Schuller presented the CERI's international research policy and disclaimed the accusation addressed to the CERI with regard to it searching for extensive control of information in education (Schuller 2004). Referring to the works developed by his centre, he explained the main points of this programme by stating that there was a limited number of experts and that they were appointed by ministries of education from different countries, that the work they produced was available to all and that he was not the head of a think tank free to define its own agenda. However, he recognised that evidence-based results and issues were subjected to various political pressures, and he focused his speech on the production of evidence and its use in educational research. He explained that educational research, contrary to universities, suffered from a deficit of legitimacy, and it was not always good, that is to say, it was not always effectively managed and disseminated. This is why he believes that the CERI worked on the issue in order to develop some possible scenarios of transformation. In referring to human capital theory, he explained that educational research was criticised for its weakness in the production of rigorous evidence related to the effects of education (Angrist 2004). However, here cognised that there can exist divergences between countries with regard to 'what works' in education. Tom Schuller used the example of randomised controlled trials to justify their implementation in the US context. He also defended the idea that experimental devices have a legitimate place in research and that the debate should not focus on the best methodology but on the mutual advantages of a mix of devices capable of strengthening evidence. The head of the CERI ended his speech by evoking the evaluations developed by the centre in its series *What Works for Policymakers and Practitioners*.

In 2007, the OECD report *Evidence in Education: Linking Research and Policy* (OCDE 2007) summarised the different contributions from experts who had attended the different CERI seminars. Tom Schuller, with his colleague Tracey Burns, drew a parallel between the mad cow affair and global warming to justify the necessity for policymakers to obtain available and real-time information on education. Taking their distance from the notion of 'evidence-based research policy', they justified the development of an 'informed-based research policy', capable of being better informed by research. Beyond these semantic nuances, the authors of the report directly mentioned the OECD report (1995) and claimed that a perfect continuity exists between the two programmes.

The objective was to solve problems caused by the lack of quality and effectiveness of educational research and its incapacity to contribute to the performance of education systems. The report attempted to overcome the divide between quantitative and qualitative methods and use evidence-based research to arbitrate decision-making and to involve practitioners and stakeholders more in the implementation of reforms. However, Tom Schuller and Tracey Burns recognised that evidence-based methods were controversial among the research community and even within the OECD, but they also pointed to the weakness of researchers' skills in quantitative methodologies and the use of databanks, their lack of knowledge in the field of assessment, experimental devices and randomised controlled trials. The authors then called for a strengthening of the use of these techniques among researchers, the development of specific centres, the extension of capacities among practitioners and policymakers in using the results and the need for better dissemination. In their opinion, educational research has to answer questions judged as being relevant by policymakers and that different brokerage agencies have to be set up. This bridge between knowledge production, mediation and use, embodied in the evidence-based research policy, is typical of the mode 2 of knowledge production which has progressively become a European research agenda.

The Mode 2 of Knowledge Production: A European Research Agenda

The objective of the Lisbon Strategy was to make the European Union 'the most competitive and dynamic knowledge-based economy worldwide, capable of a sustainable economic growth with the best employments and a greater social cohesion' and was the result of action plan started in 1993 with Jacques Delors's White Paper. If, since 1995, European social science (including education) programmes have been oriented towards problem-solving and their multidisciplinary involvement has become more relevant as claimed by European policymakers, it was only by the Fifth Framework Programme (1999–2002) that the key action of improving socio-economic knowledge by linking sciences and technology to issues in governance, European integration and systems of Welfare was affirmed (Agalianos 2006). By including more social sciences, this programme aimed to initiate a reflexion on structural trends and changes entailed by the enlargement of the European Union particularly with regard to the issues of social cohesion, immigration, welfare, citizenship and employment.

The priority of the Sixth Framework Programme (2002–2006) was devolved to governance and citizenship in the knowledge society on the basis of the objectives fixed at the Lisbon conference. Educational research was included while researchers were asked to lead projects on innovation and learning society by investigating, in particular, the dissemination of knowledge and others kinds of informal learning. More transnational and multidisciplinary focus was required in the conception of projects. They had to better fit the European agenda and to be politically relevant in providing a space of transnational collaboration between experts and representatives of Member States. The key topics were governance, lifelong learning and higher education, while ICTs would support the modernisation project. The Sixth Framework Programme clearly stipulated, at least via its first call, that educational research had to identify the challenges of the knowledge society by strengthening the links between science, education and lifelong learning policies and practices.

Since then, European policymakers have considered the knowledge economy and society as a key cornerstone in improving the quality of education and training systems (European Commission 2006). The building of a European Research and Innovation Space to fit these objectives alongside a knowledge-based policy implies an epistemic transformation of knowledge directed towards the search for a 'useful truth' for society and the economy. It is this objective which is also formulated in the conception of the mode 2 of knowledge production.

Mode 2 and European Research Programmes

The mode 2 of knowledge production is a rhetorical invention formulated by Gibbons and his colleagues in the field of the sociology of sciences (Gibbons et al. 1994), while its assumptions have been largely debated and criticised, this vision was taken on board and adopted by policymakers for research and development. The authors themselves recognised that their thesis had met a large success beyond their expectations (Nowotny et al. 2001). In inventing a new language for research, they had rescued the pure and theoretical model of science by arguing for applied and transferable research managed according to its results and uses. The mode 2 is also characterised by its transdisciplinary dimension and the claims for a certain type of research based on a wide variety of theoretical and methodological perspectives and detached from its disciplinary constituents, in order to solve problems. Scientific creativity is no longer considered from its internal dynamic but through its capacity to mobilise a variety of experts and forms of expertise. The mode 2 also considers that knowledge production spaces have to be diversified and fall outside of academia and the university landscape. Information and communication technologies can extend relationship-based networks to new institutions (think tanks, consultants, activist groups) by restructuring the borders between science and policy or between the scientific world and the layman's world. Researchers therefore have to be submitted to an external outlook and to be accountable while espousing a dialogic process in the extension and maintenance of relationships in a large and connected community. Instead of relying on peer reviews, they now have to submit their research to a quality control as producers of knowledge among others, but also as brokers and users who assert their interest in terms of the dissemination and usefulness of research findings.

While the mode 1 corresponds to the traditional approach of universities and research, the mode 2 opens the space of knowledge production to society and the economy by focusing on its contextual application. The quality of the work or research is no longer appreciated with regard to the academic community (according to the traditional peer review) but according to the efficiency and effectiveness of the work in solving problems and its practical uses. Subsequently, the mode 3 of knowledge production and the triple helix model were added to this initial definition (Etzkowitz and Leydesdorff 1997, 2000). The mode 3 characterises the coexistence of different paradigms of knowledge and innovation which is justified on behalf of a democratic pluralism. The 'mode 3' systems approach for knowledge creation, diffusion and use emphasises the following key elements (Carayannis and Campbell 2006): multilevel knowledge and innovation systems referring to stocks and flows at global and local levels coupled with clusters and networks which capitalise and disseminate them in accordance to a balance between cooperation and competition and relationships focused on performance. The triple or quadruple helix describes universities involved in applied research in relation to other public or private organisations, the media and civil society, through hybrid networks supporting new knowledge and innovation (Carayannis and Campbell 2012). The triple helix model is based on three helices: state, academia and industry (Etzkowitz and Leydesdorff 2000). Related to the sectoral classification of the OECD, the state coincides with the government sector, academia with the higher education sector and industry with the business enterprise sector. Etzkowitz and Leydesdorff propose different possible interactions between the helices: in the 'strong state' model government controls academia and industry; in the 'laissez-faire' model, each of the three helices develops quite independently, separated by clear borderlines; finally, in the model of 'trilateral networks and hybrid organisations', the dynamics of the helices can be characterised by increased overlapping and the emergence of so-called hybrid organisations at the interfaces. This pattern of amplified interaction defines the preferred scenario for the development of the advanced and knowledge-based economies. This conception of the role of innovation, resumed by the OECD and the European Commission, has led, according to Bengt-Åke Lundvall, to a certain number of distortions because of the influence of standard economics which tends to ignore the tacit and local dimension of knowledge embedded by individuals and organisations but also the complexity of learning (Lundvall 1992; Lundvall and Borras 1999).

However, the mode 2 has become a reference for the knowledge-based policies promoted by the European Commission for educational research. These conceptions are summarised in its working document *Towards More Knowledge-Based Policy and Practice in Education and Training* (2007). It explains that education and training policies need to strengthen the education–research–innovation triangle to promote a culture of assessment and useful evidence for research in order to modernise education and training systems, improve the use and impact of knowledge for effective and efficient policies and practices and enhance the quality of education to meet the Lisbon Strategy objectives. The aim is to structure the creation, application and use of knowledge for lifelong learning policies. The mode 2 of knowledge production is legitimised. According to the European Commission, the creation of knowledge in educational research raises problems of quality and relevance, while the great variety of disciplines and methodologies could potentially diminish the utility and impact in policy and practice. The staff working document provides examples of best practices at the European scale to restructure educational research via a range of programmes, agencies and institutions leading to an increase in the capacity of researchers and research units to be more useful for the knowledge economy and society. Indeed, the application of knowledge and its uses have to better contribute to improving practices and innovations beyond a posture considered as ideological and to adopt an experimental approach. The implication of policymakers and practitioners in the guidance of research is justified due to the necessity to improve its relevance. Mediation, presented as a bridge between the production of knowledge and its uses, has to involve networks, the media, websites through partnerships and agencies to ensure widespread dissemination and a better access to research results while at the same time obtaining the broadest consensus within civil society.

The document also explains that this ambition can be achieved through the development of the Seventh Framework Programme which structures European calls in the field of humanities and social sciences and by the use of European structural funds, while the lifelong learning programme has to be dedicated to the emergence of networks of brokerage agencies and experts to guide and select the most relevant educational research projects. The aim is to improve the effectiveness and efficiency of education and training systems in Europe, in parallel with the development of a European framework of indicators and benchmarks and the European harmonisation and standardisation of statistics.

In 2008, the European Commission, under its Directorate-General for Research and Innovation, produced another document dedicated to humanities and social sciences regarding scientific evidence in policymaking (EC 2008). From interviews and questionnaires addressed to a few personalities in the European research field, the document proposed to think beyond the status quo by encouraging the development of useful results for policymaking, through a strengthened dialogue between researchers and policymakers while focusing on dissemination and cooperation strategies between experts and lay persons, producing useful and relevant research findings and measuring their impact in terms of use. Its aim is to develop flexible networks between researchers, policymakers, practitioners and representatives of civil society in order to make research projects and their results more visible and accessible to a lay audience. The document argued that the complexity of the political environment and decision-making required interdisciplinary approaches and the identification of useful solutions for decision-makers. In 2010, the Research DG published a guide for social scientists and researchers in humanities with the aim of strengthening the relationships between research and policy on behalf of a more evidence-based policy (EC 2010). The document proposed to support researchers by strengthening the dialogue with policymakers and stakeholders and producing better evidence focused on problem-solving. It gave precise indications for writing 'policy briefs' which would be useful for policymaking.

The Undermined Model of Enlightenment

As one can observe through these different EC documents, the mode 2 of knowledge production has become institutionalised as the dominant model for redefining the relationships between science and policy in the fields of education and social sciences. For a long period, the 'model of Enlightenment' was the main configuration for the production of scientific knowledge (Janowitz 1972; Young et al. 2002; Pawson 2006). It formulated the relations between science, evidence and policy on the basis of a process of 'indirect dissemination', while scientific results had to inform public conscience and to change its representations of the world. This model gave policymakers the conceptual and measurement tools to give legitimacy to their decisions. However, research did not have much impact except through the accumulation of research findings and information to guide public action. The process generally included two steps (Weiss 1979): researchers had to attract policymakers' attention with regard to certain social issues (first step) and then help them to conceive problem-solving solutions (second step). This relationship model between science and policy has since faced a significant amount of criticism because it generated phenomena of 'distortion' and 'confusion' in public action. It was incapable of understanding its interlocutors and providing reliable and relevant elements to help in the decision-making process. Furthermore, some work was criticised because of their poor quality, and this reinforced the feeling of theoretical and methodological incoherence when results were disseminated.

This criticism of the 'model of Enlightenment' has also been endorsed by constructivist approaches to science. They have showed that the production of scientific facts was influenced by a plurality of actors and that it entailed debates and controversies leading to a process of negotiation and communication in policymaking. It has underlined the engagement required from policymakers, researchers and practitioners in a space of discussion, thus allowing the production of knowledge to be stabilised via different steps and dialogic procedures. The idea of a 'reasonable dialogue' between researchers and policymakers has also been expressed by other researchers to defend reformist proposals. The KNOW and POL research programme embodies this constructivist turn while calling for a better link between education research and policy in its reports (http://www.knowandpol.eu/). While mobilising researchers from eight European countries on the link between knowledge and policy, the programme aimed to characterise the multiplicity of actors involved in the production of knowledge and its different logics in terms of governance. The reports showed the importance of giving meaning to available knowledge for the governance of public action while it encouraged the development of knowledge-based tools for guiding decision-making and policymaking. While it criticised the limitation of local knowledge produced by educational research and the impossibility of accessing modes of generalisation such as statistical indicators and assessment methods, it denounced the conflict between science and expertise. Finally, the report implicitly legitimatised the mode 2 of knowledge production and its related technologies of governance and assessment. While they subtly stood out from considerations related to evidence-based research and policy, the conclusions of the programme claimed the need to implement devices for public debates which mobilise policymakers and stakeholders in reaching a consensus.

However, this programme, like the European Commission's programmes, even if they valorise the diversity of the knowledge production regimes, tends to ignore that the state has historically privileged statistical tools and experimental science against other methodologies while proposing a space of calculation distinct from people, their customs and local knowledge. These tools offered possibilities of standardisation and 'objective' technologies that allowed the population to be controlled and the development of the bureaucratic administration (Porter 1995; Desrosières 2002). If we consider the past few decades, this trust in numbers and quantification has been extended to international organisations, while a certain 'unreliability' of scientific practices has been paradoxically raised. As Ulrich Beck wrote, the 'model of Enlightenment' which affirms an unwavering truth in science and technical progress has been replaced by a reflexive model in which social sciences are subjected to criticism in the public sphere because they have not been to keep their promise of emancipation (Beck 1992). In losing their monopoly for establishing the truth regarding society and education, and by doubting their own foundations and practical consequences, social sciences, including educational research, have become the victim of the scepticism they contributed to producing while they have to learn to share knowledge production with other actors which sometimes have more powerful capacities of influence and action.

As it has been observed, social and educational sciences are more and more dependent on public opinion, and it is now the media which is raising the most important debates within society. So academics now have to position themselves between expertise and counter-expertise without being able to claim any significant reliability and legitimacy when faced with a multiplication and diversification of public forums. It entails an equalisation between experts and lay people and the development of conflicts regarding the process of rationalising public action. The limitations and precautions of scientists have given rise to a normativity claiming 'harder' methods in the observation of social and educational reality but in the end ending up with vague positions and contradictions with regard to the established evidence. In break with interpretive pluralism, some new standards and criteria have merged into a normalisation of the production of knowledge and scientific work.

In parallel, the 'linear and functionalist' model, which was heavily condemned during the 1980s–1990s, has gained some legitimacy. While it postulates for a link between evidence and policymaking, it takes natural sciences as a reference and assumes an 'instrumental' vision of science. It claims to reduce the gap between scientific knowledge and social problems faced by reformers. According to this conception, research anticipates political problems, and policymakers have to use a variety of available resources. The latter expect from research a reduction of the gap between knowledge and decision-making, itself thought as the fixation of objectives and the choice between clear alternatives. In this context, research influences choices and decision-making by providing evidence or information/knowledge capable of solving or enlightening a particular social problem. Despite some criticism and imperfections, this conception of mode 2 in the production of knowledge has become a common reference for a certain number of research programmes at the European scale but also for universities.

The European University and the Knowledge Triangle

For the past 20 years, European universities have transformed their governance and management while introducing new tools in the fields of assessment and quality, reorganised their human and material resources and transformed their professional practices and their relations to business (Maassen and Neave 2007). Some new modes of market-based regulations and performance management have been implemented, while there has been much criticism of higher education institutions which are seen to be too bureaucratic, with loosely coupled and routinised organisations, and which are not sufficiently diversified and flexible (Bleiklie 1998). More autonomy, accountability and mobility were requested by policymakers who were advocating for a modernisation project (Maassen and Olsen 2007). The higher education sector in most of European countries has undergone key reforms and incentives since the declaration of Bologna (1999) and the Lisbon Strategy which aimed to create a European Area of Higher Education and Research (EAHER).

The European Modernising Agenda After Bologna

If many studies have focused on the effects on the Bologna process as a change in the forms of higher education governance and the creation of a European space, other researchers have been looking at the links between the new modes of knowledge production advocated by the European Commission and of European higher education modernisation project (Bleikie and Byrkjeflot 2002; Bleiklie 2005).

As Roger Dale underlined (2005), when characterising the different steps of the Bologna process, policymakers were initially as interested by the impact of higher education on employability and competitiveness as by issues related to the mobility and attractiveness of talent in a context of competitive globalisation (European Commission 2009). It explains why the representatives at the Bologna conference did not primarily focus on the comparability and readability of diplomas when they created the European Credit Transfer and Accumulation System (ECTS) but were more concerned with the development of quality assurance to improve the transparency and reactivity in providing HE services for potential consumers.

If the topic of quality was again debated at the Prague and Berlin conferences, which followed Bologna, and while the contribution of European universities to competitiveness was reaffirmed, the European Commission's communication *The Role of the Universities in the Europe of Knowledge* was a new step and blueprint. The Europe of Knowledge was appearing as a strategic topic while the Commission was identifying new challenges for European universities: the internationalisation of education and research, the required cooperation between universities and industry, the multiplication of spaces of knowledge production and their reorganisation. While it was claiming efficiency, excellence and international openness, the communication proposed a new agenda for the modernisation of the universities focusing on the extension of its knowledge-related capacities and the implementation of the principles of New Public Management. These new reflections on European universities were followed by one on research during a conference at Liège: *A Vision for University-Based Research and Innovation* where the need to transform research training, to introduce more private–public partnerships and to promote interdisciplinary programmes, was evoked.

Later on, the *Mobilising the Brainpower of Europe: Enabling Universities to Make Their Full Contribution to the Lisbon Strategy* communication (CEC 2005) proposed that modernisation could be referred to as the knowledge triangle (education, research and innovation) to achieve a word-class quality and to improve the attractiveness, governance and funding of European universities. Beyond the mobilisation of brain power and attractiveness, the document stipulated that modernisation should be based on a new governance and a new regulatory framework to facilitate accountability, autonomy and incentives and to improve quality and innovation in teaching, research and services in universities.

Another communication – *Delivering on the Modernisation Agenda for Universities: Education, Research and Innovation* (CEC 2006) presented by the two commissioners for education and research, Jan Figel and Janez Poto˘cnik, respectively – affirmed that European universities had to adapt themselves to the knowledge economy, in particular by promoting the knowledge triangle and interdisciplinarity or transdisciplinarity. Later at a conference organised in Göteborg in 2009, *The Knowledge Triangle Shaping the Future of Europe, Swedish National Agency for Education*, in which the two commissioners took part, claims were put forward regarding the concept of knowledge triangles in relation to the need for improving the impact of investment in three key activities – education, research and innovation – via systemic and continuous interaction. Presented as a flexible and nonnormative model promoting the knowledge society, it not only had to facilitate the diversity of missions within European universities, which were themselves considered as international knowledge industries, but also had to involve more entrepreneurs and business. A modern university has to be characterised by its openness and autonomy while at the same time including the three sides of the knowledge triangle. In order to do so, it had to be better oriented towards problem-solving and customer satisfaction; it had to take more risks, develop links with innovative systems and clusters and put into place incentives for improving teaching and developing lifelong learning skills.

Knowledge Triangle and Third Mission

As Peter Maassen and Bjørn Stensaker explain, the knowledge triangle corresponded to emerging policies in European higher education with different adaptations among countries (Maassen and Stensaker 2011). The first aspect is quality assurance and the development of assessment methods for national systems and institutions. Since the adoption of the European standards and guidelines for quality assurance and the implementation of the Quality Assurance Register for quality assurance agencies at the meetings of Bologna and London in 2007, there has been a move towards standardisation by quality assurance in Europe. Linked to the European Qualifications Framework (EQP), it has contributed to a greater standardisation of the organisation and content of degree programmes in higher education institutions. This standardisation has been strengthened by the development of specific OECD indicators for higher education. Another trend has been the will of European policymakers to concentrate talents and resources by stimulating innovation and economy through a new research policy as can be observed through the creation of research universities in Denmark and elite institutions in Germany and Finland or in other European countries or through the creation of the European Institute of Innovation and Technology (EIT) which serves as a reference. The EIT was established on 11 March 2008. It was designed to integrate innovation, research and growth across the European Union. The idea of a European Institute of Innovation and Technology (EIT) was developed within the framework of the Lisbon Strategy based on the concept that innovation is a key driver of growth, competitiveness and social well-being. The EIT is the first EU initiative to fully integrate all three sides of the knowledge triangle (higher education, research and business) by way of so-called Knowledge and Innovation Communities (KICs). For the European Commission, the integration of all three sides and the effective transmission and sharing of knowledge, information and skills for joint exploitation are crucial to delivering the jobs and growth in Europe. The trend is to create an 'open innovation system' via networks and public–private partnerships and to strengthen links between universities and industry according to a mode of governance inspired by the mode 2 of knowledge production and/or the triple helix concept. The objective is to develop university-based research and innovation for the next 15–20 years, a large European space for research capable of mobilising brain power and enabling universities to be involved in knowledge-based policymaking.

Of course, it creates tension within Member States, and the adoption of this European strategy varies according to national context. However, we should not underestimate the influence of European recommendations and standards on national policies. In terms of research and knowledge production, one of the major effects is a greater division in academic labour within European universities between the 'teaching staff' and 'researchers' as in the case of the UK higher education system. On the other hand, the strengthening of links between research and innovation as well as the concentration of resources could lead to the development of a university-based entrepreneurship, while sources of funding will be increasingly depended on applied research, from broadened external cooperation and networks and public or private funded incentives related to innovation and technology transfer.

The application of entrepreneurship and associated principles and practices is a commonplace in literature. Etzkowitz (1991) identified the dawn of the entrepreneurial university as marking a second academic revolution by introducing the market into the heart of the university. The comparison between the introduction of a third mission of socio-economic engagement to the first academic revolution that transformed universities from purely instructional to educational and research performing institutions highlights the significance of this era of university evolution. Clark (1998) conceptualised the 'entrepreneurial transformation' of five European research universities in the direct context of these institutions searches for innovative methods to reduce their heavy reliance on governmental support and subsequent oversight. He described five key components of entrepreneurial university organisations: a strong central steering core to embrace management groups and academics; an expanded development periphery involving a growth of units that reach out beyond the traditional areas in the university; diversity of the funding base, not only by using government third stream funding but from a wide variety of sources; a stimulated academic heartland with academics committed to the entrepreneurial concept; and an integrated entrepreneurial culture defined in terms of common commitment to change. There is now considerable international literature addressing the notion of what has been termed 'the entrepreneurial university'.

Marginson and Considine's (2000) recognised the commercial engagement of universities in a mixed public and private context. They considered that the Enterprise University defines a 'new orthodoxy that favours business values and income generation'. This rhetoric identifies the increasingly important (socio) economic roles played by universities. However, while each discourse makes claims about the form of the university, they only provide generalised accounts developed from the aggregated histories of the studied institutions. Thus, while compelling in many respects, this rhetoric has often been described as generic abstractions (Tuunainen 2005) or caricatured descriptions of contemporary universities (Serrano-Velarde 2008); and the degree to which they can be universally applied has been questioned.

However, in addition to the core missions of teaching and research, the newly emphasised and frequently commercially oriented activities are now framed in what is now called a new Third Mission (Etzkowitz and Leydesdorff 1997; Laredo 2007; Mollas-Gallart et al. 2002). In the broadest terms, this mission has been defined as everything that is not traditional teaching and research (Jongbloed et al. 2008), while elsewhere this term has been more narrowly conceived in terms of knowledge and technology transfer (Hackett and Dilts 2004). In both instances, the commercial engagement of universities has become a cornerstone of national and regional innovation policies.

In light of evolving political and social situations as well as institutional contexts, there is much academic debate concerning the dynamics of these newly emphasised economic and social roles of European universities. It opposes two camps: some researchers consider that this transformation of governance and the link between universities and business is a normal consequence of the mode 2 of knowledge production and/or triple helix. They defend the idea that a new entrepreneurship has ended the boundary between the public and the private. On the contrary, other researchers are highly critical of the associated risks of this academic entrepreneurialism. For example, Slaughter and her colleagues use the notion of 'academic capitalism' to describe the extent to which market values and profitability have spread to universities but also the crisis in academic identities and autonomy (Slaughter and Leslie 1997; Slaughter and Rhoades 2004). We will later relativise this dominant idea of marketisation of higher education in Europe, but, as we shall see in chapter "The Making of a New Homo Academicus?", these evolutions call into question the position of academics in the European Higher Education and Research Space. Beyond new institutional arrangements and knowledge governance, it is important to analyse how academics themselves have participated in redefining the boundaries between science, innovation and policy via a diversity of engagements between tradition and entrepreneurship.

The Foundations of the European Epistemic Governance

In this book, we are interested in knowledge-based policy in education, e.g. a mode of governance which transforms the social role of knowledge and generates a whole new set of rules and tools supporting the work of actors and organisations. In defining the conditions of knowledge production, but also its modes of application and uses outside of the traditional scientific community, this type of policy reconfigures the relationships between educational research and policy through new techniques of control and surveillance, new techno-scientific arrangements and new post-bureaucratic regulations. In offering new options and opportunities to the academic world, this knowledge-based policy includes a moral and cultural dimension, beyond its economic aims. It challenges the historical and institutional traditions which defined the links between science and policymaking while giving a greater and new legitimacy to transnational organisations and movements.

At the same time, it legitimates the power of expertise and experts, while scientists, particularly in the field of educational and social sciences, are less recognised. Policymakers search for short-term political solutions and require utilitarian responses from traditional research. It also explains the growing influence of evidence-based technologies in education policies while scepticism and disappointment has fed the contestation of academic knowledge being considered fragile and limited.

Faced with the rise of risks and uncertainties in the decision-making process, experts and expertise have participated in the strengthening of a system of surveillance and control while at the same time being mobilised to solve controversies. Because of the multiplication of knowledge production, the boundaries between science and expertise have become blurred, while the autonomy of scientific inquiry now appears relatively minor when confronted with economic necessities in terms of growth, competitiveness and innovation.

Knowledge-based policy has therefore become increasingly interventionist in offering new modes of regulation for research. Even if the state has retained a certain power of leadership, the role of non-governmental organisations (NGO) has increased with regard to defining research strategies mobilising more and more groups from civil society. As Weingart (2008) wrote, the conception of Gibbons and his colleagues, resumed by the European Commission, in terms of 'socially robust knowledge' raises a political and epistemological question: how can we accommodate democratic decision-making procedures of representation on the one hand and the reliability, relevance and quality of scientific knowledge's claims on the other hand? While the European Commission is promoting a discourse on the democratisation of expertise, educational research is being embedded and contextualised in the knowledge economy in accordance with an epistemology which valorises knowledge outside of the research unit and the research community through a consensus between experts, practitioners and stakeholders.

In fact, as observed by Jasanoff, this procedural dimension of participation serves not only scientific aims but also political ones. Indeed, most of the technologies proposing different modes of interaction between policymakers, experts, researchers and other representatives are included in the predictive approaches (risk assessment, cost–benefit analysis, randomised controlled trials, etc.) and normative assumptions that are not truly concerned with moral and political aspects (Jasnanoff 2003). Participation alone is not enough to give meaning to interactions, while dialogue between experts and laymen is imperfectly framed because experts in different forums rely on the authority of science or specific knowledge and not really exposed to political deliberation and criticism. Therefore, the mode 2 of knowledge production raises a paradox: on the one hand, knowledge produced by experts is invading the decision-making process without any true democratic guarantees while expertise is far from being neutral, universal and unequivocal. It therefore justifies accountability and the implication of laymen in the processes of production, mediation and use of knowledge. On the other hand, the technocratic shift in policymakers giving power to expertise has led to an instrumental and ideological vision in the production of knowledge which is hindering true democratic debate. This technocratic shift, which is observable at the European level, is manifest in the strengthening of quality control and management of knowledge which structure research procedures and outputs and in the way in which issues are being integrated into the public space.

These new relationships between knowledge and policy correspond to a new 'epistemic governance' in the sense that they impact on the beliefs, ideals and motives of European actors. As Foucault wrote (1980), power is not only hierarchical but distributed through disconnected networks attempting to act on the aspirations and beliefs of people and also on their tacit conceptions of the nature of knowledge. In resuming the concepts formulated by Alasuutari and Qadir (2014), we can consider the way in which actors are engaged in policymaking and decision-making, according to an epistemic work viewing knowledge along non-directly perceptible mechanisms and techniques which define the environment of actors, who or what they are and what is acceptable or virtuous for them. The scientific and expert environment characterises a form of actors' ontology and their underlying understanding, e.g. the preconception they have of the facts and measurements upon which a policy is based. These paradigmatic premises are used to justify reforms or modernisation programmes as can be seen, for example, in the use of PISA by European Member States. This vision, which is based on an evolutionist and a cultural vision of education systems, is using expertise in the production of knowledge and considers facts and numbers as relevant, transparent and independent, particularly when they come from international organisations. From this point of view, evidence-based policies are the paragon of this ontological ordering of actors.

Another aspect of epistemic governance is the way in which actors work to define and identify each other. This characterisation of actors and identities in the policymaking process is not only a game of discourses and rhetoric as often written in the research literature on European issues. This interplay between policymakers, researchers, experts, practitioners and stakeholders includes some important rituals and a variety of modes of engagement in different activities, identifying a group or a network and a country and defending interests and strategic concerns while contributing to the legitimisation of knowledge production and decision-making. It is perceptible in the way in which the European Commission mobilises certain experts and stakeholders in their working groups in the assumption that they represent the public interest and the common good. The epistemic work is also related to the norms and ideals shared by individuals in these groups and the capacities of some of them to convince and persuade the others on behalf of great principles of justice such as equality, freedom, the well-being of children, sustainable development, etc., which belong to a shared global culture. The production of knowledge is based on a moral of reciprocal rights and obligations supported by explicit or tacit arguments and assumptions, but at the same time by forms of objective evidence as can be observed in expert groups. We shall discuss this further in chapter "'What works?' The Shaping of the European Politics of Evidence".

These actors also use material and cognitive resources which participate in the normalisation of knowledge production and the structuring of different forms of power. Epistemic governance therefore combines different modes of representation, discourses and actions on the normative, ideological, technical and scientific production of knowledge on behalf of principles of justice which are considered as legitimate in terms of accountability, political representation and responsibility. It corresponds to shared knowledge based on the interactions between researchers, experts and policymakers to give meaning to a certain social reality and to make it acceptable. It is also a social and political process for seeking the truth, based on a certain conception of evidence and defined by institutional arenas in which the participation and deliberation of practitioners and stakeholders is the prerequisite for decision-making and its justification.

In summary, the way in which different actors agree on a policy direction is based on sharing common epistemic assumptions while maintaining a certain hegemonic vision which defines the boundaries of acceptable reality. In this epistemic work, some actors have more resources than others, particularly with regard to data and knowledge, and they occupy asymmetrical positions while influencing each other. If there is no centre for epistemic governance, and if different groups can influence the policy direction at national and international scales, then epistemic work acts simultaneously on the production of evidence, either from science or from expertise, the cognitive and material environment of actors, their identification and relative positioning and the promoted norms or ideals to gain support and conviction.

Conclusion

The epistemic governance of education displays a variety of international actors and institutions which gradually transform the modes of knowledge production and their assessment. Embedded within the European agenda for research, the knowledge triangle, legitimised by the theory of mode 2 and its developments, is considered as the only regulation capable of developing innovation and sustaining economic growth and employment. Even though European countries maintain specific traditions in terms of knowledge regimes, the reconfiguration of relationships between science and policy corresponds to transnational move which shifts the boundaries of the academic world and, as it is demonstrated by the PISA survey, raises expert networks which impose a new definition of education and research policies. In this first part of this book, we provide a description and an analysis of this transnationalisation in studying the manner this politics produces knowledge but also new forms of standardisation and evidence which contribute to redraw the background of academic activities and work. Without ignoring differences from one country to another, we make the assumptions that a strong trend leads to deconstruct the Enlightenment model, on which was based the academic tradition until now, and to institutionalise a utilitarian and neo-positivist epistemic regime.

References

Agalianos, A. (2006). Crossing borders: The European dimension in educational and social science research. In J. Ozga, T. Seddon, & T. S. Popkewitz (Eds.), *Education research and policy. Steering the knowledge-based economy* (pp. 43–78). New York: Routledge World Yearbook of Education.

Alasuutari, P., & Qadir, A. (2014). Epistemic governance: An approach to the politics of policy-making. *European Journal of Cultural and Political Sociology, 1*(1), 67–84.

Angrist, J. D. (2004). American education research changes tack. *Oxford Review of Economic Policy, 20*(2), 198–212.

Apple, M. W. (2006). *Educating the "right" way: Markets, standards, God, and inequality.* New York: Taylor & Francis.

Ball, S. J. (2012). *Global Education Inc. New policy networks and the neoliberal imaginary.* Routledge: London.

Beck, U. (1992). *Risk society: Towards a new modernity* (p. 1992). London: Sage.

Becker, H. S. (1973). *Outsiders: Studies in the sociology of deviance.* New York: Free Press.

Bell, D. (1973). *The coming of the post-industrial society: A venture in social forecasting.* Middlesex: Penguin.

Bleiklie, I. (1998). Justifying the Evaluative State. *New Public Management Ideals in Higher Education: European Journal of Education, 33*(3), 299–316.

Bleiklie, I. (2005). Organizing higher education in a knowledge society. *Higher Education, 49,* 31–59.

Bleiklie, I., & Byrkjeflot, H. (2002). Changing knowledge regimes: Universities in a new research environment. *Higher Education, 44*(3), 519–532.

Bottani, N., & Tuijnman, A. (1994). International education indicators: Framework, development and interpretation. *Capítulo, 1,* 21–35.

Bowker, G. C., & Star, S. L. (1999). *Sorting things out: Classification and its consequences.* Cambridge, MA: MIT Press.

Callon, M. (1986). Some elements of a sociology of translation: Domestication of the scallops and the fishermen of St Brieuc Bay. In J. Law (Ed.), *Power, action and belief: A new sociology of knowledge?* (pp. 196–223). London: Routledge & Kegan Paul.

Callon, M., Lascoumes, P., & Barthe, Y. (2009). *Acting in an uncertain world: An essay on technical democracy.* Cambridge, MA: MIT Press.

Campbell, J. L., & Pederson, O. K. (2011). Knowledge regimes and comparative political economy. In D. Béland & R. Cox (Eds.), *Ideas and politics in social science research* (pp. 167–190). New York: Oxford University Press.

Carayannis, E. G., & Campbell, D. F. (2006). *Knowledge creation, diffusion, and use in innovation networks and knowledge clusters: A comparative systems approach across the United States, Europe, and Asia.* Connecticut/London: Wesport/Greenwood Publishing Group.

Carayannis, E. G., & Campbell, D. F. J. (2012). Mode 3 knowledge production in quadruple helix innovation systems. 21st-century democracy, innovation, and entrepreneurship for development. *Springer Briefs in Business, 3,* 21.

Carvalho, L. M. (2014). The attraction of mutual surveillance of performances: PISA as a knowledge-policy instruments. In T. Fenwick, E. Mangez, & J. Ozga (Eds.), *Governing knowledge. Comparison, knowledge-based technologies and expertise in the regulation of education* (pp. 58–72). New York: Routledge World Yearbook of Education.

Castells, M. (1996). *The rise of the network society.* London: Blackwell.

CEC (2006). *Commission of the European Communities, Delivering on the modernization agenda for universities: Education, research, innovation.* Communication from the Commission COM 2006/208, Brussels CEC.

Chitty, C. (1989). *Towards a new education system: The victory of the new right?* London: Falmer Press.

Clark, B. R. (1998). *Creating entrepreneurial universities: Organizational pathways of transformation.* Oxford: Pergamon.

Cobb, R. W., & Ross, M. H. (Eds.). (1997). *Cultural strategies of agenda denial: Avoidance, attack, and redefinition*. Lawrence: University Press of Kansas.

Council of the European Union (2005, November 24). Resolution of the council and the representatives of the governments of the member states, on mobilising the brain power of Europe: Enabling higher education to make its full contribution to the Lisbon strategy. *Official Journal of the European Union 2005/C 292/1, 48*.

Dahrendorf, R. (1995). *A history of the London school of economics and political science 1895–1995*. Oxford: Oxford University Press.

Dale, R. (1999). Specifying globalisation effects on national policy: Focus on the mechanisms. *Journal of Education Policy, 14*, 1–17.

Dale, R. (2000). Globalisation and education: Demonstrating a "common world education culture" or locating a "globally structured agenda for education"? *Education Theory, 50*(4), 427–448.

Dale, R. (2005). Globalisation, knowledge economy and comparative education. *Comparative Education, 41*(2), 117–151.

Dale, R., & Robertson, S. (2009). *Globalisation and Europeanisation in education*. Oxford Symposium Books.

Denham, A., & Garnett, M. (1998). *British think-tanks and the climate of opinion*. London: University, College London Press.

Denham, A., & Garnett, M. (2004). A "hollowed-out" tradition? British think-tanks in the 21st century. In D. Stone & A. Denham (Eds.), *Think-tank traditions: Policy research and the politics of ideas* (pp. 232–246). Manchester: Manchester University Press.

Derouet, J.-L., & Normand, R. (2010). Caesars and Rubicon. The hesitations of French policymakers in identifying a third way in education and training. *Journal of Educational Administration and History, 43*, 97–121.

Desrosières, A. (2002). *The politics of large numbers: A history of statistical reasoning*. Harvard: Harvard University Press.

EC (2010). Europe 2020, a strategy for smart, sustainable and inclusive growth, CPM 2020, Final, Brussels.

Etzkowitz, H. (1991). The entrepreneurial university and the emergence of democratic corporatism. In H. Etzkowitz & L. Leydesdorff (Eds.), *Universities and the global knowledge economy: A triple helix of university-industry-government relations* (pp. 141–152). London: Cassell.

Etzkowitz, H., & Leydesdorff, L. (1997). *Universities and the global knowledge economy: A triple helix of university-industry-government relations*. London: Continuum.

Etzkowitz, H., & Leydesdorff, L. (2000). The dynamics of innovations: From national innovation systems and "Mode 2" to a triple helix of university-industry-government relations. *Research Policy, 29*, 109–123.

European Commission. (2006). *Delivering on the modernization agenda for universities: Education, research and innovation*.

European Commission. (2007). *Towards more knowledge-based policy and practice in education and training*. Commission Staff Working Document. European Communities.

European Commission. (2008). *Knowledge for growth European issues and policy challenges*. DG research. http://ec.europa.eu/invest-in-research/pdf/download_en/knowledge_for_growth_bat.pdf.

European Commission. (2009). *Knowledge for growth. Prospects for science, technology and innovation*. Selected papers from Research Commissioner Janez Potoˇcnik's Expert Group. http://ec.europa.eu/invest-in-research/pdf/download_en/selected_papers_en.pdf.

Foucault, M. (1980). *Power/knowledge: Selected interviews and other writings 1972–1977*. London: Harvester Press.

Gibbons, M., Limoges, C., Nowotny, H., Schwartzman, S., Scott, P., & Trow, M. (1994). *The new production of knowledge, the dynamics of science and research in contemporary societies*. London: Sage.

Grek, S. (2012). Learning from meetings and comparison: A critical examination of the policy tools of transnationals. In G. Steiner-Khamsi & F. Waldow (Eds.), *Policy borrowing and lending in education* (pp. 41–61). New York: Routledge World Yearbook of Education.

Hackett, S. M., & Dilts, D. M. (2004). A systematic review of business incubation research. *The Journal of Technology Transfer, 29*(1), 55–82.

Henry, M., Lingard, B., Rizvi, F., & Taylor, S. (2001). *The OECD, globalization, and education policy*. Oxford: Pergamon-Elsevier.

Husén, T. (1968). Lifelong learning in the 'educative society'. *Applied Psychology: An International Review, 17*, 87–98.

Husén, T. (1974). *The learning society*. London: Methuen.

Husén, T., & Kogan, M. (Eds.). (1984). *Educational research and policy: How do they relate?* Oxford: Pergamon Press. Rectifier texte chapitre 1 tu les as mis inversés.

Hutmacher, W., Cochrane, D., & Bottani, N. (2001). *In pursuit of equity in education: Using international indicators to compare equity policies*. Dordrecht: Springer Science & Business Media.

Janowitz, M. (1972). *Sociological models and social policy*. Morriston: General Learning Systems.

Jasnanoff, S. (2003). Technologies of humility: Citizen participation in governing science. *Minerva, 41*, 223–244.

Jones, K. (2001). Travelling policy/local spaces: Culture, creativity and interference. *Education and Social Justice, 3*(3), 2–5.

Jongbloed, B., Enders, J., & Salerno, C. (2008). Higher education and its communities: Interconnections, interdependencies and a research agenda. *Higher Education, 56*(3), 303–324.

Lange, B., & Alexiadou, N. (2010). Policy learning and governance of education policy in the EU. *Journal of Education Policy, 25*(4), 443–463.

Laredo, P. (2007). Revisiting the third mission of universities: Toward a renewed categorization of university activities? *Higher Education Policy, 20*(4), 441–456.

Latour, B. (1987). *Science in action: How to follow scientists and engineers through society*. Cambridge, MA: Harvard University Press.

Lingard, B. (2010). Policy borrowing, policy learning: Testing times in Australian schooling. *Critical Studies in Education, 51*(2), 129–147.

Lundvall, B.-Å. (1992). *National innovation systems: Toward a theory of interactive learning*. London: Pinter Publishers.

Lundvall, B.-Å., & Borras, S. (1999). *The globalising learning economy: Implications for innovation policy*. Luxumbourg: Office for Official Publications of the European Communities.

Maassen, G., & Neave, P. (2007). The bologna process: An intergovernmental policy perspective. In P. Maassen & J. P. Olsen (Eds.), *University dynamics and European integration* (pp. 135–154). Dordrech: Springer.

Maassen, P., & Olsen, J. P. (Eds.). (2007). *University dynamics and European integration*. Dordrecht: Springer.

Maassen, P., & Stensaker, B. (2011). The knowledge triangle, European higher education policy logics and policy implications. *Higher Education, 61*(6), 757–769.

Marginson, S., & Considine, M. (2000). *The enterprise universities: Power, governance and reinvention in Australia*. Cambridge: Cambridge University Press.

Martens, K., & Wolf, K. D. (2009). *Boomerangs and Trojan horses: The unintended consequences of internationalising education policy through the EU and the OECD* (pp. 81–107). Netherlands: Springer.

Mazon, B. (1988). *Aux origines de l'EHESS. Le rôle du mécénat américain*. Paris: Éd. du Cerf.

Meyer, H. D., & Benavot, A. (2013). *PISA, power, and policy: The emergence of global educational governance*. Oxford: Symposium Books.

Meyer, J. W., Boli, J., Thomas, G. M., & Ramirez, F. O. (1997). World society and the nation-state. *American Journal of Sociology, 103*(1), 144–181.

Mirowski, P., & Plehwe, D. (2009). *The road from Mont Pelerin*. Cambridge, MA: Harvard University Press.

Mollas-Gallart, J., Salter, A., Patel, P., Scott, A. & Duran, X. (2002). *Measuring third stream activities: Final report to the Russell Group of Universities*. Brighton: SPRU. Available at http://www2.lse.ac.uk/economicHistory/Research/CCPN/pdf/russell-report_thirdStream.Pdf

Normand, R. (2011). *La mesure de l'école. Une arithmétique politique des inégalités*. Paris: Peter Lang.

Normand, R. (2013). Governing population: The emergence of a political arithmetic of inequalities in education: A comparison between the United Kingdom and France. In M. Lawn (Ed.), *The rise of data: Historical perspectives* (pp. 139–157). Oxford: Symposium Books.

Normand, R. (2015). The "French Pinnacle" of PISA. A boundary object between translations and irreversibility. In M. Lawn & R. Normand (Eds.), *Shaping of European education. Interdisciplinary approaches, series studies in European education* (pp. 61–89). London: Routledge.

Novoa, A. (2014). Comparative research in education: A mode of governance or a historical journey? In T. Fenwick, E. Mangez, & J. Ozga (Eds.), *Governing knowledge. Comparison, knowledge-based technologies and expertise in the regulation of education*. New York: Routledge World Yearbook of Education.

Nowotny, H., Scott, P., & Gibbons, M. (2001). *Re-thinking science. Knowledge and the public in an age of uncertainty*. Cambridge: Polity.

OECD. (1995). *Educational research and development*. Trends, issues and challenges.

OECD. (1996). *The knowledge-based economy OECD*.

OECD. (2000). *Schooling for tomorrow*. OECD scenarios OECD.

OECD. (2001). *Knowledge management in the learning society*. Paris: OECD.

OECD. (2003). *Knowledge management. New challenges for educational research*. Paris: Publications de l'OECD.

OECD. (2007). *Evidence in education*. OCDE: Linking Research and Policy.

Ozga, J., Dahler-Larsen, P., & Segerholm, C. (2011). *Fabricating quality in education: Data and governance in Europe*. London: Routledge.

Pawson, R. (2006). *Evidence-based policy. A realist perspective*. London: Sage Publications.

Pollard, A. (2010). *Professionalism and pedagogy: A contemporary opportunity: A commentary by the Teaching and Learning Research Programme and the General Teaching Council for England*. London: TLRPo. Document Number.

Pons, X. (2011). What do we really learn from PISA? The sociology of its reception in three European countries (2001–2008). *European Journal of Education, 46*(4), 540–548.

Porter, T. A. (1995). *Trust in numbers: The pursuit of objectivity in science and public life*. Princeton University Press: Princeton.

Radaelli, C. M. (1999). The public policy of the European Union: Whither politics of expertise? *Journal of European Public Policy, 6*(5), 757–774.

Rizvi, F., & Lingard, B. (2010). *Globalizing education policy*. Abingdon: Routledge (Taylor & Francis).

Robertson S. -L. (2005, May). Re-imagining and rescripting the future of education: Global knowledge economy discourses and the challenge to education systems. *Comparative Education, 41*(2), 151–170.

Rochefort, D. A., & Cobb, R. W. (Eds.). (1994). *The politics of problem definition: Shaping the policy agenda*. Lawrence: University Press of Kansas.

Schuller, T. (2004). *International policy research: "Evidence" from CERI/OECD*. Paper presented at the European Conference on Educational Research, University of Crete, 22–25 Sept 2004, http://www.leeds.ac.uk/educol/documents/00003633.htm.

Schuller, T. (2006). International policy research: 'Evidence' from CERI/OECD. In J. Ozga, T. Seddon, & T. S. Popkewitz (Eds.), *Education research and policy. Steering the knowledge-based economy* (pp. 78–90). New York: Routledge World Yearbook of Education.

Serrano-Velarde, K. E. (2008). Quality assurance in the European higher education area. *Higher Education Management and Policy, 20*(3), 1–18.

Simola, H. (2005). The Finnish miracle of PISA: Historical and sociological remarks on teaching and teacher education. *Comparative Education, 41*(4), 455–470.

Slaughter, S., & Leslie, L. L. (1997). *Academic capitalism. Politics, policies and the Entrepreneurial University*. London: John Hopkins University Press.

Slaughter, S., & Rhoades, G. (2004). Academic capitalism in the new economy: Challenges and choices. *American Academic, 1*(1), 37–59.

Snow, D. A., Rochford, E. B., Jr., Worden, S. K., & Benford, R. D. (1986). Frame alignment processes, micromobilization, and movement participation. *American Sociological Review, 51*(4), 464–481.

Stone, D. (1996). *Capturing the political imagination: Think tanks and the policy process*. London: Psychology Press/Franck Cass.

Stone, D., Denham, A., & Garnett, M. (1998). *Think tanks across nations*. Manchester: Manchester University Press.

Tröhler, D. (2013). The OECD and cold war culture: Thinking historically about PISA. In H. Meyer & A. Benavot (Eds.), *PISA, power, and policy: The emergence of global educational governance*. Oxford: Symposium Books.

Tuunainen, J. (2005). Hybrid practices? Contributions to the debate on the mutation of science and university. *Higher Education, 50*(2), 275–298.

UNESCO. (2005). *Towards knowledge societies*. Paris: UNESCO.

Waldow, F. (2013). PISA under examination: Changing knowledge, changing tests, and changing schools. *Comparative Education, 49*(4), 536–537.

Weingart, P. (2008). How robust is "Socially Robust Knowledge"? In M. Carrier, D. Howard, & J. Kourany (Eds.), *The challenge of the social and the pressure of practice: Science and values revisited* (pp. 131–145). Pittsburgh: Pittsburgh University Press.

Weiss, C. H. (1979). The many meanings of research utilization. *Public Administration Review, 39*(5), 426–443.

World Bank. (2003). *Lifelong learning for a global knowledge economy*. Washington, DC: World Bank.

Young, K., Ashby, D., Boaz, A., & Grayson, L. (2002). Social science and the evidence-based policy movement. *Social Policy and Society, 1*, 215–224.

Zhao, Y., & Meyer, H.-D. (2013). High on PISA, low on entrepreneurship? What PISA does not measure. In H. Meyer & A. Benavot (Eds.), *PISA, power, and policy: The emergence of global educational governance*. Oxford: Symposium Books.

The Politics of Standards and Quality

Far from being limited to marketisation, the building of the European space of life-long learning is a response to the consequences of globalisation (Lawn and Lingard 2002). It has created new processes of regulations and evaluations and has generated initiatives from which the consensuses or compromises have gone beyond that of states. Quality politics are supported by an economic, political and technical trans-nationalisation. The aim of this governance is to restructure the European space and to organise new relationships between diverse actors concerned by the production of standards. The latter is different from the hierarchical control we have become accustomed to with the traditional bureaucratic state. Of course, the development of quality politics was characterised at the national level with the apparition of the Evaluative State and later by the development of assurance quality procedures. It has also been linked to Europeanisation through connecting actors and networks and institutionalising standards via a governance by numbers. The Europeanisation project brings together national actors, and it tends to blur traditional boundaries between the state and society while transforming the rules of representation. Cosmopolitan arenas bring together policymakers, experts, researchers, professionals and stakeholders even if resources and powers remain largely asymmetric. This cosmopolitism is welcomed by experts but also by transnational organisations and agencies which disseminate standards, technics, indicators and data towards the states and local authorities through the implementation of national or local policies.

Therefore, the politics of quality serve multiple aims within the Europeanisation process. The design of indicators and data has led to comparable education policies in a large space and according to different scales. This comparison of standards is an incentive for competition between countries but also for measuring progress in the convergence of policies and their alignment within the European agenda. Comparisons, as proven by PISA, serve as a common reference for policymakers implementing reforms. Different levels and supranational arrangements have to be

© Springer International Publishing Switzerland 2016   63
R. Normand, *The Changing Epistemic Governance of European Education*,
Educational Governance Research 3, DOI 10.1007/978-3-319-31776-2_3

considered to understand the European standardisation and the building of quality standards. All the sectors within the scope of the lifelong learning strategy are involved in the process (basic education, higher education, vocational education and training), while international organisations (the World Bank, OECD, UNESCO) multiply reports in the promise of educational quality for all. Quality politics have to serve the knowledge economy since it has been promoted by the Lisbon Declaration (cf. first chapter). It is also the result of globalisation which has led to a restructuration of both information flows and decision-making places according to scale politics, thus diminishing the importance of nation–states. Networks are superseding the traditional forms of political representation. The fixity of a territory and its institutional hierarchies has been replaced by the mobility of persons and the circulation of ideas and tools at the supranational scale. Quality politics correspond to a travelling policy, emancipated from borders between countries and even from Europe, modelling education and training systems despite some national and local hybridisations. This import/export game relies on networking governance in which policymakers and experts exchange best practices as they find a legitimacy for their actions. These politics are also anchored in an epistemological legitimacy. It is largely conceptualised by the theory of human capital which considers that the comparison of education systems is a good means of improving economic productivity and competitiveness. Furthermore, it gains legitimacy from new psychometrics and their international surveys on student and adult skills. It supports the postulates of evidence-based research mapping 'that works' in education. The building of a European and common space of measurement, as global quality politics, belongs to a 'government by numbers', thus leading to an increase in the role of expertise as well as transforming the relationships between science and policy.

In this chapter, we shall expose the foundations of this standardisation policy and its effects on education via the use of sociological research findings. We will then characterise the politics of progressively building standards at the European scale and buying into the lifelong learning strategy and knowledge economy. We shall then illustrate, using the case of higher education as a basis, the multiple logics and quality of conventions governing standards. The end of the chapter shall be devoted to the effects of standardisation on the definition of a new human agency handling standardised environments.

The Politics of Standards: Objects, Metrics and Expertise

If we resume Bowker and Star's definition (1999), it is possible to define standardisation as a process of constructing uniformities across time and space, through the generation of agreed-upon rules. Standards enable people to work at distance beyond communities of practice. They are based on metrics and designed by external institutions as professional organisations and agencies and by the state itself (Timmermans and Epstein 2010). Standards are norms which compare individuals and actions in a common language shared by evaluators, policymakers and stakeholders. They simplify and unify social reality by using technologies of comparison and governance at distance. This common representation of standards has increased constraints on actors but also with regard to certain possibilities of action and interaction (Ponte and Gibbon 2005; Ponte et al. 2011). Standards take their shape from classifications, indicators and other instruments of measurement which set boundaries and exclude some groups or individuals. However, standards and methodological procedures, if they have participated in shaping the world, are also negotiated and revised according to conventions and values related to a group or an institution. Networks of experts and expertise play an important role in setting up standards and integrating them into specialised and technical knowledge even if other actors are involved. They contribute in defining the boundaries of what is measurable and objective for governing institutions. In education, as elsewhere, organisations and international agencies mobilise different epistemic communities to participate in the design of tools and guidelines for each country.

Properties and Dimensions of Standards

For our purpose, we have classified standards into four important subtypes (Timmermans and Berg 2003). Design standards set structural specifications: they define the properties and features of tools and products. Such standards are explicit and are more or less detailed specifications of individual components or social and/or technical systems, ensuring their uniformity and their mutual compatibility. Standards in curriculum and assessment correspond to this first definition. Terminological standards, such as the International Standard Classification of Education (ISCE), ensure stability of meaning over different sites and over time, and they are essential for the aggregation of individual elements into larger wholes. Performance standards set outcome specifications. For example, a performance standard can specify the maximum level of achievement rates deemed acceptable for education policy (as measured by indicators and benchmarks). The last category is procedural standards, which specify how processes are to be performed. Such standards delineate the steps that are to be taken when specified conditions are met as in Quality Assurance in Education (QAE).

Some previous studies have shown that the definition of standards relies on the authority and legitimacy given to expertise and expert knowledge not being easily understandable to laymen. Experts conceive instruments and procedures by confining themselves into a technicality which avoids them having to give arguments and justifications (Brunsson and Jacobsson 2000; Jacobsson 2000). The promulgation and enforcement of standards is a central type of social regulation. Standards may productively be substituted for other forms of authoritative rule. When organisations or states are weak and cannot coerce behaviour through direct orders, standards can fill the gap by coordinating activities. And although standards are often promulgated by experts, they may come to function as an alternative to expert authority – a way of embedding authority in rules and systems rather than in credentialed professionals. At the same time, regulations via standards can serve as an alternative to regulations through social norms and conventions.

Other researchers have explained the normative dimension of standards. In a perspective of governmentality inspired by Michel Foucault's theory, standards are considered as technics of surveillance and control contributing to the implementation of a new rationality shaping behaviours within organisations and social life (Higgins and Larner 2010a, b; Henman and Dean 2010; Miller and O'Leary 1987). Busch demonstrated (2011) how standards emerged with the development of scientific instruments and procedures, particularly in maritime explorations, calculating time and space, or in fighting against disease, or in developing accountancy technics or in railway transportation. Standards have been historically linked to quality control producing reliable information and knowledge in serving the objectives of governance and management. Busch describes, with regard to education, that statistics and tests were used to promote efficiency and standards in defining teaching methods, time schedules and disciplinary protocols borrowed from industry. Today this standardisation has been extended to school choice and voucher systems. He also argues that standardisation is present within the medical world which has adopted procedures and protocols shaping the work of physicians and their relationship with patients.

In his explanation about the genesis of standards, Lawrence Busch draws an interesting parallel with the market. He notes that, for neo-liberals, the market is the most effective and efficient governing mechanism. By difference with the state which needs central planning, the market is based on a different epistemology. Central planning requires that the planner understands all the variables and their interaction to produce results. By contrast, the market does not need to know a given price because it reveals prices in accordance with circumstances (bad weather, transport difficulties, lack of supply, etc.). It makes the market attractive for a lot of neo-liberal thinkers. But in a global market, with international firms and a great volatility of prices and profits, while the state intervention is limited, another regime has been progressively invented using standards, certifications and accreditations as flexible means of regulation. While the interest for standards dates back from the nineteenth century, their use has become an imperative for the global neo-liberalism. Standards play an increasing role because they replace legal frameworks forged by states and statist regulations. They enable companies to discipline supply and to reduce pressure and competition on prices. They can also provide standardised products but also more expensive differentiated ones regarding the market segmentation. But standards by themselves are insufficient to constitute a new governance regime and they need other features found in legal regimes. So, standardisation has been developed according to a tripartite standards regime: standards, certifications and accreditations. For years, a complex network of institutions has emerged at global level to define and certify standards which were used by the market to inform buyers and sellers, while accreditation organisations were created to recognise certifying organisations and to give them legitimacy. In limiting the state interference in its business, the tripartite standards regime involves collectively a range of international actors in a form of hybrid governance which depends on the state but, at the same time, escapes from its regulation because it is self-organised and regulated by multinational companies and certifying/accrediting bodies. It also concerns, as we will see later, the global higher education area.

In the field of public health, Timmermans and Berg describe how standards strongly influence medical practices in specifying the types of drugs and protocols which have to be used by physicians at the hospital (Timmermans and Berg 1997). Many actors (pharmaceutical companies, patients, physicians, regulatory authorities, the legal system, etc.) participate in the definition of standards through complex games of conflict, negotiations and compromise. Politics transforms human populations into standardised objects and exposes them to scientific scrutiny, administrative routines and commercial objectives in order to conciliate principles of efficiency with some universalistic principles of care and well-being. The setting of standards can be imposed authoritatively by the state or through a consensus between stakeholders. It can be determined by various motives: security, efficiency, market forces, reallocation of resources, etc.

Standardisation and Actor–Network Theory

Through different accounts on standardisation, actor–network theory (ANT) studies the way different actors (scientists, experts, normalisers, etc.) deploy technics and mobilise other actors to govern at distance, beyond local spaces, from calculative devices and processes of translation (Latour 1987; Callon 1986). Tara Fenwick and Edwards wrote (2010) that ANT describes the way in which human and non-human elements are enacted as they become assembled through interwoven networks spread across space and time. It studies the micro-interactions through which different 'actants' are performed into being and managed to hold together. Networks produce force and other effects: knowledge, identities, rules, routines, behaviours, technologies, instruments, regulatory regimes, reforms, etc. ANT explains how some networks and connections work and become stable and durable by linking people and things while others fail. ANT has advanced several important concepts to analyse these processes: symmetry is a mean to not distinguish among non-human and human energies and form (objects, nature, technology, texts, concepts, etc.) that exercise influence in assembling and mobilising networks, translation refers to negotiation that works to shape or change elements and link them to extended chains of interconnected activity and enrolment and mobilisation mean processes that include and exclude elements from the chains and direct activity to performance. ANT is useful to analyse the centrality of artefacts in education policies. It can trace the negotiations and performances through which educational standards achieve and maintain some durable forms as a consequence of social–material relations in which they are located and performed. It can also consider rifts and disjuncture in prescriptions of educational standards and their implementation by recognising ambivalences, oscillations and transgressive enactments. ANT explains also that standards and powers are understood as emerging effects through a series of complex interactions and how conflicting values are assembled in a same agency. Its explanations go beyond the politics of language and the negotiations of ideologies in standard debates to focus on the ways that material objects and actions are implicated in the plays of standards formation.

ANT has been used in education to characterise the variety of sociotechnical assemblages which technologise and systematise education policies through spaces of commensurability and calculability induced by the development of such instruments as PISA or evidence-based policy frameworks (Fenwick and Edwards 2010; Gorur 2011a, b). We have also mapped networks of experts and epistemic communities who and which elaborated the international instruments of measurement, particularly the indicators of the Open Method of Coordination (OMC) (Normand 2009, 2010). Other researchers have used ANT to analyse socio-material assemblages linked to standardisation in teaching and learning activities and to study the place of non-human actors and objects in social interactions and in the shaping of identities (Fenwick and Landri 2012).

As we will see in the following pages, standards and standardisation have had important consequences in the building of the European space of education and the implementation of the knowledge economy. In creating some equivalences not just by sharing ideas and discourses but also by designing permanent and sustainable objects, such as statistics, standardisation transforms the modes of governance by involving complex networks of non-statist actors.

The Knowledge Economy and the European Space of Statistics

In promoting the knowledge society and knowledge economy since the Lisbon conference, the European Commission wanted to develop standards to breathe life into the European space of education (Lawn 2011). The conception of indicators and benchmarks by different groups of experts was well accepted by national policymakers who considered it as a means of strengthening cooperation between countries and improving education systems' efficiency and quality. The first meetings used school quality as a basis for discussion, while experts were solicited to develop indicators and to borrow knowledge accumulated by the OECD and Eurostat with the INES programme, as we have seen in chapter "An Epistemic Governance of European Education". The establishment of a quality assurance framework, including 16 indicators, was an important step for the coordination between countries

(European Commission 1999, 2001a, b, c). In the field of higher education, the Bologna conference, in setting up a system of harmonisation and comparison between diplomas in Europe, was a means for advancing the cause of standardisation. The creation of ECTS was a major policy enactment, even if some previous reflections had been conducted at the European conference of university presidents and quality agencies.

Standards Through the Open Method of Coordination

The Lisbon Strategy was a landmark for the implementation of standards within European education systems and in meeting the challenges of the knowledge economy according to official documents (European Commission 2000, 2001b). It also defined objectives for the investment in human capital and the promotion of mobility at the European scale. The Open Method of Coordination, with its indicators and benchmarks, was the main instrument for designing common standards for education policies. The European Council asked the Commission to write a report on the 'concrete future objectives of education and training systems' (Council of the European Union 2001). It defined 13 objectives to be reach by 2010 and proposed a common framework (European Commission 2002). The aim was to improve the quality of European education systems along with their accessibility and openness. It was approved by the ministers and quality was becoming a reference for education, while the OMC was measuring progress with regard to the objectives fixed at Lisbon. The idea was to facilitate exchanges of information and best practices between European policymakers through mutual cooperation and learning (European Commission 2001b). Consequently, governance by standards and quality was developed to structure exchange networks based on measurement technologies and statistical reports supporting political decision-making in European countries. The OMC was relayed by the Standing Group on Indicators and Benchmarks (SGIB) which was created to develop comparative measurements between education systems and to facilitate exchanges and the sharing of best practices (Lange and Alexiadou 2007). The definition of common standards in Europe was definitely based on expertise. The SGIB conceptualised 29 indicators related to different topics: age of teachers, ratio of pupils to teaching staff, rate or completion of upper secondary education and improvement in low-performing students attaining reading literacy; reading, mathematics and science performances; public expenditure on education; participation in lifelong learning; etc. In addition to performance indicators, the SGIB work programme scheduled the creation of five benchmarks (European Commission 2004):

1. EU average of no more than 10 % of early school leavers
2. Increase of at least 15 % in graduates in mathematics, science and technology and decrease in gender imbalance
3. Completion rate of upper secondary education of at least 85 % of 22-year-olds

4. Decrease of at least 20 % from the year 2000 in the percentage of low-achieving 15-year-olds in reading literacy in the EU
5. EU-level participation in lifelong learning of at least 12.5 % of the adult working-age population (25–64 age group)

During the following years, the European Commission and the European Council discovered there was a significant gap between the indicators fixed by the Lisbon Strategy and the current reforms implemented by the Member States (European Council 2004). They claimed that the reforms should be accelerated, while a group of experts, led by Wim Kok, the former prime minister of the Netherlands, decided to revise the strategy midterm. The Kok report suggested urgent measures aligned to indicators and benchmarks and argued that the European Commission had to revise its objectives by targeting key areas of education policy: key competencies, ICTs, vocational education and training, social inclusion and active citizenship (Kok 2004). The European Commission, expecting an effective implementation of benchmarks, suggested improving the investment in human capital and developing vocational training and apprenticeships, reducing the dropout rate, developing incentives to share the costs between the public and the private and facilitating lifelong learning. It recommended raising quality standards in education and training, encouraging mobility and flexibility for students and trainees and developing non-formal and informal education (European Commission 2005). Following the Kok report, the Open Method of Coordination was simplified, while states had to produce an annual report about any initiatives taken in reforming their education systems.

In 2007, the Commission, on the basis of the work carried out by the Eurydice European Unit, European Centre for the Development of Vocational Training (Cedefop) and Centre for Research on Education and Lifelong Learning (CRELL), decided that 30 key indicators would be put into place (European Commission 2007) to cover main policy areas: improving equity in education and training, promoting efficiency in education and training, making lifelong learning a reality, key competencies among young people, modernising school education, modernising vocational education and training and modernising higher education and employability. In another report, the Commission declared that the revision of the Lisbon Strategy had to focus on knowledge, innovation and the optimisation of human capital (De la Fuente 2003).

Let us now scrutinise these measurements of the Open Method of Coordination for education and training. The indicators and benchmarks were centred around eight key policy domains, each domain being related to one or several indicators: making education and training fairer, promoting efficiency in education and training, making lifelong learning a reality, mastering key skills for young people, modernising school education, modernising vocational education and training and modernising higher education and employability. However, this categorisation looked like a response to a progressive technocratic approach. To understand the scope of these indicators, they must be related to demographic challenges and to the European employment strategy as they contribute significantly to the orientation of the European lifelong learning policy. In this light, participation in pre-school education (equity) and the completion rate for upper secondary education (lifelong learning) are aimed at boosting the productivity of young people until they become adults. Similarly, investment in education and training (efficiency and modernisation) and the returns on investment from education and training (employability) are in the vein of human capital theories. The participation of adults in lifelong learning (lifelong learning) and learning or improving adult skills (employability and lifelong learning) reflects the objective of sustaining the productivity of older workers. The population's educational attainment (employability), the rate of higher education graduates and the transnational mobility of students in higher education (modernising higher education) are proof of the Commission's desire to develop and strengthen the talent pool in competition with the USA, China and Southeast Asian countries. The reading literacy, mathematics, science, ICT, indicators, etc. (key skills for young people) fulfil the need for international comparisons of educational achievement which are now regarded by economists as the most appropriate measurement of productivity and the quality of educational systems. A lot of the OMC indicators tend to formalise the principles of human capital theory through numbers.

Standardisation and Its Agencies

This implementation of the European Commission's political agenda and its project to standardise European policies were also relayed by several data-producing agencies. The Centre for Research on Education and Lifelong Learning (CRELL), created in 2005, is a research centre with a specific expertise in the field of economics, econometrics and statistics. It cooperates closely with Eurostat and the OECD. The centre based in Ispra (Northern Italy) was set up by DG EAC's statistical unit to develop indicators and benchmarks for Member States to make progress in the attainment of the Lisbon objectives. CRELL econometrists and statisticians are most often high-level experts who have already worked for the European Commission or other major international organisations or sometimes simply have an affinity with human capital economists. There are close links between CRELL and European Expert Network on Economics of Education (EENEE) which was created by DG EAC. CRELL provides its expertise to DG EAC and helps them prepare their annual reports and write briefs, which DG EAC, in turn, uses with their groups of experts. CRELL also organises seminars, conferences or workshops specialising in the measurement of lifelong learning in cooperation with the OECD. CRELL is also coordinated by EC's Joint Research Centre (JRC). JRC management has been placed under the aegis of the European commissioner for research and consists of institutes spread all over Europe. JRC is in charge of bringing scientific support to research programmes aligned with European policies in fields as varied as the environment, health, energy, technology, conducting materials, etc. JRC considers that econometric and statistical tools are essential for assessing the efficiency of policies in areas such as growth, competitiveness, the internal market and education. Building on the competences, it has developed in data analysis, modelling and information quality; it promotes an effective contribution to statistics, macroeconomic modelling, financial econometrics, sensitive analysis, knowledge and multi-criteria social assessment.

In Ispra, CRELL is hosted by the Econometrics and Applied Statistics Unit, one of JRC's networked institutes. The econometrics unit is more specifically in charge of developing econometric tools for the analysis and assessment of European policies in relation with several of EC's directorates-general (economic and financial affairs, internal market and services, research, information society and media, enterprise and industry). The mission of the Institute for the Protection and Security of the Citizen (IPSC) is to provide research results and to support EU policymakers in their effort towards global security and towards the protection of European citizens from accidents, deliberate attacks, fraud and illegal actions against EU policies. To that end, it has developed information technologies and sophisticated engineering systems with the aim of developing international data analyses.

Educational statistics is not only managed by this agency but also by other institutions such as international organisations. Andrew Barry suggests that it is necessary to take into account the connections between technological areas which fall beyond national borders as they produce standards or measurement instruments which are transferable across space or time (Barry 2001). This standardisation process, whether it applies to statistical items or to other technologies, remains essential for the harmonisation of European policy and for the construction of a 'calculation space'. Therefore, European institutions are not solely in charge of the harmonisation process. The European Commission only delegates responsibilities to other actors in the tacit understanding that standards and measurement instruments are developed on a voluntary basis. The harmonisation process has not given rise to a centralised European government but instead relies on such scattered institutions and agencies, both in the public and private sectors, as laboratories, expert groups or networks, standardisation committees or ministerial departments (Lawn and Grek 2012). They mobilise experts from the OECD, the US Educational Testing Service (ETS), the American National Center for Education Statistics (NCES) and other institutions such as the Australian Council for Educational Research (ACER) and Cito (a Dutch testing and assessment company). The International Association for the Evaluation of Educational Achievement (IEA), which was quite a small association when these international surveys became more prominent, has changed since the 1960s. It recently joined forces with the ETS through its IEA Data Processing and Research Centre in a joint venture, the IEA-ETS Research Institute, which aims to develop and set up large-scale assessments, train experts and policymakers in its field, collect data and disseminate the outcomes of international surveys from TIMSS (mathematics and science), Progress in International Reading Literacy Study (PIRLS), the International Adult Literacy Survey (IALS) and PISA (reading, mathematics and science).

Sotiria Grek argues that before the European Commission took over PISA and transferred the OMC indicators and benchmarks, the OECD, via the DeSeCo project (1997–2005), had sought to design a conceptual framework to identify key competencies, strengthen international assessments and define overarching goals for education systems and lifelong learning (Grek 2012, 2013). Prior to the development of the Programme for the International Assessment of Adult Competencies (PIAAC), the OECD had also conducted two international adult skills surveys: IALS (1994–1998) and ALL (2002–2006). In examining their development as key elements in influencing education policy directions in Europe, Sotiria Grek demonstrated how these projects have mobilised a large number of experts, statisticians and national policymakers in a series of meetings throughout Europe. She describes a world of travel, exchanges and collaboration and a place where new friendships can be forged. However, these exchanges most often take place in an increasingly competitive field, where large international research organisations strive to secure the limited and diminishing funding available from national governments for the conduct of these studies. The development of adult literacy studies shows that international comparative testing is one of the prime instruments in the steering and exchange of knowledge in education in Europe. It is a major movement in the introduction of knowledge in policy for which expertise is central in legitimising new interactions between science and government.

Standards, Statistics and Classifications

In addition to international surveys, Eurostat, the European Commission's Directorate of Statistics, has worked in the past decades with other institutions to develop its lifelong learning statistics and its systems for comparing countries and regions (EUROSTAT 2007). It is a way of standardising the collection and production of statistical information and led to the designing of the European Statistical System (ESS) which harmonises data between Member States. Eurostat has proposed that Member States adopt common methodologies in consolidating data for different areas of public policies beyond education. Standardisation was also part of successive revisions of the International Standard Classification of Education (ISCED) of which the aim was to facilitate the compilation of data and their comparison. The European shaping of statistics is based on quality standards defining categories and classifications used for the collection of data and the design of indicators.

As we can see, the production of European statistics is subject to realistic requirements: metrological realism forces statisticians to design the least biased possible measurement instruments and to produce relevant and reliable data, as well as user realism because statistics are used by European policymakers and may be presented to other stakeholders in a public discussion (Desrosières 2002). However, as suggested below, these European statistics shape a particular representation of education and training by relating technical instruments (nomenclatures, classifications, indicators) to new categories of knowledge and actions specific to a lifelong learning policy. In their study on the International Classification of Diseases, a system managed by the World Health Organization, Geoffrey Bowker and Susan Leigh Star suggested that lists are a very effective means of coordinating information and work widely across time and space (Bowker and Star 1999). But classification schemes and statistical nomenclatures give rise to conflictual definitions because the different stakeholders – civil servants, statisticians, experts and researchers – develop different moral and political conceptions. These systems are the result of a permanent but evolving negotiation and depend not only on the solving of technical problems but also on the will to be as close as possible to reality. Classifications and nomenclatures are technologies which impose universal schemes to social actors in how they structure the information collected from very heterogeneous areas. We will illustrate our point with three examples in the area of education and training.

The 2001 'Report of the Eurostat Task Force on Measuring Lifelong Learning' had already identified the principles of a statistical classification of learning activities related to formal, non-formal and informal education (Eurostat 2001). This classification has since been used in a handbook published by Eurostat's Education and Culture unit (Eurostat 2006). Lifelong learning is regarded as an intentional activity performed by young or adult individuals to improve their knowledge and skills in a more and less formalised environment. Formal education, the first statistical category, characterises intentional learning on the basis of a set schedule and duration, in a hierarchical structure with successive course levels and enrolment requirements within established educational institutions. Non-formal education, the second statistical category, includes all types of taught learning activities on a teacher–student(s) basis without there necessarily being any spatial or temporal proximity. The last category, informal learning, corresponds to self-learning in the family, the workplace or daily life.

According to Eurostat, the UNESCO-designed international classification – ISCED97 – is helpful for classifying formal and non-formal education, but it cannot cover all lifelong learning categories. The new classification promoted by Eurostat aims to measure the time and money spent in learning and to combine this data with information collected on informal learning as it is perceived by individuals. This is why in 2001 Eurostat departments were already planning to conduct surveys on how individuals invested their spare time in learning (Time Use Surveys) and on its relative share of the household budget (Household Budget Surveys). Time Use Surveys take the form of a questionnaire in which the surveyed individual is asked to estimate the average time spent in activities as varied as attending seminars and conferences, visiting exhibitions, using a computer and surfing on the Internet, listening to the radio or watching TV and learning with colleagues or friends. In parallel, Household Budget Surveys collect information on the personal financial investment devoted to learning. Data collection should be extended to private individuals and companies in order to cover all lifelong learning categories. For Eurostat, this data should be oriented towards learners and take account of all their needs in the field of formal, non-formal and informal knowledge acquisition.

The second example concerns the reviewed architecture of qualifications at the European level (Deane 2005). For Eurostat statisticians, the classification of learning activities is too narrowly linked to that of qualifications. The Commission has for several years argued for the accreditation of non-formal and informal learning and has encouraged Member States to adopt common principles and procedures at national, regional and local levels. The idea is to link the accreditation of learning to the expression of individual rights via a credit transfer system. In 2006, the European Qualifications Framework (EQF) laid the foundations for the accreditation, transfer and recognition of formal, non-formal and informal skills. This accreditation is regarded as a step forward towards the identification, assessment and recognition of a comprehensive range of skills that individuals develop throughout their lives in different fields (education, work, leisure).

Based on learning outcomes, standards lead to the design of assessments and procedures to define validation criteria. For formal education, they take the form of exams or tests. For informal education, accreditation can centre on interviews with individuals, the building of a portfolio, skills check-up, observations or simulations of an activity and evidence of professional practices. This relation between the classification of learning activities and that of qualifications undermines the importance of diplomas in the recognition of individual skills. The European Statistical System has three major challenges regarding data development. First, it has to measure the learning process to transform instruction into formal education. The second challenge is to develop more relevant statistics to cover all aspects of lifelong learning, especially those related to course offer, funding, recruitments, diplomas, adult education and further vocational training. The third challenge concerns the measurement of the cumulative effects of formal, non-formal and informal learning activities on the indicators of human, financial and social capital via the use of a longitudinal approach.

Governing by Numbers: New Political Technologies

The rise of the knowledge economy in Europe can be explained by the development of international comparisons of performance and productivity between education systems and the standardisation activities imposed on numerous actors in the areas of evaluation, diplomas, curriculum and ICTs. Standards lead to perpetual adjustments involving public and private actors. The process is a voluntary one and includes a mix of regulations and innovation, but it is also considered as a key element in the lifelong learning policy. As we have seen above, this standardisation, through the design of indicators, benchmarks and other tools, is supported by European centres of calculation extending information systems across Europe. However, this standardisation is fluidly, smoothly and weakly regulated by states. It is soft governance requiring voluntary engagements and self-management as is the case for European projects. The European governance of education also facilitates policy learning by making agreements, collecting data and organising clusters from which experts and policymakers share the same objectives. We will present these different dimensions of policy learning in the following chapter.

Standardisation as a Global Post-bureaucratic Regime

Through the design of statistics in Europe, instrumental at-distance governance implements a complex mix of state and non-state institutions, market actors and international networks challenging the sovereignty of states. Jenny Ozga (2011) distinguishes post-bureaucratic from conventional bureaucratic regimes, by suggesting that each presupposes a specific kind of knowledge and way of using it. While bureaucratic modes of government require established bodies of knowledge to be translated into vertical relations, post-bureaucratic modes of governance attempt to turn actors' autonomy and reflexivity into means of governing. Therefore, instead of considering the state at the centre and the nation as an autonomous entity, for which knowledge is produced by a small number of professionals and academics, post-bureaucracy is polycentric and it is simultaneously international, transnational, subnational and national. One can observe the involvement of private interests, edu-business and philanthropic organisations both nationally and globally (Ball 2012), which is central to what Ball and Junemann (2012) refer to as 'network governance', creating 'heterarchies' that mix together bureaucracy, markets and networks in new ways. Stephen Ball (2009) wrote that heterarchy, as a notion more relevant than network for him, is an organisational form somewhere between hierarchy and network that draws upon diverse horizontal and vertical links that permit different elements of the policy process to cooperate (and/or compete) while individually optimising different success criteria. It replaces or combines bureaucracy and administrative structures and relationships with a system of organisation replete with overlap, multiplicity, mixed ascendancy and/or divergent-but-coexistent patterns of relation, which operates at and across 'levels' (local, subnational, national and international). The characteristics of heterarchies are that different kinds of power relations may exist between the same elements at the same time. Policy heterarchies display various relationships and asymmetries (partnerships, contracts, inspection, competition, performance management and regulation, sponsorship) with actors playing different roles, using different capabilities and exercising different forms of power.

As a result, standardisation is made up of a multiplicity of actors taking part not only in the policy process but in the production of knowledge. Under post-bureaucracy, knowledge is pluralistic, flexible and provisional and it is always policy and future oriented (Ozga 2011). Above all, it is comparable and can travel fast; it derives its legitimacy not only from scientific knowledge but also from know-how and experience (Grek and Ozga 2010). The use of experts and expert knowledge produces, through the creation of data and measurement tools, standards with advanced technological devices rendering educational facts commensurable and state intervention transparent while strengthening the competition between education systems. Beyond the use of instruments and in addition to the legislative arsenal linking Member States to the European Union, soft governance is supported by expert groups, networks or clusters. They develop transversal modes of cooperation through alliances or different forms of participation which have been encouraged by the European Commission in order to persuade and convince Member States and their representatives to adopt specific standards in their national policy (Sellar and Lingard 2013, 2014). This incentive power, based on a large mobilisation of experts, practitioners, stakeholders and policymakers in European programmes, is an important driver in achieving the Lisbon Strategy.

Standards and the European Area of Big Data

Using the actor–network theory, Radhika Gorur entered into the 'PISA Laboratory' to observe how scientists classify and categorise the world according to categories borrowed from psychometrics and mathematical modelling, while data and scientific statements are embedded into material devices. PISA's bureaus form a centre of calculation in which data is combined in different ways to produce coalescing knowledge based on specific practices and technical choices. It is therefore possible to consider scientific evidence as an assemblage, a reality performed into being, rather than a representation of a pre-existing truth. It converts PISA knowledge from a 'matter of fact', something that is beyond dispute, into a 'matter of concern', a political object. In this assemblage, psychometricians perform a PISA of statistical sophistry within the limitations of large-scale testing, commensuration and standardisation. Subject experts praise PISA as a pedagogic innovation honouring the application of knowledge over curriculum. Country representatives see PISA as a patriotic advantage in achieving high scores. The OECD considers PISA as a standard to provide policy imperatives. PISA is ontologically variable as it mobilises a diversity of worlds, representations and modes of ordering. Taking PISA as an illustration, we can assume a new architecture is emerging in which the knowledge of experts and professionals invents, from project to project, from website to website, new ways of formalising, standardising and universalising education policies. It is a fragmented and complex governance at the European level involving a wide variety of actors according to different places and scales. This pluralism of actors has enabled the European Commission to shift from bureaucratic, hierarchical and traditional forms of state intervention to ensure modes of coordination by the market and networks. It is particularly true for the definition of quality standards in higher education as we will see further.

This standardisation, relatively invisible at the state level, creates changes in political behaviour and tools, while it is justified on behalf of democratisation, increased participation and transparency. Standards rely on a procedural process:

they are negotiated and revised regularly on a voluntary basis which is different from state norms submitted to structured ways of political representation and debate. They enable agencies and expert networks to reach a consensus and to define new recommendations. As indicators and benchmarks, they facilitate the governance of the European space of education through a certain reliability of data and the possibility to measure and compare achieved goals. Standards reduce uncertainty by offering soft, networking and at-distance governance, delegating more responsibility to non-governmental actors and involving both public and private professionals.

These performance standards have been relayed by the development of systems of evaluation and insurance quality in European countries according to the principles of accountability. Stephen Ball has shown how such technologies of governance as accountability, the market and performance management have orientated the political agenda (Ball 2013). This assemblage of political technologies corresponds to the surveillance and control of educational professions subjected to audits and New Public Management (Power 1999). Data is essential in the creation of these infrastructures, while statistics have entered into the era of 'big data' which will result in important epistemological and political consequences for education. The technological trend in politics, through frameworks and infrastructures, defines a rationality which masks the power in place as well as asymmetric positions between actors.

This government by numbers has also had some rescaling effects and has deterritorialised education policies through a 'global panopticism' which has facilitated the extension of neo-liberalism and the marketisation of education systems (Lingard et al. 2013). It is also a biopolitical project for managing populations through techniques of measurement that enable nation–states to position themselves and their education systems within the global market place. Testing and related technologies are very important in the reconstitution of the new neo-liberal versions of educational accountability which have resulted in real implications regarding teachers' work in classrooms. If, at the beginning, accountability was top-down, putting strong pressure on schools, today it tends to take multiple forms, becoming more horizontal and requiring a stronger involvement of actors.

Towards a New System of Accountability

The transformations of these modes of calculation are the consequences of criticism addressed to certain school comparison methods and evidence-based measures. The variety of local contexts and the difficulties in making actions and systems commensurable have not just revealed the imperfections of large-scale assessments, but their actual methodology has been contested. The complexity and hybridisation of policies challenges the design of standardised measurements. This reality is taken into account by international organisations. In a recent note, the OECD proposed new forms of accountability (Hooge et al. 2012).

Instead of a common vertical top-down accountability, which enforces compliance with laws and regulation, the policy brief proposed the implementation of a horizontal accountability which engages multiple stakeholders in addition to the teaching profession in the educational decision-making processes and their implementation. It is a means of expanding the notion of accountability to a multi-leveled approach which includes data from school performance measures but also develops assessments and gets feedback from other sources. This policy, which involves students, parents, communities and other stakeholders in the formulation of strategies and multiple devices for evaluation, aims to legitimise a quality approach in the services provided by schools.

This new approach has been studied by Jenny Ozga and her colleagues (Ozga et al. 2011; Ozga 2012). While analysing the practices of Quality Assurance and Evaluation (QAE) in several European Northern countries (Finland, Sweden, Denmark, Scotland and England), the research team showed that QAE is structured by the international evidence-based policy movement and the development of indicators and benchmarks (Grek et al. 2009). QAE has transformed educational debates from a normative discussion into an expert discussion about statistics. In line with these changes, people in schools have to make choices and assume a collective responsibility in getting data on their own in order to orientate the school project. The traditional forms of judgement and data collection have been transferred to individuals or groups in charge of the implementation of Quality Assurance and Evaluation (QAE) frameworks and technologies through a multiple accountability process. This has been followed by the changing roles of the inspection bodies which have shifted from inspecting and controlling schools and teachers to new tasks of supporting, coaching, and advising them on how they can improve. Therefore, QAE instruments applied at the local level have become a means of promoting soft governance without renouncing to comparability, of converting teachers to the interest of accountability and of changing their professional practices while disconnecting the issues of evaluation from the public debate. In this process, the local is rebuilt by the centre, in the sense that the autonomy and responsibility of actors are defined in relation to measurement tools and information systems governed by the Central State which thus reaffirms its control by fixing targets and performance indicators. However, QAE creates tensions among inspection bodies which have to be positioned among these externally defined technics of control and regulation (Grek et al. 2013; Grek and Lindgren 2014). They have to apply new rules and implement the evaluation and self-evaluation of schools in order to share their expert knowledge with the members of the school community. If the introduction of quality transforms durably inspection practices while participating in the international circulation of standards at the European level, as shown by the peer learning activities within the Standing International Conference of Inspectorates (SICI), it renews their conceptions of control by converting them to audit-based approaches and proximity in their relationships with schools.

Standards, Quality and Tools in Higher Education

The notions of quality and evaluation in higher education are nothing new. As Guy Neave has argued, the Evaluative State, with the increase in the number of students, quickly assumed responsibilities for controlling legality and mastering expenditures (Neave 1988). Neave distinguishes between evaluation serving the maintenance of the system and evaluation defining strategic objectives of change (Neave 1994). The former relates both to the control of the annual budget and the allocation of human and material resources. The latter fixes long-term performance-based objectives, particularly the access and inclusion of students, the fight against exclusion and dropouts, the transformations of the school provision and the cost and balance of the teacher/student ratio. This new evaluation is defined *a posteriori* as the control of a product, process or output rather than an input. It is the result of new relationships between higher education and the economy, while higher institutions have been converted to educating the masses. Evaluation has become a powerful means of regulating and rationalising the state's intervention with regard to setting quality-based objectives and criteria. This quality framework introduces strategic control within higher education institutions.

Quality Insurance and Accountability After Bologna

In the middle of 1980s, control by quality standards was implemented in the UK, a leading exponent of this policy. In the other European countries, the issue of quality has been limited to the limitation of expenditure, while at the same time there has been a strong demand for accountability and institutional autonomy. The issue of performance then emerged with the institutionalisation of quality through a series of meetings organised in 1987 by the European Association for Institutional Research (EAIR) which sought to promote self-evaluation mechanisms related to innovation-related problems. The Consortium of Higher Education Researchers (CHER) was also an important actor in legitimising quality management in European higher education and advancing the idea of the imperative transformation of higher education institutions. These meetings between professionals were followed by other formal and political meetings, while the European Commission was searching to enhance external and systematic evaluation in higher education institutions. The *European Pilot Project for Evaluating Quality in Higher Education* brought together 17 countries and 46 institutions in the middle of the 1990s to design new knowledge, to transfer it to other countries and to set up discussions on evaluation. Progressively, quality was considered as an object of measurement through data collection, while Total Quality Management models were disseminated.

Even if there are *bona fide* differences in Europe between higher education systems, a same trend can be observed through the development of mixed systems combining subjective elements and data considered as being objective.

Self-evaluation is often combined with performance indicators, while evaluation between peers and the visits of external experts remain the most widespread forms of evaluation. But the European higher education systems are facing an increasing demand for accountability; and quality assurance methods have been widely disseminated during the past decade particularly with regard to teaching and student learning. Quality assurance approaches are not only associated with managerial control in academic organisations, they are also considered as drivers for transparency and openness while they are becoming increasingly subjected to external agencies. If the definition of academic quality remains linked with being published and excellence and such prestigious institutions as Oxford or Harvard, the new quality policy, by using standards and objective criteria, is challenging this traditional vision to promote a service-based relationship and is setting up step-by-step controls in regard to precise objectives and measurements. By using both external control and internal quality frameworks and procedures, evaluators claim an 'objective' approach guaranteed by standards upon which performance is measured and compared. Many higher education institutions in Europe have established quality assurance systems to regulate their activities. As Michael Power explains, this extension of the audit process has paradoxically created a crisis of a lack of trust with regard to the institution itself, while indicators and control procedures aim to give guarantees of reputation and effectiveness in order to satisfy consumers, students, parents and business.

The issue of quality was widely supported and praised at the Bologna conference of which the aim was to make the European Higher Education and Research Area a major driver for the development of the knowledge economy. The creation of this harmonised space was to make Europe more attractive and competitive, while diploma structures were harmonised to enhance European student mobility. But the Bologna process, because of its extension, was not capable of developing quality assurance by itself. This is why the European strategy was pursued through the development of comparable criteria and methodologies, particularly with regard to student learning and curriculum. A 'Joint Quality Initiative' group was established to design a common and comparable qualification framework for higher education in which skills and profiles would be aligned from one national system to another. The Dublin Descriptors were important for the standardisation process. In identifying the key competencies which had to be mastered by students at different stages, they provided a standard curriculum. Furthermore, in the 2000s, the Tuning Project sought to harmonise teaching structures and programmes from teaching disciplines on the basis of comparable quality standards, by creating a link between learning outcomes, skills and the European Credit Transfer System (ECTS).

In parallel, accreditation procedures were launched in the majority of higher education systems from the European East-Centre. In Europe, several external assessments were implemented in higher education institutions under the supervision of the European Rectors' Conference and the OECD Institute for Higher Education Management (Knight and de Wit 1999). During these years, Member States have given priority to the development of assessments and quality insurance in higher education system, particularly through the creation of national agencies. The implementation of quality insurance mechanisms in higher education has strengthen the certification of universities and diplomas, while higher education institutions have been put in competition with other providers, particularly private institutions escaping from control by the state. According to many reports, the use of new digital technologies has been considered as a means to diversify diploma delivery and supports according to different learning levels. Interactions between academics and students (virtual/non-virtual) and types of media (text, picture and sound, multimedia), teaching contents and curricula had to be assessed in relation to the same objectives: developing qualifications and meeting the demand. The definition of knowledge and skills had to narrowly associate professionals in the design of qualification and certification frameworks able to include new forms of recognition for diplomas.

The experiment of quality insurance was also supervised by the OECD institutional management programme which was implemented from 1994 to 1998 by the Academic Cooperation Association (ACA) through an international project on higher education quality and internationalisation. This project was continued with the European University Association, while the International Association of University Presidents set up a 'task force' on accreditation and focused its 1999 annual conference on the issue of quality and internationalisation. This orientation and reflections have been taken up by the European Commission which has created the European Network for Quality Assurance in Higher Education (ENQA) in the same year. This creation has followed a recommendation from the Council of Ministers made in September 1998. The aim was to promote cooperation between actors involved in quality insurance approaches in higher education after the pilot project led the Commission and recommendations from the European Council and Bologna conference. Member States have been recommended to introduce insurance quality assessment-based methods and common principles already experimented in pilot projects during the years 1994–1995. Quality insurance agencies as well as higher education associations have been invited to adhere to the ENQA. A steering group has been charged to implement an action plan, to disseminate information beside members and to organise regular meetings like workshops and conferences.

Frameworks, Rankings and Benchmarks: Tools of Quality

In 1998, after the Lisbon Declaration instituting the recognition of qualifications in the European Higher Education Area, a working group on transnational education has been created under the supervision of the UNESCO and the European Council. It has to elaborate a code of 'best practices', a set of principles to be respected by institutions involved in the provision of education services at the global level. This 'ethical' code had to be completed by recommendations concerning qualification assessment abroad. Procedures and criteria had been conceived by the European Network of Information Centres (ENIC). In addition to this code well implemented in different English-speaking countries, European higher education institutions have been invited to accept the principles of accreditation and quality audits by external agencies. The model was inspired by the UK Quality Assurance Agency which had developed a quality insurance system through a cooperation with several universities and transnational programmes and harmonisation of foreign diplomas in Europe, East Asia and Middle East (Middlehurst 2001).

This quality policy created the European Qualifications Framework (EQF) in terms of knowledge and skills and contributed to the foundation of evaluation and accreditation systems in Europe. The European Network for Quality Assurance in Higher Education was particularly active in the development of networks and cooperation between national quality assurance agencies (ENQA 2005). It was part of the creation of EQF, and it involved its experts in the process but also provided information and tools for its members. In setting up standards and guidelines, ENQA sought to promote quality assurance methods and programmes for higher education institutions in Europe and to develop measurement tools (rankings, benchmarks, etc.) for the comparison of systems.

At a global level, international rankings, such as the most famous one, the Shanghai Jiao Tong University Institute of Higher Education [SJTUIHE], ushered in a new era for higher education of global competition between national and higher education institutions (Marginson and van der Wende 2007). The Shanghai Jiao Tong and the second most well-known instrument, the Times Higher Education Supplement, were published in the beginning of the 2000s. Today, policymakers take into account this comparative data when they make decisions about higher education policies and the allocation of resources. These rankings give credence to the idea that universities' performance has to be displayed via 'league tables' and to take the comprehensive research-intensive university as an example (Marginson 2007). At the same time, they discard other university models without considering the size of higher education institutions. Research is mainly valued at the international level because it generates attractiveness for researchers and students and for policymakers it sustains innovation and economic competitiveness. Ranking data is mainly quantitative and based on research findings like Nobel Prizes and Fields Medals in mathematics.

Those studies which have analysed the methodology of rankings are generally critical (Hazelkorn 2009, 2011). They show deep differences from one system to another with regard to principles, conceptual approaches but also the availability and reliability of data. From this perspective, there is no objective measurement but a diversity of tables created worldwide. They do not use the same data and indicators, and ponderations differ from one ranking to another. Despite these biases, rankings highlight definitions of academic quality according to the same standards, and they are used to build an international reputation with some spin-off effects on higher education governance. They are now fully part of the international higher education landscape and have extended quality assurance into measurements of word-class excellence. In doing so, they have orientated higher education and research policies and led countries to restructure and concentrate their resources and to increase the visibility of their institutions. Despite the criticism rankings have attracted, national systems use them because they are considered to be easily readable and accessible, they offer a simple measurement of research performance, and they justify political choices in governance and in the allocation of budgets (Hazelkorn 2007, 2008). International organisations (the OECD, the European Commission) are very active in the development of these comparative instruments, while tables inform stakeholders and give the impression of transparency promoted by accountability policies.

Benchmarking also plays an important role in quality approaches by formulating standards which, like rankings, are highly influential. As Isabelle Bruno has demonstrated, benchmarking was rationalised in the industrial world at the turn of the 1980s by engineers from the multinational company Xerox, and it was later invested by some scientists' approaches to management (Bruno 2009). What is at stake is not only getting obeisance from subordinates but reaching a consensus regarding 'objectively' fixed targets, motivating freely consented actions under exogenous and non-hierarchical, objective and non-interpersonal pressure. Benchmarking is a mode of government promoting initiative, self-evaluation, responsibility, voluntarism and personal engagement. Instead of subjecting people to orders and rules, it leads to them acting on their own initiative. It is a means of governing the real through an empirical method searching for 'best practices' differently from accountancy technics or commercial negotiations. In fixing targets which need to be reached, benchmarking opens up a space of potentialities and competition while best performances are sought everywhere and worldwide. The government of benchmarking assigns quantified objectives claiming realism by probing data, evidence-based management or management by facts.

Consequently, in higher education, benchmarks are powerful instruments of at-distance coordination for managers and policymakers, while systematically collected data allow them to determine ways of improving their own institutions. Benchmarks can be defined in different departments or faculties to compare performances for competitive and/or cooperative purposes. They are means of guiding consumer choice in the higher education market. ENQA has widely disseminated the principles of benchmarking by setting up categories and comparative scales and promoting best practices. This extension of benchmarks in Europe can be explained by a search for quality and continuous improvement justifying changes within organisations and professions. Benchmarks are used to achieve certain standards, to implement regulatory systems, to transform organisations and to enhance the dynamics of innovation. They are also used to exchange best practices and to develop peer learning activities.

Even if it based on powerful instruments that incite worldwide competition, education quality cannot be reduced to this market logic. Of course, the development of a global market in higher education is a reality, but in many countries the state continues to regulate and assess higher education institutions. Of course, quality reveals prices and consumer preferences, for example, when students and parents accept to pay higher fees for services, they find more in tune with their needs and revenues. And, measured by rankings, this accentuates the marketisation of higher education institutions in worldwide competition to attract the best students. But quality, as demonstrated by research in the economics of conventions, corresponds to socio-institutional arrangements and modes of coordination which are different from those of the market (Eymard-Duvernay et al. 2005; Boltanski and Thévenot 2006). For example, quality measured by quantitative criteria and statistics materialises a search for efficiency and equity with regard to the development of the Evaluative State. The implementation of New Public Management includes components which are different from the market logic, and this has led to changes affecting work conditions and professions. Furthermore, quality produces an impact on the reputation of higher education institutions which are not engaged in a competitive environment. Some of them are attractive because they have a marketable tradition or an intellectual and scientific history. This plurality of quality conventions demonstrates how valorisation of quality depends on context, type of institution, modes or coordination and governance, accountability instruments and methods of certification and accreditation. If rankings and benchmarking strengthen the market logic regulating universities, other aspects related to ethics, collegiality, learning, self-development and well-being and identity are more difficult criteria to measure, but they are also decisive with regard to choices and preferences. Quality therefore refers to different conventions and modes of coordination from which people justify their action and do not always identify quality in an instrumental manner. Paradoxically, it explains the success and miracle of quality standards, as we have already observed in the case of PISA, which espouse a range of definitions of quality and help to converge stabilised compromises from diverse interpretations and expectations.

From Standardisation to Normalisation: The Fabrication of a New Agency

As we have seen above, the actor–network theory (ANT) is useful for analysing standardisation and standards, particularly the relations between calculation instruments and knowledge production. Numbers are objects interacting and categorising a certain vision of the world and an at-distance control through heterogeneous networks (Latour 1987; Law 1992). In investigating the roles of non-humans in these networks and data circulation, ANT has demonstrated operations of mediation and translation between standardisation and politics, thus reducing the extent and complexity of knowledge produced in research units and embedded in sociotechnical devices. Knowledge production is registered in inscriptions, collections of objects and material forms assembled and manipulated by individuals and institutions, thus

giving consistency to standards. Standardisation is relatively contingent and operates from chain to chain according to arrangements and compromises between
diverse actors. From conception to implementation, it is a long-standing process of
mobilisation, networking and empowering.

Standardisation and Different Regimes of Justice

As we have seen in the previous pages, standardisation aims to conciliate two logics: a logic of regulation and a logic of objectivity. A logic of regulation is where
standards serve to fix objectives and to implement education policies. A logic of
objectivity is where standards are linked to tests, indicators and benchmarks which
objectivise these policies through statistics and numbers. However, standards serve
other aims. They are used to coordinate tasks and activities beyond individuals: for
example, a principal can ask a group of teachers to take into account standards and
to improve their effectiveness. Standards therefore have a function of coordination
action. Standards also deliver information. For example, a benchmark gives information about the position of universities in relation to their competitors. Or an indicator can be used to compare the evolution of the number of students per faculty.
Standards relate to different formats of information linked to different logics of
regulation and coordination of action between individuals, groups and organisations. Standards also serve the evaluation process. They can help produce a judgement on a situation in time and space and propose equivalences between different
entities, for example, PISA score comparison.

Our reflection on standards has borrowed some concepts from the ANT but also
from the theory of conventions studying the production of standards and their use
(Boltanski and Thévenot 2006). These two French sociologists have demonstrated
how experiences among social actors are related to different hardships as they are
committed to their social environment. By mobilising different worlds and logics of
action, according to cognitive and material resources, they carry a sense of justice
and common good into the public space, particularly when they are confronting
other human beings. This encounter generates disputes because of the diversity of
common goods within society, but compromises can be found to avoid potential
conflicts and violence. Even if these compromises are unstable and revisable, some
of them have been embedded in institutions for a long time, and they are more difficult to challenge. However, denunciations and justifications serve to dismantle and
build compromises as changes occur in society. It accounts for social arrangements
among individuals dependent on experienced situations; their moral competences
are mobilised for the common good, and they are recognised and identified by the
group and form a commitment taken from several principles of justice (Boltanski
and Thévenot 2006). This sense of justice is not imposed by a predefined frame but
through discussion and deliberation, a space of justification and criticism, one
which can provoke an agreement on the action to be carried out.

Boltanski and Thévenot (2006) identified six types of common good that can be distinguished in relation to the 'cognitive' 'worlds' or 'spheres' shared by academics – those that determine the intellectual dimensions of their practice: the *Inspired* (I), *Domestic* (D), *Civic* (C), *Opinion* (O), *Market* (M) and *Industrial* (Ind) worlds[1] (see in the table below).

'Worlds of Justice', as Presented in Boltanski, L. and Thévenot, L. (2006)

	Inspired	Domestic	Civic	Opinion	Market	Industrial
Mode of evaluation (worth)	Grace, noncon-formity, creativeness	Esteem, hierarchy	Public interest	Fame	Price, gain	Effectiveness
Format of relevant information	Emotional	Oral, exemplary	Formal, official	Semiotic	Monetary	Measurement and criteria, statistics
Elementary relation	Passion	Trust	Solidarity	Recog-nition	Competition	Functional link
Human qualification	Creativity, ingenuity	Authority	Equality	Celebrity	Desire, purchasing power	Professional competency, expertise

So, regimes of justice and diversity of goods are important features of interactions between actors and give structure to their lives. The theory of Luc Boltanski and Laurent Thévenot is useful in specifying how evaluation and standardisation relate to different orders of worth: an industrial worth when evaluation is targeting effectiveness, a market worth when evaluation is putting people and resources in competition with each other, a civic worth when evaluation is highlighting a reduction in inequalities, etc. Boltanski and Thévenot use a notion of evaluation which goes far beyond its usual meaning: they consider modes of valuation, in the sense that judgement from standards has to be put into the perspective of a plurality of valuations for the common good. Standards and standardisation deploy different orders of worth in terms of justification. One can invoke standards on behalf of students' well-being, an increase in performance, maintaining a university's prestige, equality of opportunities, the tradition of curriculum, etc. Standards therefore draw up a global political order and they are the result of arrangements, and compromises between different actors emphasise such or such

---

[1] I will apply this codification to the rest of this chapter, to avoid introducing too many concepts. The juxtaposition of two 'worlds' is denoted by a forward slash (e.g. the world of domesticity versus the world of the market: D/M), and the compromise between two worlds is denoted by the abbreviation 'compr' (e.g. a compromise between the world of domesticity and the world of the market is represented as: D compr. M). I also refer readers to the appendix, for an elaboration on the characteristics of the different worlds.

conception for the common good. They allow several forms of evaluation to be oriented according to this perspective.

These arrangements and conventions are not only discourses or principles of justice. They are produced by prior investment to give them a certain consistence and solidity. Standards have an objective dimension: they are material assemblages. As we have already shown above, the politics of standards is made of invested forms and solidified objects contributing to the creation of conventions but also to regulations and coordination between individuals, groups and organisations. However, standards do not count just on their material equipment: they count by their degree of objectivity. This objectivity relates to different degrees of evidence highlighted by expertise but also by statistics probing information. The development of the evidence-based education is a classic example of this standardisation. Standards are increasingly justified by randomised controlled trials or meta-analyses which legitimise a new knowledge production mode while at the same time undermining ethnographical approaches and case studies in educational research. This new production of knowledge has led to the design of standards and normative guidelines which aim to regulate and conform to practices (on behalf of evidence-based research and policy). This regulatory objectivity is more than just a simple material assemblage. It has created a new agency between the person and his/her professional environment. Authors such as Mead (1934) or Cooley (1909) have described the notion of agency within a scheme of practices related to the production of citizens as a collective while also they undermine the role of primary groups as a vital cog for the development of morality and the self, sentiments and ideals. Mead breaks down the construction of the self into social processes of communication and community: agency is composed by socially organised principles of interaction and communication which represent the 'community'. And it is also the effect of standards to equip this agency and to embed objectivity in core practice through calculative and normalising devices.

Standards and Normalised Human Agency

According to these assumptions, it is of interest to make a distinction between standardisation and normalisation. Standardisation ensures a comparison in time and space for regulatory and coordination tasks and for information and evidence purposes. Normalisation refers to a disciplinary work of standards as Foucault and, subsequently, Tom Popkewitz, conceptualised through the notion of 'devices' for the former and the 'typification of human beings' for the latter. This creation of a modern, technocratic and reflexive self is a 'fabrication process' as Popkewitz (2007) explained. Modernist politics, by playing down their own-created exclusion ways and by inverting the relation subject–object from an instrumental vision, have prevented the creation of symbolic spaces and negotiation of meaning by educational and training actors. Ideally, in European politics, citizens break from the different stages shaped by compulsory schooling in order to establish a professional life cycle of lifelong learning in which tests constantly play a necessary role. The individual has to plan his or activity by himself or herself, which is not possible for children as they do not have the capacity to do so (Popkewitz 2012). Thus, lifelong learning development calls for a break with traditional school patterns in order to integrate a new way of life according to new learning commitments and its standardised environment, which thus provokes a risk and incertitude gap but can also shape a liberal individual who is capable of expressing choices and preferences from the market.

Popkewitz (2012) has shown that agency finds its boundaries in typified shapes and schemes of political, cultural and social practices which order human beings suitable of becoming investigation objects of their own professional and social situation. Through standardisation, the implementation of human reason as a changing agent introduced two opposing registers: a form of freedom granted to people according to a promise of emancipation versus a social, bureaucratic and technocratic administration of their lives. Popkewitz (2010) showed that human beings are fabricated not by taking into account their agency, but according to a rational and instrumental view. Epistemological principles which ordain the programme of modern reason define an agency by ignoring the diversity of social ways of life. Thus the agency resists the inscription of human beings within a typology, a standard or a technique, even if science and technique can claim useful knowledge and a better plan for lifelong learning politics in order for individuals to be better taught. According to Popkewitz (2012), this fabrication process presents two correlated meanings: firstly, it maintains a fiction about what human beings should be; secondly, it sees them as ontological subjects of 'reality' within which they exist and about from which it is necessary to reproduce a work of transformation.

Laurent Thévenot (2009) shares Popkewitz's conclusions. In his opinion, standardisation includes an arrangement with a material environment through a set of engagements but also in the search for common good expressed in a diversity of quality conventions. One can understand the politics of standards through this link between personal and collective engagements and the standardisation process aiming at a diversity of the common good. As demonstrated by Laurent Thévenot, firstly, the politics of standards reduce the plurality of the common good and principles of justice to the worth of instrumental effectiveness which prevents the recognition of other modes of evaluation related to creativity, innovation, cultural differences, social inclusion and other modes of vocal expression outside the accountability regime. Secondly, it assumes an objective state of knowledge regarding practice by attributing measurable properties to the human agency, and it underestimates the tacit and distributed dimension of action and cognition in the classroom. Thirdly, significant investment is needed to ensure functions of information, regulation and coordination, while at the same time it engages stakeholders and practitioners through an irreversible and endogenous normalisation which undermines their capacities of reflexivity and self-accomplishment.

Standards are shaping human agency and form a practical engagement in an environment. Therefore, this process of normalisation tends to ignore the plurality of practicalities and narratives from which people give meaning to their engagement in the world. This normalisation ignores the multiplicity of types of attachment that human beings have with their environment in favour of linking them to externally defined functionalities and claiming them to be objective. This complexity of agency requires meanings to be negotiated as a consequence of numerous interactions, through a diversity of logics of action, and not only classifications or taxonomies being stabilised in the same manner as words in a dictionary. Standardisation demands that individuals build up their own self according to an ideal of justice which takes root in the tradition of our liberal societies, marked by autonomy and accomplishment offering the perspective of a salvation for education and work. But this freedom conferred to individuals disregards the activation of their capacities within a standardised environment where a collective constraint surrogates standards and reduces the possibility of exploring and exchanging with others. Responsibility allocated to individuals is less a moral essence than an instrumental one because they have to be accountable for their effectiveness and subjected to exigencies of standardised assessment of knowledge and skills. In the end, lifelong learning politics fabricate 'human types' according to a grid which makes them become visible and calculable objects: these politics are useful for a kind of population whose government's main aim is to improve competitiveness and investment in human capital (Popkewitz 2012).

Conclusion

The politics of standards has considerably transformed the governance of education systems in Europe while restructuring modes of knowledge and evaluation via new instruments. Quality is not defined at state levels but by international networks and expert centres producing standards and recommendations for best practices. In this chapter, we have focused on compulsory schooling and higher education, but other sectors of lifelong learning policy deserve consideration even though we have not had the time and space to look into them further: lifelong learning guidance for which new frameworks and procedures have been recently defined and vocational education and training (VET), which at its onset used quality approaches and ICTs as an important driver for standardisation. Quality serves the process of Europeanisation while imposing a normative definition of education in terms of classification, criteria, procedures and indicators in order to build a European system of statistics and benchmarks for the Open Method of Coordination. This government by numbers is essential for structuring modes of knowledge production and thus legitimising a new orientation of policies in compliance with the European agenda. We must not forget, while analysing the structuring role of objects, as measurement instruments, the flexible and contextualised uses of these numbers as well as the variety of actors producing them. Standardisation aims not only to harmonise practices and policies, but its effects are reformulated and translated into heterogeneous actions and categories of thought. The relative convergence of national systems by standards has been achieved through diversified modes of coordination and the valuation of the common good, and, paradoxically, it explains the success of quality. Even if it responds to different values and visions, the politics of quality has succeeded in implementing standards because it has given policymakers and stakeholders a vision they judge to be clear, reliable and relevant for guiding their behaviour. This soft normalisation process seems to be defining today a new regulatory objectivity and a new agency framing and changing academic work as we shall see in more detail in chapter "The Making of a New Homo Academicus?".

References

Ball, S. (2009). Academies in context: Politics, business and philanthropy and heterarchical governance. *Management in Education, 23*(3), 100–103.

Ball, S. J. (2012). *Global education inc: New policy networks and the neo-liberal imaginary.* London: Routledge.

Ball, S. J. (2013). *The education debate*. Bristol: Policy Press.

Ball, S. J., & Junemann, C. (2012). *Networks, new governance and education*. Bristol: Policy Press.

Barry, A. (2001). *Political machines: Governing a technological society*. London: A&C Black.

Boltanski, L., & Thévenot, L. (2006). *On justification: Economies of worth*. Princeton: Princeton University Press.

Bowker, G. C., & Star, S. L. (1999). *Sorting things out: Classification and its consequences.* Cambridge, MA: MIT Press.

Bruno, I. (2009). La recherche scientifique au crible du benchmarking. *Revue d'Histoire Moderne Contemporaine, 5,* 28–45.

Brunsson, N., Jacobsson, B., et al. (2000). The contemporary expansion of standardization. In N. Brunsson, B. Jacobsson, et al. (Eds.), *A world of standards* (pp. 127–137). Oxford: OUP.

Busch, L. (2011). *Standards: Recipes for reality*. Cambridge, MA: MIT Press.

Callon, M. (1986). Some elements of a sociology of translation: Domestication of the scallops and the fishermen of St Brieuc Bay'. In J. Law (Ed.), *Power, action and belief: A new sociology of knowledge?* (pp. 196–223). London: Routledge & Kegan Paul.

Cooley, C. H. (1909). *Two major works: Social organization. Human nature and the social order.* Glencoe: Free Press.

Council of the European Union. (2001). The concrete future objectives of Education and training systems (February) (5980/01/ EDUC 23), reported to the Stockholm European Council in March 2001.

De la Fuente, A. (2003), Human capital and growth in a global and knowledge-based economy, part II: Assessment at the EU country level, *Report for the European commission, DG for Employment and Social Affairs.*

Deane, C. (2005). Transparency of qualifications: Are we there yet? *European Journal of Education, 40*(3), 279–293.

Desrosières, A. (2002). *The politics of large numbers: A history of statistical reasoning.* Cambridge, MA: Harvard University Press.

European Association for Quality Assurance in Higher Education (ENQA). (2005). *Standards and guidelines for quality assurance in the European higher education area.* Helsinki, Finland (Funded with support of the European Commission, Directorate-General for Education and Culture). http://www.enqa.eu/files/BergenReport210205.pdf.

European Commission. (1999). *Evaluating quality in school education: A European pilot project.* Luxembourg: Office for Official Publications of the European Communities.

European Commission. (2000, March 23–24). *Lisbon European council meeting – presidency conclusions*. Brussels: General Secretariate of the Council.

European Commission. (2001a). *European report on quality of school education – 16 quality indicators. Report based on the work of the working committee on quality indicators.* Luxembourg: Office for Official Publications of the European Communities.

European Commission. (2001b). *Making a European area of lifelong learning a reality. Communication from the Commission.* COM (2001) 678 final, 21 Nov 2001.

European Commission. (2001c). *Recommendation 2001/166/EC of the European parliament and of the council of 12 February 2001 on European cooperation with regard to the qualitative assessment of school education* [Official Journal L 60 of 01.03.2001]. http://europa.eu/legislation_summaries/education_training_youth/lifelong_learning/c11038b_en.htm.

European Commission. (2002). *Education and training in Europe: Diverse systems, shared goals for 2010. The work programme on the future objectives of education and training systems.* Luxembourg: Office for Official Publications of the European Communities.

European Commission. (2004). *Progress towards common objectives in education and training: Indicators and benchmarks.* Commission Staff Working paper, pp. 114, SEC (2004).

European Commission. (2005). *Mobilising European brains, which... Mobilising the brainpower of Europe: Enabling universities to make their full contribution to the Lisbon strategy.* COM (2005) 152 final 20 April. Brussels: European Commission.

European Commission (2007) *A Coherent framework of indicators and benchmarks for monitoring progress towards the Lisbon objectives in education and training.* Brussels, 21 February. 61 final Communication from the Commission.

European Council. (2004). Conclusions of the council and of the member states' representatives meeting within the council on common European principles for the identification and validation of non-formal and informal learning (May), (9600/04/EDUC 118 SOC 253).

EUROSTAT. (2001). *Report on the eurostat task force on measuring lifelong learning.* Luxembourg: Office des publications officielles des Communautés européennes.

EUROSTAT. (2006). *Classifications for learning activities-manual. EUROSTAT/F-4, education, science and culture statistics.* Luxembourg: Office des publications officielles des Communautés européennes.

EUROSTAT. (2007). *Europe in figures: Eurostat yearbook 2006–2007.* Luxembourg: Office des publications officielles des Communautés européennes.

Eymard-Duvernay, F., Favereau, O., Orléan, A., Salais, R., & Thévenot, L. (2005). Pluralist integration in the economic and social sciences: The economy of conventions. *Post-Autistic Economics Review, 34*(30), 22–40.

Fenwick, T., & Edwards, R. (2010). *Actor-network theory in education.* London: Routledge.

Fenwick, T., & Landri, P. (2012). Materialities, textures and pedagogies: Socio-material assemblages in education. *Pedagogy Culture & Society, 20*(1), 1–7.

Gorur, R. (2011a). ANT on the PISA Trail: Following the statistical pursuit of certainty. *Educational Philosophy & Theory, 43*(5–6), 76–93.

Gorur, R. (2011b). Policy as assemblage. *European Educational Research Journal, 10*(4), 611–622. http://dx.doi.org/10.2304/eerj.2011.10.4.611.

Grek, S. (2012). What PISA knows and can do: Studying the role of national actors in the making of PISA. *European Educational Research Journal, 11*(2), 243–254.

Grek, S. (2013). Expert moves: International comparative testing and the rise of expertocracy. *Journal of Education Policy, 28*(5), 695–709.

Grek, S., & Lindgren, J. (Eds.). (2014). *Governing by inspection.* London: Routledge.

Grek, S., & Ozga, J. (2010). Re-inventing public education the new role of knowledge in education policy making. *Public Policy and Administration, 25*(3), 271–288.

Grek, S., Lawn, M., Lingard, B., Ozga, J., Rinne, R., Segerholm, C., & Simola, H. (2009). National policy brokering and the construction of the European education space in England, Sweden, Finland and Scotland. *Comparative Education, 45*(1), 5–21.

Grek, S., Lawn, M., Ozga, J., & Segerholm, C. (2013). Governing by inspection? European inspectorates and the creation of a European education policy space. *Comparative Education, 49*(4), 486–502.

Hazelkorn, E. (2007). The impact of league tables and ranking systems on higher education decision making. *Higher Education Management and Policy, 19*(2), 1–24.

Hazelkorn, E. (2008). Learning to live with league tables and ranking: The experience of institutional leaders. *Higher Education Policy, 21*(2), 193–215.

Hazelkorn, E. (2009). Rankings and the battle for world-class excellence. *Higher Education Management and Policy, 21*(1), 1–22.

Hazelkorn, E. (2011). *Rankings and the reshaping of higher education. The battle for world-class excellence.* HoudMills: Palgrave MacMillan.

Henman, P., & Dean, M. (2010). E-government and the production of standardized individuality. In V. Higgins & W. Larner (Eds.), *Calculating the social: Standards and the reconfiguration of governing* (pp. 77–93). Basingstoke: Palgrave Macmillan.

Higgins, V., & Larner, W. (Eds.). (2010a). *Calculating the social: Standards and the reconfiguration of governing.* Basingstoke: Palgrave Macmillan.

Higgins, V., & Larner, W. (2010b). From standardization to standardizing work. In V. Higgins & W. Larner (Eds.), *Calculating the social: Standards and the reconfiguration of governing* (pp. 205–218). Basingstoke: Palgrave Macmillan.

Hooge, E., Burns, T., & Wilkoszewski, H. (2012). *Looking beyond the numbers: Stakeholders and multiple school accountability.* Paris: OECD.

Jacobsson, B. (2000). Standardization and expert knowledge. In N. Brunsson, B. Jacobsson, et al. (Eds.), *A world of standards* (pp. 40–49). Oxford: Oxford University Press.

Knight, J., & de Wit, H. (Eds.). (1999). *Quality and internationalisation of higher education.* Paris: OECD.

Kok, W. (2004, Nov). *Facing the challenge: The Lisbon strategy for growth and employment.* Report from the high-level group chaired by Wim Kok. http://ec.europa.eu/growthandjobs/pdf/kok_report_en.pdf.

Lange, B., & Alexiadou, N. (2007). New forms of European union governance in the education sector? A preliminary analysis of the open method of coordination. *European Educational Research Journal, 6*(4), 321–335.

Latour, B. (1987). *Science in action: How to follow scientists and engineers through society.* Cambridge, MA: Harvard University Press.

Law, J. (1992). Notes on the theory of the actor-network: Ordering, strategy, and heterogeneity. *Systems Practice, 5*(4), 379–393.

Lawn, M. (2011). Standardizing the European education policy space. *European Educational Research Journal, 10*(2), 259–272.

Lawn, M., & Grek, S. (2012). Europeanizing education: Governing a new policy space. In *Symposium Books.* Symposium Books. PO Box 204, Didcot, Oxford, OX11 9ZQ, UK.

Lawn, M., & Lingard, B. (2002). Constructing a European policy space in educational governance: The role of transnational policy actors. *European Educational Research Journal, 1*(2), 290–307.

Lingard, B., Martino, W., & Rezai-Rashti, G. (2013). Testing regimes, accountabilities and education policy: Commensurate global and national developments. *Journal of Education Policy, 28*(5), 539–556.

Marginson, S. (2007). Global university rankings: Implications in general and for Australia. *Journal of Higher Education Policy and Management, 29*(2), 131–142.

Marginson, S., & Van der Wende, M. (2007). To rank or to be ranked: The impact of global rankings in higher education. *Journal of Studies in International Education, 11*(3–4), 306–329.

Mead, G. H. (1934). In C. W. Morris (Ed.), *Mind, self, and society.* Chicago: University of Chicago Press.

Middlehurst, R. (2001). University challenges: Borderless higher education, today and tomorrow. *Minerva, 39*(1), 3–26.

Miller, P., & O'Leary, T. (1987). Accounting and the construction of the governable person. *Accounting, Organizations and Society, 12*(3), 235–265.

Neave, G. (1988). On the cultivation of quality, efficiency and enterprise: An overview of recent trends in higher education in Western Europe, 1986–1988. *European Journal of Education, 23*(1–2), 7–23.

Neave, G. (1994). The politics of quality: Developments in higher education in Western Europe 1992–1994. *European Journal of Education, 29*(2), 115–134.

Normand, R. (2009). Expert measurement in the government of Lifelong Learning. In E. Mangenot & J. Rowell (coord), *What Europe constructs: New sociological perspectives in European studies*. Manchester: Manchester University Press.

Normand, R. (2010). Expertise networks and tools of government: The fabrication of European policy in education. *European Educational Research Journal, 9*(3), 408–423.

Ozga, J. (2011). Researching the powerful: Seeking knowledge about policy. *European Educational Research Journal, 10*(2), 218–224.

Ozga, J. (2012). Governing knowledge: Data, inspection and education policy in Europe. *Globalisation, Societies and Education, 10*(4), 439–455.

Ozga, J., Dahler-Larsen, P., Segerholm, C., & Simola, H. (Eds.). (2011). *Fabricating quality in education: Data and governance in Europe*. Londres: Routledge.

Ponte, S., & Gibbon, P. (2005). Quality standards, conventions and the governance of global value chains. *Economy and Society, 34*(1), 1–31.

Ponte, S., Gibbon, P., & Vestergaard, J. (Eds.). (2011). *Governing through standards: Origins, drivers and limitations*. Basingstoke: Palgrave MacMillan.

Popkewitz, T. (2007). *Cosmopolitanism and the age of school reform: Science, education and making society by making the child*. New York: Routledge.

Popkewitz, T. (2010). Comparative studies and unthinking comparative "thought". The paradox of reason and its "abjection". In M. Larson (Ed.), *New thinking in comparative education, honoring Robert Cowen* (pp. 15–28). Rotterdam: Sense Publishers.

Popkewitz, T. (2012). Numbers in grids of intelligibility: Making sense of how educational truth is told. In H. Lauder, M. Young, H. Daniels, M. Balarin, & J. Lowe (Eds.), *Educating for the knowledge economy? Critical perspectives* (pp. 169–191). London: Routledge.

Power, M. (1999). *The audit society: Rituals of verification*. Oxford: Oxford University Press.

Sellar, S., & Lingard, B. (2013). The OECD and global governance in education. *Journal of Education Policy, 28*(5), 710–725.

Sellar, S., & Lingard, B. (2014). The OECD and the expansion of PISA: New global modes of governance in education. *British Educational Research Journal, 40*(6), 917–936.

Thévenot, L. (2009). Governing life by standards: A view from engagements. *Social Studies of Science, 39*(5), 793–813. doi:10.1177/0306312709338767.

Timmermans, S., & Berg, M. (1997). Standardization in action: Achieving local universality through medical protocols. *Social Studies of Science, 27*(2), 273–305.

Timmermans, S., & Berg, M. (2003). *The gold standard: The challenge of evidence-based medicine and standardization in health care*. Philadelphia: Temple University Press.

Timmermans, S., & Epstein, S. (2010). A world of standards but not a standard world: Toward a sociology of standards and standardization. *Annual Review of Sociology, 36*, 69–90.

'What Works?' The Shaping of the European Politics of Evidence

Introduction

Evidence-based policy (EBP) aims to respond to one question: what works in the fields of health, education, justice and welfare? It is part of the trend of evaluating public policies, but it corrupts it by its extreme instrumentalism and decisionism (Majone 1989). EBP has been imposed as a 'gold standard', while its experimental features are affirmed. This 'political experimentalism' is at the crossroad of science, expertise and policy and is institutionalised as a discourse of truth with a criticism addressed to education research. It legitimises institutions and technologies that entail other modes of intervention from the Welfare State.

Indeed, from one country to another, several epistemic regimes have supported these policies. An epistemic regime can be defined as a collective action that explicitly or implicitly transforms stable forms of knowledge and instruments of evaluation while legitimising new actors sharing the same norms, interests and conventions for a certain vision of the relationships between science and policy. This regime is not linked to disciplines, but includes some features of the mode 2 regime in the sense that it is supported by instrumentation and 'interstitial' arenas which engage non-scientific actors (experts, policymakers, companies, foundations, associations). An epistemic regime introduces a new division of labour which transforms the modalities of evidence and the norms of truth while embedding the production of knowledge in information systems related to the digital economy. Of course, the difference between national and institutional contexts in the production and standardisation of scientific knowledge must not be underestimated, as we have seen in chapter 'Introduction'. But here, we shall mainly describe the trajectories of the evidence-based policy in education at the international and European level. Beyond the translation and hybridisation of some national patterns, some mechanisms of appropriation and the imitation between states and international organisations shall be analysed as well as the circulation of this epistemic regime and its instrumentation into a science of government.

© Springer International Publishing Switzerland 2016

R. Normand, *The Changing Epistemic Governance of European Education*,
Educational Governance Research 3, DOI 10.1007/978-3-319-31776-2_4

As has been proven for international indicators (Normand 2010; Lawn and Normand 2014; Henry et al. 2001), technologies of evidence have been transferred between and borrowed from countries. Beyond this international policy borrowing, this chapter shall focus on the policies which institutionalised and introduced these technologies into the state's very core, in particular through the implementation of New Public Management and changes in welfare. From examples taken from health and education, we shall explain how some arguments, devices and types of mobilisation have contributed to the success of these new technologies. At the same time, the chapter shall describe the epistemic restructuring of science and the emergence of a mode of 'regulatory objectivity' which produces hierarchies of evidence in educational research (Cambrosio et al. 2007; Jasanoff 2011).

In the following pages, I shall state the epistemological foundations of technologies of evidence. They legitimise a new mode of production of scientific knowledge and address a criticism of social sciences which have been accused of being incapable of adopting the same quality.[1] This new 'experimentalism' shall then be presented in a description of the social epistemology of the politics of evidence. I shall then show how it was transformed from health to education. In the next part of this chapter, I shall put into perspective the use of this political technology in the UK Third Way programmes, focused on an 'at-risk' population and the debate it raised in education. The last part shall be dedicated to the study of the shaping of global evidence-based policymaking from local configurations in New Zealand to transnational networks linking local devices with worldwide collaborations and international programmes.

The Social Epistemology of the Politics of Evidence

The epistemology developing technologies of evidence strongly challenges the academic tradition of social sciences. Firstly, it institutionalises a 'hierarchy of evidence' through which randomised controlled trials (RCTs) occupy the first rank alongside quasi-experimental devices, systematic reviews of research literature and metadata analyses. Ethnography and case studies via interviews and observations are placed at a lower rank.

---

[1] This research was achieved through a participation in an expertise programme entitled *Evidence-Informed Policy in Education in Europe* (EIPEE) coordinated by the EPPI-Centre of London in cooperation with the French Institute of Education and the French Ministry of Education (specifically, its directorate-general of schools). I participated in several meetings bringing together experts, education ministries, agencies and stakeholders working for the European Commission. I also studied the official reports of the OECD and the European Commission and analysed several official websites of national and international organisations. This work helped me write a thesis regarding the accreditation for supervising research in France entitled *En quête d'évidence. Les sciences sociales et la mesure de l'État dans l'éducation et la santé* [In Quest of Evidence. Social Sciences and the Measurement of the State in Education and Health] (2011, Sciences Po Paris).

Furthermore, technologies of evidence legitimise the mode 2 of knowledge production (Gibbons et al. 1994). According to this approach, as we have seen previously, the production of knowledge is improved by breaking down the barriers of disciplinary compartmentalisation, the heterogeneity of methods and the fragmentation of research findings. Despite this 'functionalist' model, which was severely criticised during the 1980s–1990s, it has since gained a certain legitimacy (Weiss 1979). Assuming a direct link between the production of evidence and decision-making, and taking into account the model of natural sciences as a standard, it claims to reduce the gap between scientific knowledge and the social problems faced by reformers in pushing constructivism back.

Evidence-Based Policy as a New Experimentalism

The experimental approach is praised as it brings producers and users of knowledge closer together in a function of 'mediation' inspired by health monitoring systems which nevertheless are far from guaranteeing the transparency they claim. Research findings have to be translated into platforms, websites and other media to better inform policymakers and practitioners and to associate them in the knowledge production and transfer. This 'brokerage' function tends to be developed through the creation of numerous 'portals'. One of the best known is the *Educational Evidence Portal* in the UK. International organisations such as Cochrane and Campbell, the *Evidence for Policy and Practice Information and Co-ordinating Centre* (EPPI-Centre), the *Social Care Institute for Excellence* and the *National Institute for Clinical Excellence* are also brokerage agencies in the fields of health, education and social welfare.

This new 'political experimentalism' aims to challenge the 'model of Enlightenment', the dominant configuration in the production of knowledge even if links between science and policy are quite old. In fact, the state often used statistical tools and experimental science because they provided a space of calculation distinct from people, their customs and local knowledge (Desrosières and Naish 2002; Porter 1995). Statistics offered possibilities for the standardisation of devices and for the quantification of people which were very useful in the development of centralised and bureaucratic administrations. It is easy to observe how, during the past few years, this trust in numbers and quantification has been reinforced inside state and international organisations particularly through the technology of benchmarking. This positivist recovery was affirmed in a context of criticism against social and educational sciences (Beck 1992). Doubting their own foundations and their practical consequences, they have become the victims of a scepticism they themselves had contributed to producing. Their reflexive and critical model has increasingly been challenged by other forms of production of knowledge, particularly expertise which claims a greater credibility and legitimacy. It is important to explain how this recovery was made possible.

To understand the creation and dissemination of the evidence-based policy, we have to look back at the changes in the modes of evaluating federal programmes during the Kennedy–Johnson administration in the USA. During the 1970s, large-scale surveys and planning were abandoned for the rationalisation of budgetary choices (RCB). It emerged in an ideological climate hostile to social and educational sciences. In both health and education, randomised controlled trials (RCTs) and a hierarchy of evidence were promoted and were challenging the usual evaluation techniques. This approach, which corresponded to an experimental conception of the social survey, used natural sciences as a model in order to reduce the gap between scientific knowledge and the implementation of reforms while at the same time producing recommendations which were considered to be useful for policy-makers and practitioners.

In the beginning of the 1970s, a science of evaluation was born but with different trends. Donald T. Campbell, a psychologist, published a paper noticed by specialists in this field of research (Campbell 1969). He called for the USA and other nations to adopt a new experimental approach for social reforms. For Campbell, certain 'true' experiments are required to subject groups of individuals to a treatment and then to compare the said group with a control group. In order for the evaluation of public policy to be validated, it had to expose certain individuals to different randomised treatments fitting the principles of the experimental approach. His book proposed to extend 'the logic of the laboratory' to the whole US society. Along with the statistician Julian C. Stanley, he published another book which made claims for a new standard for social sciences in which the social scientist would become the 'methodological servant of the experimental society' (Campbell and Stanley 1963).

But other specialists of the evaluation of public policies, such as Lee J. Cronbach, Michael Scriven or Daniel Stufflebeam, rejected the idea that experiments were the best way of evaluating a public action programme (Alkin 2004). For those advocating the pluralistic approach, evaluation should help policymakers raise the right questions in an accessible language by providing useful and transparent information to improve programmes. Contrary to the experimental approach, this form of pluralistic evaluation claims it is comprehensive. It is not limited to the measurement of outcomes and the determination of causal variables, but it requires a vast range of judgements and information gathered from a diversity of actors. It is democratic and pluralistic in the sense that it encourages widespread participation and deliberation.

During the 1980s–1990s, US federal agencies, in charge of the evaluation of public programmes in welfare and health, mainly promoted the experimental approach and focused short-term findings which they considered to be better adjusted to the measurement of effectiveness. Evaluators had to specify the expected outcomes from clearly quantified objectives. A distinction was established between experimental device and control device. Evaluation had to fit requirements of uniformity and stability of the treatment during the experiment, and at the same time it was designed from samples considered to be statistically representative.

On his side, the US administration went very far in the dissimulation of evidence and propaganda (Berliner and Biddle 1995). A systematic circumventing strategy appeared with the publication of the report What Works: Research About

Teaching and Learning (1986). The document, considered as a research literature review, was published with great fanfare by the US Department of Education, and it was accompanied by a foreword from State Secretary Bennett and a dedication from President Reagan. In the middle of summer 1986, 300,000 copies were circulating. Presented as the summary of 'eminent researchers' work, measuring the impact of teachers and parents on school achievement, it was a propagandist document praising the merits of the conservative administration policy. At the same time, there were attempts to make some evidence disappearing because they were judged compromising. A first affair involved the National Science Foundation (NSF). One of its employees had prepared a biased study suggesting that the nation would soon lack of scientists and engineers. The rapport gave the opportunity for the head of the Foundation to orchestrate a vigorous campaign about the obvious crisis faced by the USA. Many versions of the document were reproduced and disseminated among the NSF high executives, while assessment by peers was scrupulously avoided and contradictory data were ignored. In 1992, the affaire was disclosed and the Foundation had to provide explanations to the US Congress. The second affair emerged with the publication of the Sandia report, an analysis of the education system initially conducted by a service from the US Department of Energy. The paper had circulated among researchers and policymakers at the US Department of Education, and it gave the opportunity of a special session at the US Congress. The research findings were contradicting the policy led by Bush and his administration. But the heads of the Department of Education required to not publish the report, and it was revised by the National Science Foundation and the National Center for Education Statistics. The report was discretionally published in the Journal of Educational Research without the list of its authors but after that Bush had missed his re-election in 1992.

RCTs and Experiments: From Social Policy to Education

This reinforcement of methodological requirements in evaluation was accompanied by a more conservative climate towards social issues. While the margins of power of the Federal State were being restricted because of the economic crisis, social programmes were put under pressure with regard to their performance and effectiveness. The General Accounting Office, the organisation in charge of evaluations and audits at the US Congress, was promoting controlled experiments with members of parliament, governmental agencies and the federal administration. Consequently, randomised controlled trials (RCTs) were extended to economic and social areas like the actions of the police and justice. For example, the Spouse Assault Replication Program developed controlled experiments to evaluate the impact of warrants for arrest on the diminution of offences.

Controlled trials also served to evaluate the incentives of social reforms on the behaviour of 'at-risk' youths. Different programmes were launched: *New Chance*, the LEAP (*Learning, Earning, and Parenting Program*) in Ohio, the *Learnfare* in

Wisconsin, the *Teenage Parents Demonstration Project* in New Jersey and Illinois. In the field of education, one of the most important experiments was the evaluation conducted in Tennessee. From 1985 to 1990, the Project STAR or *Tennessee Student/Teacher Achievement Ratio* experiment was a large-scale controlled experiment measuring the effect of the reduction of class sizes on school achievement (Mosteller and Boruch 2002). Its findings were used to demonstrate to teacher trade unions that additional public expenditure in education was a source of waste. But this evaluation was also a landmark for economists of education promoting the theory of human capital and controlled experiments.

The Project STAR (Tennessee Student/Teacher Achievement Ratio) experiment, developed between 1985 and 1990, has been qualified by Frederick Mosteller, an eminent representative of the statistical theory at the Harvard University, as the 'most great experiment ever achieved in the area of education' (Mosteller and Boruch 2002). STAR was a large-scale controlled experiment assessing the effect of class size on student achievement. During the 1980s, in the USA and particularly in the South states, governments had introduced a legislation to improve student performance after the publication of the report A Nation at Risk (1983). The 'movement for excellence' had extended the school day and strengthened requirements for grade promotion. Skills tests had been institutionalised, while policymakers wanted to develop merit-based pay for teachers, sanctions and rewards for failing schools and accountability programmes (Normand 2009). Many famous governors like Bill Clinton for Arkansas and Lamar Alexander for Tennessee were strongly involved in these educative reforms.

Lamar Alexander, who has become later the state education secretary for George Bush Sr, had been re-elected for a second mandate as the governor of Tennessee. Considering education had to be the first lever of reforms, it implemented the Better School Program (1983) and presented it during a TV discourse. One of its components was the creation of a career scale for teachers including a system of remuneration and performance. But this bill was rejected by the Senate Education Committee because of a vindictive opposition of the Tennessee Education Association (TEA), the main teacher trade union representing 36,000 members. In 1984, Lamar Alexander proposed another version to the legislative assembly with a less ambitious system of performance-related pay. But there was a debate between the members of the parliament about class size during the vote. A proposal had been written under the influence of trade unions to reduce the class size from 25 to 20 per teacher. Steve Cobb, a democrat who was supporting Alexander's policy, had read the research literature on the issue, particularly the meta-analysis of Glass (1982), which suggested there was not linear relationship between the class size and student achievement. Consequently, Cobb explained that this measure would cost a lot for the community and it would not produce any difference in student results. After many debates, Alexander promulgated the 1984 Act implementing a performance-related pay for teachers, but he encourages at the same time an experiment on class size: the Project STAR. In fact, under the pressure of trade unions, the Congress and the Senate had finally adopted a legislation inciting to reduce the class size during the first grades of schooling in using different grants which increased state expenditures because of the increase in the number of teachers per student. To assess the cost and effects of this measure, it was decided to lead a pilot survey by recruiting 200 additional teachers with a reduction of class size to 15 in more than a hundred of classrooms. During 3 years, the Department of Education was in charge of the assessment, and he gathered researchers from Tennessee to plan a controlled experiment.

The experiment assessed different configurations of classrooms: small classes with 13–17 students, normal classes with 22–25 students (the law prohibited to go beyond 25 students) and normal classes with pedagogical assistants. In comparing student performance for each type of classroom, researchers assessed relative gains in test scores. All the state school districts were invited to join, but they had to accept the principle of hazard allocation of teachers and students. At the beginning, 180 schools from 50 districts (out of a total of 141) expressed their interests, but only 57 could meet the experiment's requirements. The data showed that small classes had obtained better results for the first grades, but there were no differences for the other grades, even when the teacher was supported by a pedagogical assistant. The experimentation had costed 3 millions of dollars each year, but it was less compared to the cost of systemically reducing class size: a reduction from 22 to 15 students per classroom would have cost 300 millions of dollars because of additional teachers. The Project STAR results were used by the government to demonstrate to trade unions that additional educational expenditures were a source of waste, and this experiment became a methodological reference for the human capital economists sharing the same theoretical and positivist conceptions.

Policy Travelling from Health to Education

We are now describing the way evidence-based technologies have travelled from medicine to education in the USA. It is not the first time that medicine is used as a reference by educational research. Hygienic science and eugenics have strongly influenced child studies during the last century. Assessment techniques in education, like arts of testing, have been inspired by the medical world. More recently, research on cognitive psychology or neuroscience programmes have developed linkages with medicine. However, it is a specific configuration illustrated here which fuelled debates in educational research. We explain how evidence-based methods in medicine have been globally institutionalised on behalf of a golden standard and how this paradigm has been resumed and promoted in US education policies.

The Search for a Global Standard in Medicine

The principles of the evidence-based policy were firstly designed and developed in the medical sector under the influence of the pharmaceutical industry (Marks 1999). During the 1990s, the epidemiologist David Sackett, one of the eminent figures of this movement, noticing the variety of treatments used by physicians, proposed new methods to test medical interventions, to evaluate their clinical and scientific validity and to educate physicians in the use of systematic reviews of research literature. He presented 'controlled randomised trials' as a methodological 'gold standard' for medicine (Timmermans and Berg 2003). In addition to this work, official reports ordered by foundations and governmental agencies pointed out the failure of medical care, the problems caused by the increase in medical expenditure and the necessity to use ICTs in diagnoses (Berg 1997).

For some professionals and policymakers, evidence-based medicine offered a lot of advantages. It reassured practitioners about the effectiveness of treatments and the associated risks. Governmental agencies can define recommendations and design best practice guidelines to improve the effectiveness and quality of healthcare. Epidemiologists defended the expansion of a health monitoring system to alert public authorities about the health problems faced by the 'at-risk' population. And US courts could use the findings of evidence-based medicine to judge good or bad medical practices in conflicts opposing physicians and patients (or their associations). During this period, the Agency for Healthcare Policy and Research was created. Its objectives were to promote and disseminate the guidelines provided by evidence-based medicine. Centralised by an agency, the National Guideline Clearinghouse, its role was to transform the knowledge of physicians and medical practice.

At the same time, in the UK, the National Health Service (NHS) launched an R&D programme to look into changing the production of evidence in medical care. The British authorities proposed to Iain Chalmers and his colleagues that they develop randomised controlled trials in natal and prenatal clinic. From this experience, they created the Cochrane Collaboration to develop systematic reviews at the global scale (Timmermans and Kolker 2004). Collaborative review groups or CRGs, organised through networks, began to assemble experts and scientists in charge of the quality of evaluation protocols, the compilation of resources and training colleagues. Within a few years, the Cochrane Collaboration had created dozens of centres worldwide and developed huge databanks and a randomised controlled trials register for delivering best practice recommendations. An infrastructure, similar to the Cochrane organisation, was also created in the fields of education, welfare, crime and justice: the Campbell Collaboration. Set up in the USA, in the wake of Donald T. Campbell's ideas, the Collaboration developed its own databank entitled C2-SPECTR or Campbell Collaboration Social, Psychological, Educational and Criminological Trials Register which stored randomised controlled trials and included systematic reviews of literature extended to the field of welfare policies: education, justice, crime, social work, etc.

Box: Key Personalities and International Organisations in the Area of Evidence-Based Policy

Archie Cochrane (1909–1988) was a Scottish physician known for his book *Effectiveness and Efficiency: Random Reflections on Health Services* (1972) who defended the use of randomised controlled trials to make medicine more effective and efficient. This defence of evidence-based medicine led to the development of the Cochrane Database of Systematic Reviews, the creation of the Cochrane Centre at the University of Oxford and the creation of the Cochrane Collaboration. Archie Cochrane participated in the Spanish Civil War before being an ambulance driver in the Second World War and was a prisoner of war. This experience had a deep impact on him and persuaded him that some medical interventions were ineffective and they had to be supported by evidence. He was then involved in the defence of the adoption of scientific methods within the medical community and launched pioneer studies on randomised controlled trials when he joined the National School of Medicine in Cardiff, Whales.

Donald Thomas Campbell (1916–1996) was a US social scientist. After his doctorate in psychology at the University of Berkeley, he worked in several US universities before becoming the president of the American Psychological Association. He created the field of evolutionist epistemology by generalising Karl Popper's philosophy of sciences and also defended the postulate that public policies could be improved by experiments. This defence of the experimental method was expressed in a large number of articles and in his book *Experimental and Quasi-Experimental Devices for Research* (1966) which became a reference for the experts in the evaluation of public policies in the USA.

Iain Chalmers (1943–) is a British researcher in the field of healthcare and one of the founders of the Cochrane Collaboration. Between 1978 and 1992, he was the first head of the national unit of prenatal epidemiology at Oxford University. He developed a digital bank of controlled trials and a series of systematic reviews on randomised trials in the field of prenatal health. He was then appointed director of the Cochrane Centre and became the editor of the James Lind Library which documents the history and evolution of therapeutic trials. This library has passed strategic agreements with a certain number of international organisations under the auspices of the Cochrane Collaboration.

David Sackett (1934–) is considered as one of the three founding fathers of clinical epidemiology, with Archie Cochrane (the UK) and Alvan Feinstein (the USA). Clinical epidemiology is a research based on the methods of epidemiology (and other sciences such as biomedical statistics, behavioural sciences and the economics of health) applied to the study and management of health problems. In particular, it aims to reduce bias in clinical research and

(continued)

to design or implement randomised controlled trials. In 1967 Sackett occupied the first worldwide chair of clinical epidemiology and biomedical statistics at the McMaster University, Hamilton, Ontario, Canada. He has contributed to the development of evidence-based research methods through numerous books and articles before being invited in 1994 by the UK National Health System to create the first centre of evidence-based medicine in Great Britain and became a professor in the Department of Clinical Medicine at the University of Oxford.

The *Cochrane Collaboration* is an international network of practitioners, researchers and associations of patients in the field of public health. It aims to collect evidence-based research results to improve the quality of research and inform decision-making. This work led to the building of international benchmarks to guide health policies and to ensure the quality and effectiveness of healthcare through a partnership between researchers, the pharmaceutical industry, practitioners and patients. The objective is also to provide drugs which have previously been tested clinically in the field in order to assess potential risks and therapeutic benefits. http://www.cochrane.org/

The *Campbell Collaboration* is an international research network which produces systematic reviews on the effects of social interventions in crime, justice, education, international development and social work. It aims to contribute to social change by improving the quality of public and private services worldwide. It prepares, maintains and disseminates methods and data with the objective of improving knowledge for decision-making and practice. This information based on evidence to policymakers and practitioners should lead to better results in the implementation of public policies. http://www.campbellcollaboration.org/

US Think Tanks and Evidence-Based Research in Education

During the 1980s, after several budget cuts in education, and in a climate of scepticism regarding large-scale programmes, the US Office of Educational Research and Improvement (OERI) played an active role in restructuring educational research. Researchers were accused to being insufficiently trained in evaluation in comparison to physicians and the pharmaceutical industry. This is how the OERI influenced the Academy of Sciences which produced a damning report on the quality of educational sciences and put forward claims for the adoption of more rigorous methodologies linked to coherent and explicit modes of reasoning and ones which were more understandable for both practitioners and policymakers. This criticism addressed against educational research and social sciences was supported by a complex network of neoconservative think tanks and foundations capable of disseminating numerous ideas which were important for the neoconservative political agenda (Spring 2005). In these networks, policymakers like Chester Finn or advisers like Diane Ravitch, because they had worked for a long time in the federal government or for US foundations, were successful in penetrating the general media in a manner which academics or researchers could not. In 1982, they create the Educational Excellence Network within the Hudson Institute, a network supported by the Thomas B. Fordham Foundation. The Educational Excellence Network flooded the public arena with incessant political recommendations, briefs, bills and reports. Finn and Ravitch always considered that federal programmes were under the control of a federal elite and that the financial support of educational research centres was leading to an excessive leftist politicisation. That is why they were very active in developing the policy of evidence.

Other think tanks sought to identify researchers who could produce findings to give legitimacy to their action. They funded academic chairs, conferences and congresses capable of disseminating the ideas of Milton Friedman, the economist at the origin of vouchers, and those of the Austrian economist Friedrich Hayek, who was highly critical of bureaucracy, planning and social sciences. We can also mention two other key permanent relays of conservative ideas in education: the Heritage Foundation and the American Enterprise Institute. The creation of the Heritage Foundation came from a proposal by Pat Buchanan, who himself was responding to the request made by President Nixon just after his election, to create an institute promoting republican ideas and developing talent among conservative intellectuals (Denham 1996). In 1995, the foundation published Chester Finn and Diane Ravitch's report about reforms in education. The American Enterprise Institute focuses more on giving scholarships to researchers and intellectuals who defend conservative theses. In the end, the Hoover Institution became, under the leadership of W. Glenn Campbell, a centre welcoming conservative ideas and publishing the works of researchers like Gary Becker, Milton Friedman or Friedrich Hayek (Smith 1991, pp.184–189).

The development of conservative think tanks can be explained by the revenge of circles close to presidents Reagan and Bush who wanted to have more influence in opposition to the dissemination of liberal ideas from other think thanks such as the Institute for Policy Studies, the Brookings Institution or the RAND Corporation. The latter are typical of the kind of institution which accompanied the developments of technocratic thought and the Keynesian policies of the Kennedy and Johnson administrations (Smith 1991, pp. 146–166; Ricci 1993, pp. 149–181). The reaction of conservatives can be explained by the fear that the 'establishment' was weakening the impact of their ideals in American society and that social sciences were disseminating a rationalistic and relativist mindset that was undermining the attachment of US people to tradition. The creation of those institutions was a good means of becoming an intellectual force capable of producing a solid criticism of political liberalism and its allies.

In 1998, under the influence of interest groups, the US Congress voted an annual budget of 150 billion dollars to fund education reforms based on evidence. In the beginning of the 2000s, a bill, calling for more rigour in educational research and the development of randomised controlled trials, was examined.[2] Even if it is was not adopted in the end, it gave birth to a coalition of experts and researchers, close to the US New Right, defending the policy of evidence (the Coalition for Evidence-Based Policy).

Among its members were Robert Boruch, a well-known expert in the technologies of evidence, at the origin of the creation of the Campbell Collaboration; Diane Ravitch, a neoconservative spokeswoman; and Robert Solow, an economist representing economic orthodoxy. The coalition lobbied like-minded US policymakers and members of the parliament, but also the National Science Foundation, to promote technologies of evidence in welfare and health policies. The *No Child Left Behind Act* (2001), which defined the new objectives of education federal policy, resumed these recommendations. This Act, in force in the USA, stipulates that educational research has to test hypotheses and to use such experimental or quasi-experimental devices as randomised controlled trials. In 2002, the Institute of Education Sciences (IES[3]) was created, and it continues to prescribe today some evidence-based standards and 'best practices'.

The IES has conceived user-friendly guides for practitioners and researchers enabling them to identify and implement pedagogical best practices based on rigorous evidence of effectiveness as they are provided by randomised controlled trials. These guides describe the necessary steps for a scientific approach and propose a series of standards which researchers and practitioners have to apply to rigorously assess the effectiveness of practices in schools. The document mentions a range of existing works in the area of health and education. Practitioners are invited to search for additional information on a website (What Works Clearinghouse) which presents an inventory of 'best practices' and provides to practitioners, policymakers and researchers scientific data on 'what works' in education. This website affirms to be supported by high-quality assessments and reproducible interventions (educational programmes, products, practices and policies) to increase student achievement. For this, the IES has entered into contracts with different organisations or associations, particularly the Coalition for Evidence-Based Policy, but also think tanks as the RAND Corporation or universities as the University of Pennsylvania where Robert Boruch works. In August 2002, the US Department of Education signed a contract of 18. 5 millions of dollars with the international Campbell Collaboration to create a partnership with the American Institutes for Research animating the website What Works Clearinghouse.

---

[2] (*Scientifically Based Education Research, Evaluation, and Statistics and Information Act*, 2000).
[3] The IES replaced the National Institute of Education (NIE) and the Office of Educational Research and Improvement (OERI).

Political Technologies of the Welfare State

This background overview of the US evidence-based policy in education and health shows that these technologies convinced policymakers searching for short-term answers and who were eager to reduce public budgets dedicated to research. These new technologies of evidence, as we shall see, contributed significantly in transforming the UK Welfare State. The latter used new measurement instruments to evaluate individual and collective risks in social intervention programmes in health and education. This new Welfare State no longer claims its action on behalf of the collective solidarity or mutualisation of risks. Instead, it seeks to find evidence about the economics and its effectiveness in the treatment of social problems. By taking a certain distance from the mode of pluralistic evaluation, which is not compatible with the urgency of decision-making and the short-term duration of a political mandate, British authorities privileged a new mode of production of evidence facilitating the mobilisation of 'stakeholders' in the elaboration of consensus and techniques aiming to reach a certain 'objectivity' in the treatment of social issues. Therefore, *evidence-based policymaking* (EBPM) redefined the relationships between science and policy.

In the 2000s, the National Health System's policymakers believed that issues of education, welfare and crime were linked to problems of public health. International organisations such as Campbell and Cochrane were invited to participate in a large project, the *Wider Public Health Project*, to collect evidence about health policies. This evidence-based policy was widely included in the modernising agenda of the New Labour Party. Researchers, analysts and policymakers wished to identify 'what works'. In 1997, *the New NHS* White Paper proposed to reform the public health system, while the Labour government was explaining that health services and the treatment of patients had to be profitable and to be based on evidence regarding their effectiveness.

Evidence-Based Policy as a Project of Modernisation

The government then facilitated the creation of a series of official organisations to explore and disseminate 'what works' in health, education and social welfare. The National Institute for Clinical Excellence's role is to carry out evaluations and to formulate national guidelines. In the field of welfare, the Social Care Institute for Excellence produced similar data and tools. The Evidence for Policy and Practice Information and Co-ordinating Centre, created in 1993, launched a journal entitled *Evidence & Policy* to promote the widespread use of new modes of production of evidence. The objective of the centre is to conduct systematic reviews of research literature, to develop methodological tools, to implement procedures and training sessions on evaluation and to maintain a databank for users and policymakers.[4] Its methods were borrowed from the Cochrane Collaboration and the Campbell Collaboration. In education, the EPPI-Centre focuses its actions on schools and students and manages knowledge according to different standards in order to make research findings accessible and compliant with the criteria of evidence-based research. Each review of literature had to specify the adopted protocol and the inclusion/inclusion criteria from which data is extracted from the databank. A review of literature is generally carried out in two steps: the first step is to map out the area of research to be analysed with keywords in order to obtain an initial descriptive account and the second is a more detailed exploration from which the most important studies are extracted. These areas of investigation are numerous: teaching, evaluation and learning, leadership, gender, inclusion, student skills, professional development of teachers, etc.

If the notion of 'evidence' did not directly appear in the *Modernising Government* White Paper (Cabinet Office 1999), technologies of evidence had been disseminated since 1999 in conferences and publications under the supervision of the Economics and Social Research Council (Parsons 2002). The idea that policy had to be led by the evidence of 'what works' progressively appeared in governmental reports (Cabinet Office 2001a, b; National Audit Office 2001, 2003). The notion of *evidence-based policymaking* (EBPM) became remarkably successful with policymakers, while public services were being transformed to better respond to the need of users in terms of effectiveness and quality (Davies et al. 2007; Sanderson 2002). This technocratic and instrumental conception of public action was then closely linked with accountability policies and performance management, two pillars of the Third Way (Le Galès and Faucher-King 2010).

Progressively, EBPM became a key element in the strategy of Tony Blair's cabinet and that of the National Audit Office in charge of the evaluation of social policies with regard to their relevance, cost and effectiveness as stated by the principles of New Public Management (Hall et al. 2013). The introduction of comprehensive spending reviews (CSRs) or public service agreements (PSAs) had to 'galvanise' the provision of public services and lead to 'major improvements of results'. This new logic of evidence aimed to replace a partial and short-term vision of politics among ministerial cabinets by a more rigorous and systematic approach with regard to public expenditure. These hopes were largely dashed (Wells 2007). But there was a profound change in the political culture of national policymakers: they pushed aside political values to replace them by a 'scientific objectification' of 'what works' to legitimise decision-making. This new orientation was a real break with the British political model or 'Westminster model'. Instead of a centralised exercise of power shared with members of parliaments according to the traditional mechanisms of political representation, the dispersion of the state's authority among networks and non-governmental agencies reinforced the requirement for evaluation and evidence.

---

[4] EPPI-Centre, or Evidence for Policy and Practice Information and Co-ordinating Centre, is a part of the Social Science Research Unit of the Institute of Education at the University of London. Since 1993, it has promoted its advance in the implementation of systematic reviews in the fields of social sciences and public policies.

As has been shown by the British case, evidence-based policy is contemporaneous of a new apprehension of risks justifying the action of the state. The traditional approach of social insurances, linked to redistribution, was being challenged, while the responsibility of risk was transferred to individuals according to a workfare logic (Jessop 1993). In Great Britain, as in Europe, the types of risk linked to insecurity at work and employment have been extended to education and health. Other forms of the state's social intervention have emerged (flexicurity, social inclusion, the principle of precaution) (Clarke and Newman 1997). With the progress of genetics, health risks are being re-evaluated from individual characteristics, and a predictive medicine approach has raised some deontological and ethical issues. In education, the diagnosis of 'students at risk', who are likely to fall into deviance, crime or addiction, corresponds to the same rationale (Riele (te) 2006). In the UK, welfare programmes put 'educative pressure' on the familial structure by linking the amount of allocations to the efforts made by parents with regard to their children's schooling (*Learnfare*) or to the constitution of a 'stable' family limiting the number of children (*welfare*).

Governing and Measuring People 'at Risk'

In the field of social statistics, the traditional and descriptive approach is slowly being replaced by the design of more individualistic and determinist models. While statistical tools of the Welfare State have aggregated individual data to the general characteristics of a population, in the name of solidarity and mutualisation of risk, the personalisation of hazards tends to challenge the balance and principles of the insurance society such as the mechanisms of statistical control over people.

These new measurements of the Welfare State, through the technologies of evidence and risk factor criteria, have strongly influenced decision-making and the public health debate. The testing of 'individuals at risk' corresponds to a public health policy in which 'health monitoring' becomes the new device for governing populations (Jorland et al. 2005). This diagnosis of factors of individual risk underestimates the effect of social background to valorise an individual probability which makes the individual responsible for his or her behaviour or pathology. So it becomes up to the person, considered as autonomous, to take charge of his or her capital in health via information and incentives generated by the prevention policy (Cribb and Gewirtz 2012).

These new social state's measures are particularly visible in the field of risk behaviours. This area of social intervention has been invested by epidemiological methods related to licit or illicit psychoactive use of drugs, non-protected sexual relationships, unsafe driving, wrong eating habits, school dropout, suicidal ideation, abuses, sleep disorders and low self-esteem. To these measurable factors of risk, some demographic, social and cultural features are added as well as opinions, dispositions and behaviours registered often on psychometric scales. In applying the epidemiological approach and tools to the study of human behaviours, this new paradigm of research aims to prevent risks while it develops multifactorial analyses of causalities focused on the individual. These measurement or risk factors have become at the core of decision-making and debates in public health. To adopt effective and preventive programmes, the epidemiology proposes to study the variation of a disease in relation to modifying factors in the continuity of previous research work demonstrating the link between smoking and lung cancer. But identifying individual risk factors tends to relativise social environment effects to consider an individual probability which makes the individual responsible of his/her behaviour or pathology. So, it is the person, judged autonomous, who has to take charge of his/her health capital in regard to information and incentives produced by preventive policies.

According to this preventive medicine, the practitioner has to enter patients' individual features into a statistical model and, from parameters provided by different epidemiological studies, to assess the life expectancy and probability of contracting diseases. The epidemiological paradigm goes beyond the field of public health to be devolved to religious practice, vote and even ethnic background on school achievement. Biologists, political scientists, psychologists and sociologists develop logistic models by estimating the same odd ratios. The discovery of new risk factors is enhanced by methodological innovation in metrology and computerisation. That is why the list of 'objective risks' related to health and well-being is increasing and includes more and more heterogeneous factors linked to social behaviours, psychological states or lived experiences. Epidemiology often considers social variables as biological variables with the idea that health inequalities would be embodied and correspond to the own individual biological patrimony.

It tends to rehabilitate certain laws or social reproduction or contagion: some statistical modes related to 'behavioural epidemics' postulate that social behaviours (drug uses, collective practices, fashion) are disseminated in a population not by the intermediary of a pathogenic agent but by the imitation of or conformity to a group; they come to consider that the victim is a passive agent against whom public authorities can intervene to limit the disease spreading. In that sense, the development of genetics has hardened measurement by establishing statistical relationships between genetic factors and the appearance of criminal behaviours. Within the education area, the label 'students at risk' tends to replace traditional categories of 'disadvantaged', 'deprived', 'poor' and 'marginalised' which serve generally to characterise students facing difficulties in school achievement (Lubeck and Garrett 1990; Riele te 2006). It concerns generally students who did not succeed in their secondary schooling. In the UK, under the New Labour policy, sociological categories of cultural capital and social capital have been implicitly used to specify the situation of this 'at-risk' young people, disconnected from their families and society (they would lack social capital) and unknowing what to do with their life (lack of identity capital), while they do not value or reject education (lack of cultural capital) (Levitas 2004). The economic dimension is most often ignored in these analyses which prefer conceptualising 'youth at risk' in terms of individual and familial disorders.

Epidemiologists also analyse youth behaviour problems and psychologies by associating their biological features with those related to their social identity. These variables tend to underestimate the social and cultural environment, as their personal narrative, to provide evidence on negative aspects often related to their familial instability. Some strong incentives are put forward to maintain these young people, maladjusted and unprepared for the labour market, in the education system. The category 'dropouts' is largely used by experts and policymakers for characterising major risks in the 'loss of human capital'. If the main factor of risk remains the 'non-achievement of secondary education', other characteristics are used to establish a causality between the individual and his/her social failure. International surveys develop list of different variables as poverty, ethnic minority status, familial status, weak knowledge of the major language, type of school, geographic isolation and community features. The individual variables are most often self-esteem and motivation, but physical (as illness or disability), behavioural (indiscipline, pregnancy, drug use), familial (lone parenthood, conflicts, sexual abuse) or socioeconomic (parents' level of revenue and education, fixed home or not) factors are also registered. As in heath, the range of factors in education is large and gives place to many variables and factorial analyses.

The Great Debate and Controversy in Education

In 1996, during the annual conference of the Teacher Training Agency, David Hargreaves,[5] an eminent researcher in education, gave a lecture which echoed widely in the UK scientific community (Hargreaves 1996). A professor of Educational Sciences at the University of Cambridge, he resumed in his lecture the criticism he had addressed against sociology of education and extended his reasoning to education research which he accused of being incapable of serving the UK education system. To support his arguments, he established a comparison with the area of health in which evidence-based medicine was emerging. He then asked the Teacher Training Agency to improve the dissemination of research findings to teachers and to give them the possibility of carrying out their own projects instead of relying on academic research with little direct and beneficial impact on teaching practices.

David Hargreaves defended the idea that educational research, contrary to medicine, has no prestige and could not adopt the same technical language. The majority of research is not cumulative while small-scale surveys produce no relevant and conclusive findings. The reproduction of experiments which, according to this famous professor, was more than necessary in social sciences due to cultural and contextual variations was lacking. Researchers in education prefer to spend their time in disputes on the philosophy and methodology of social sciences. This attitude

---

[5] A former chief inspector of London's schools, he was one of the leaders in the criticism of teacher training which he considered to be unadjusted due to its academic feature.

undermines the foundations of research which cannot claim to get funding from these postulates. By contrast, medicine is capable of formulating a diagnosis and prescribing effective treatments. Therefore according to Hargreaves, there is no difference between researchers and practitioners, and research in medicine is not private, esoteric and irrelevant as it is in education. Incapable of producing results regarding the effectiveness of teaching practices, educational researchers have failed to create a body of knowledge which is as solid as that found in medicine. Educational research, dominated by a linear model (fundamental research–applied research–dissemination), has not succeeded in disseminating its findings, in transforming its practices and in proposing a valid demonstration. Hargreaves considered that researchers were only accountable to themselves while they were incapable of reaching the standards of engineering or pharmaceutics. In the conclusion to his lecture, he proposed to adopt a national strategy for educational research which would define short-term and long-term priorities and introduce mechanisms of coordination between funding agencies tied to accountability. He thought that practitioners and policymakers had to play a more important role in the choice of research programmes and researchers had to include these requirements in their projects so that they could become accountable for their research findings. Hargreaves judged than it was necessary to establish a national forum to associate stakeholders with the political agenda of educational research.

Alis Oancea analysed the discourses of the new orthodoxy of evidence and the criticism addressed to educational research, by distinguishing topics and levels of analysis of this denunciation (Oancea 2005). He organised it into three categories: the diagnosis of the quality, the explanation of dysfunctions and the solutions to be implemented. The arguments in favour of reform called for a clarification of concepts, a better methodology to prevent bias, training programmes for researchers, changes in the research agenda with a stronger involvement of users, better dissemination of best practices, the strengthening of partnerships and links between research and practice, changes in the funding process, the development of systematic reviews, the transformation of evaluation by peers, the creation of structures of coordination and the steering of research.

The debate between the pros and cons was embedded in frontal oppositions related to the accumulation of scientific knowledge (reproduction, dissemination, interdisciplinarity); the need to harmonise research procedures (in terms of coordination, commensurability, codes of best practices); rationality in linking policy, practice and research; and the adoption of a teleological or normative vision (improvement of practices, prescriptions, planning, scientific determinism). Researchers opposed to the evidence-based policy denounced this 'new orthodoxy' which is based on a linear and cumulative vision of knowledge and a truncated conception of 'accountability'. Some of them qualified this policy as hidden 'instrumentalism', 'positivism' or an attempt to reinstall 'strong sciences' and 'rationalism'. Others criticised the 'maximisation of objectivity' which undermines values, emotions and subjectivity, the centralism of methodologies to assess quality, the uselessness of lists of accountability criteria, the behaviourist description of practices, the 'diktat' of the UK Department of Education and the adoption of a scientist language.

One of the major opponents of evidence-based policy is the sociologist Martyn Hammersley, an ethnographer and specialist in qualitative methodology. He opposed the solutions proposed by David Hargreaves during his lecture; he defined his critical stance in two books (Hammersley 2002, 2007) in which he answered the three arguments advanced by Hargreaves: education research is not sufficiently cumulative, it does not contribute to the improvement of teaching practices and it has to imitate the methods used in medicine. If Hammersley recognised that it was necessary to make research findings more cumulative, he refuted, however, the criteria of assessment proposed by Hargreaves that pressure on research would better serve the interest of practitioners and policymakers. In his opinion, assessment based on the criteria of evidence-based research has introduced a methodological monism undermining the quality of research itself. He also considered that it was very difficult to reduce the social complexity of learning to a positivist measurement, a standardised treatment or controlled experiments. This political pressure and attempts to control have negative effects on the long-term production of knowledge which was capable of effectively informing teaching practices. The reduction of budgets and the multiplication of short-term requirements would have a negative impact in the end.

Hammersley also criticised the postulate that research, through its instrumental conception, had to indicate to practitioners the best technique for solving problems by subjecting teaching to a scientific theory in which teachers study the most adjusted techniques. He believes that the work of psychologists, philosophers and sociologists has shown that pedagogy is more a practice than a technique and that it corresponds to a diversity of judgements in situation which cannot be reduced to the application of predefined rules. Knowledge is mobilised by teachers in the classroom, from judgements and assessments they try to implement and which are difficult to operationalise from measurable results. This practical feature of teaching is reinforced by the fact that teachers work with group of students and not with patents like physicians. Therefore, if educational research can contribute to improving practices, it can only do so by creating an environment in which knowledge modifies its conceptions and situations guiding its action.

Hammersley rejected the comparison made by Hargreaves between medicine and education: in the former, there is a gap between researchers and those who use their work. Research is mainly conducted in the laboratory and does not involve clinicians much. Furthermore, sociologists such as Becker have demonstrated that clinical experience is used to legitimate choices of treatment outside of scientific rules and procedures. Another work has underlined the pragmatic dimension of clinicians who trusts more their intuition and proximal acquaintances than abstract knowledge and principles. It has also been proved that evidence-based medicine has some limitations: the research literature varies in quality and some scientific areas are easier to cumulate than others. Some gaps make it difficult to normalise practices and can lead to false conclusions on the relative effectiveness of certain treatments. There are also numerous biases in systematic reviews which tend to underestimate negative results and to create distortion in the judgement of clinicians. These methods are mainly used to control costs and budgets in medicine and this explains why so many physicians are opposed to them.

In his reply, Hargreaves explained that physicians and teachers are applied professionals and they have similar postures in the way they make complex judgements (1997). The difference is in the fact that physicians use research on practice to inform and improve decisions while this is not the case for teaching. Hargreaves also doubted that teachers were able to use rich and diversified judgements and considered they follow rules and routines to obtain better results with less effort. Even if they had tacit knowledge and numerous judgements, it did not create any difference with physicians who do not necessarily apply the universal laws of natural sciences. Hargreaves therefore rejected the accusation of positivism and claimed that medicine, like teaching, is sensitive to the context of situations. The difference is that physicians have an infrastructure of knowledge to which they can refer to in their clinical judgements. Hargreaves argued that teachers, like physicians, were more interested in 'what works?' than 'why it works?', but contrary to medicine, they cannot find a scientific explanation in their professional activities because of a lack of shared knowledge base for validated experiments. Using several examples, Hargreaves defended the relevance of randomised controlled trials in social sciences and considered that it did not undermine the professionalism of teachers but that it could strengthen their skills and stimulate the debate with researchers about the quality of research.

Since this original controversy, other criticisms have been made against the evidence-based policy in education. Maggie McLure analysed in detail the systematic reviews conducted by the EPPI-Centre and which were strongly supported by UK policymakers (McLure 2005). She showed that the language used to describe and justify this methodology is a mix of old scientific positivism (systematisation, reliability, rigour, reproduction) and a rhetoric from the audit culture (transparency, quality, insurance, standards). But the EPPI-Centre's approach maintains a discourse of mistrust against academics and researchers who it accuses of not being sufficiently cautious, of being undemocratic, furtive, unskilled, chaotic, egocentric, etc. However, the work of the technicians/experts who design these systematic reviews was closely studied by McLure. They follow very rigid protocols and use tools to extract keywords from data to synthetise online reports. They not only have to conform to the epistemology of evidence, they are also subjected to a neo-Taylorist regime and a managerial discipline which characterise work within the EPPI-Centre.

These technicians are prisoners of a terminology which forces them to use taxonomies and to calibrate a rhetoric far from the scientific discourse. So, some terms generally associated with cognitive and intellectual practices of research, such as 'analysis' or 'interpretation', have disappeared from reports. The lexicon used denies any textual structure of research which is considered as an obstacle to be bypassed when writing extracted and aggregated material. Strangely enough, reading is absent from the process. No study identified as being relevant is really read: in fact, the method can be considered as a huge algorithm for not reading. The definition of a protocol and the criteria to judge the quality of research impede diversion and adjacent reading as it is impossible to extend the corpus once the procedure has been codified and launched. Extractions from databanks and digital research lead to a significant number of studies not fitting the required criteria and consequently they are not registered. Often, when there is no summary, the simple reading of the title is sufficient to decide whether the research will be deleted from the list. Furthermore, technicians/experts who review research literature have time and organisational constraints which do not allow them to be as exhaustive as they would have expected to be at the launch of the protocol.

According to McLure, experts or technicians cannot avoid drawing conclusions on education policies and teaching practices. Unfortunately, these conclusions are often related to their own experience or convictions rather than a synthesis of data they have produced. In fact, even if they are not allowed by the protocol to use their own rhetoric style but instead to objectively assembly data and though their readers have to navigate through empty and stereotyped sentences, some experts authorise themselves to use arguments or sometimes a conceptualisation of a criticism which tries to conform to the conventions of academic work. But some of these conclusions are lukewarm or trivial when they do not give place to rhetorical manoeuvres to arrive at conclusions which conform to current policy expectations. Consequently, the EPPI-Centre's protocol does not eliminate the processes of interpreting and judging literature reviews, but it makes them less visible and transparent while outrageously simplifying educative issues and their solutions and destroying important aspects of research: reading, writing, reflection, interpretation, argumentation and justification.

Hargreaves's statements were aimed at policymakers, particularly Chris Woodhead who was the chief inspector of schools and head of the Ofsted, the UK inspection agency. He also criticised the claimed value of sociology of education and affirmed that academics were only producing poorly written research findings. Two reports were published at the request of the UK Department of Education. The first one, led by James Tooley,[6] considered, from the review of research articles, that a lot of them were faulty (Tooley and Darby 1998). In the introduction, Chris Woodhead claimed that the majority of articles were second-hand findings and that a lot of money had been wasted funding them. Funded by the Ofsted which wanted to raise standards in classrooms, the study resumed Hargreaves' criticism and defined the best criteria for the evaluation of research: a serious contribution to theoretical knowledge, being relevant in practice and upstream and downstream coordi-

---

[6] James Tooley, professor of educational sciences at the Manchester University and head of education in the most important New Right think tank, the Institute of Economic Affairs.

nation. The second report, the Hillage report, written by researchers from the Institute for Employment Studies at the Sussex University, went further in discussing the quality and utility of research (Hillage et al. 1998).

Following Hargreaves' suggestions calling for the creation of an independent forum and national strategy, the authors of the second report considered that educational research was too often disconnected from teaching practices and inaccessible to teachers. They recommended making research more relevant for the members of the education community, better disseminating high-quality results towards users and the public; contributing to solidify the existing body of knowledge; strengthening links between research, policy and practice; giving a greater coherence to research programmes; requiring better relevance and reliability; and implementing quality insurance mechanisms to better control public expenditure. The report detailed what should be the new modes of relationships between policy and research: more partnerships and mediation and an improvement in the quality of an evidence-based policy.

The UK government took a series of initiatives to enable educational research to be able to identify the best effective practices for raising standards. It sought to promote 'centres of excellence' by allocating specific funds to institutions involved in priority areas, by supporting systematic reviews and randomised controlled trials to better achieve these new strategic objectives. After the creation of the EPPI-Centre, the National Educational Research Forum (NERF) was launched in 2001 to define priorities in the funding of educational research so that it better responds to the needs of users. NERF produced an ambitious document for its national strategy. The Forum had to demonstrate that R&D could play a major role in responding to the needs of education policy, in anticipating change and in strengthening the links between research and educative programmes. According to Stephen Ball, this document was ridiculous and depressing because of its caricatured conception of research and its apparent ignorance of its main constituents while wanting to be the starting point of national consultation (Ball 2001). The document proved the political will to implement a 'governance by quality' and to strengthen the steering of research by non-governmental agencies for accountability purposes. It proposed to standardise the objectives and procedures of research while however at the same time recognising the diversity of types of educational research and the objectives pursued by different programmes. NERF also proposed setting up national priorities and assessing the skills of researchers. During this period, the Economic and Social Research Council created the Teaching and Learning Research Programme (TLRP) to better respond to policymakers' expectations regarding the effectiveness of research and its capacity to be accountable with regard to 'what works'. The aim was to federate and to fund researchers focusing on the learning and improvement of outcomes involving stakeholders. It was the result of strong political pressure to better align teaching practices to evidence-based research and to strengthen accountability. In the end, the programme took up a significant share of the public funds dedicated to educational research.

The Globalisation of Evidence-Based Policymaking

Until now, we have considered the emergence and development of evidence-based policy from the US and UK point of view, by showing how, in health and education, these new technologies have contributed to redrawing the modes of social interventions of the state and undermining the place and position of social and educational sciences. But these configurations go beyond the national context and are now on a global scale. The third part of this chapter will aim to describe this frame of scales from the local to the global (Sassen 2006). Globalisation is not just a simple interdependence between states. As we have seen in the first chapters of this book, it articulates actors and intra-statist processes with global networks and digital technologies which tend to promote a government by numbers and standards guiding decision-making at the local level (Ozga et al. 2011). This multi-scalar globalisation entails transnational dynamics which are embedded in local devices. I shall present here the extent of the international circulation of the evidence-based policy in the area of education. I have studied the connections which were set up between policymakers and experts, the operations of translation and transfer by international organisations such as the OECD and the gradual inclusion of problematics of evidence in the European strategy for lifelong learning. To illustrate some connections from the local to the global, I will begin with the case of New Zealand, which was a political laboratory in the design and implementation of evidence-based technologies, both in education and health, and it served as a model for international organisations. I will then show how New Zealand's policy extended into a project funded by the European Commission and one which mobilises a large number of stakeholders.

The New Zealand Evidence-Based Policy

In the beginning of the 2000s, the New Zealand evidence-based policy was developed from work on the design of indicators for the education system to define a new strategy for education policy. A Strategic Research Initiative was initiated by the Ministry of Education so that commissions could work together for systematic reviews of research literature to better inform decision-making. These first reviews of the literature helped to identify key topics but also to show that some data and research findings were lacking if the national strategy was to be adjusted, in terms of learning and improving student results. The Ministry wanted to strengthen the relevance of this work by using more rigorous methodologies adapted to its strategy. The idea was to adopt a method to capitalise knowledge produced by research at the global level and to develop regular syntheses to inform practitioners and policymakers.

In 2002, the New Zealand Ministry of Education implemented a project entitled *Iterative Best Evidence Synthesis Programme* (BES) which aimed to reinforce access to and use of evidence-based research by practitioners (Alton-Lee 2007). The objective was to identify, assess and synthesise 'what works' in education, in particular improving effectiveness and student results. In order to do so, syntheses were regularly worked out on the basis of a capitalisation of international research findings. While the project was under the responsibility of its Chief Education Adviser, Adrienne Alton-Lee, the New Zealand Ministry created a national group including writers of syntheses, quality insurers and methodologists, teacher representatives, researchers and political advisers. Some more specialised groups were institutionalised to developed evidence-based methodologies.

The BES programme was well supported by teachers' trade unions, while syntheses were applied to various areas like teaching and learning, training and school management. Today, the programme continues to develop online resources and proposes support for professionals in research and training by linking difficulties in student learning with health and welfare issues. It explains why this policy strongly focuses on the relatively poor and marginalised Maori people. Some practical guides and recommendations were addressed to all the New Zealand educational stakeholders. Collaborations between researchers, policymakers and professionals were strongly supported according to the principles held by the mode 2 of production of knowledge. The New Zealand Ministry of Education assumes a brokerage function in the implementation of the evidence-based policy.

This programme has benefitted from strong recognition worldwide, while New Zealand has had very good results in international surveys such as PISA, the new global instrument for the benchmarking of education policies. This is why the New Zealand experience influenced the OECD in the production and promotion of an international expertise on evidence-based policies.

The OECD/European Commission Joint Strategy

The OECD expressed its interest for the technologies of evidence by organising an initial workshop in Washington DC, in April 2004, under the aegis of the Centre for Educational Research and Innovation (CERI), the US Institute of Education Sciences and the Coalition for Evidence-Based Policy. The OECD/CERI defended the idea that policymakers need relevant and rigorous educational research. The seminar proposed to reflect on the needs and constraints addressed by the 'policy of evidence', to explore the sources and reasons for resistance to experiments and to study the practical results obtained in different countries. The discussion focused on randomised controlled trials. On the US side, the OERI coordinated further research syntheses of 'what works' (*What works: Research About Teaching and Learning*, 1985), and the Institute of Education Sciences was very active in the development of randomised controlled trials and systematic reviews. Among the papers discussed, one was an excerpt of the lecture given by Phil Davies, a member of Tony Blair's cabinet, during the first annual conference of the Campbell Collaboration, while another document presented three examples of the use of randomised controlled trials synthesised by Ann Oakley, the future head of the EPPI-Centre.

The meeting was held on 14–15 September 2005 at The Hague (the Netherlands). It aimed to explore how 'bridges' could be built between researchers, policymakers and practitioners, by using evidence-based research to improve education policies. Participants had to design an analytical framework and to specifically discuss brokerage agencies which, like the EPPI-Centre in the UK, were seeking to improve the links between research and political expectations. Participants were invited to talk about experiments led by different national agencies and programmes: the EPPI-Centre, the What Works Clearinghouse in the USA, the Iterative Best Evidence Synthesis led by Adrienne Alton-Lee in New Zealand and the work of the Campbell Collaboration in its C2-SPECTR project. During the welcome session, Tom Schuller, head of the CERI, intervened with David Gough, who had just become the new head of the EPPI-Centre. The working document resumed the conclusions of the CERI on knowledge management (OECD 2003).

The last meeting was held in London (6, 7 July 2006) under the auspices of the UK Department of Education and the Teaching and Learning Research Programme (TLRP)).[7] Nineteen representatives from OECD countries attended the meeting as well as David Pascal Dion, at the time the director of the European Expert Network on Economics of Education (EENEE) for the European Commission (General Directorate of Educaiton and Culture). The objective was to discuss and reflect about the implementation of 'evidence-based policies', to expand and support programmes of experiments and to make general recommendations. In his introduction, Tom Schuller resumed the issues that had been established by the CERI to demonstrate the usefulness of evidence-based research in improving the performance of education systems in the rankings of international surveys. David Pascal Dion was looking at the possibilities of introducing technologies of evidence in the European lifelong learning strategy.

The OECD report: *Evidence in Education: Linking Research and Policy* (OECD 2007) resumed the different contributions of experts in this series of seminars, without producing any recommendations for Member States. Distancing itself from the 'evidence-based' work which was highly controversial within the educational research community, it justified the necessity to develop an 'informed-based research policy', e.g. a policy better 'informed' by research. Beyond these semantic differences, the two authors evoked the problems posed by the lack of quality and effectiveness of educational research and its incapacity to improve the performance of education systems (Burns and Schuller 2007). The report suggested bypassing the divide between quantitative and qualitative methods to use evidence-based research to arbitrate in decision-making and to involve practitioners and stakeholders in the implementation of reforms.

In March 2007, the Directorate-General for Education and Culture of the European Commission organised an international conference along with the German Ministry of Education and Research entitled *Knowledge for Action – Research*

---

[7]TLRP, Teaching Learning Research Programme, aiming to canalise educational research on the 'what works?' issue.

Strategies for an Evidence-Based Education Policy (DIPF 2007). While the head of the DG EAC, Odile Quintin, attended the meeting with other lecturers presenting successful evidence-based policies, Tom Schuller gave an overview of the series of seminars and OECD's latest report. In the same year, the DG EAC drafted a report entitled *Towards More Knowledge-Based Policy and Practice in Education and Training* (European Commission 2007) which valorised the work carried out by the OECD on 'evidence-based policies'. This DG EAC document concluded that some ideas had to be proposed to Member States in order to help them develop policies and practices based on evidence in their education systems. It also gave examples of programmes and experiments: the UK Teaching and Learning Research Programme, the EPPI-Centre and some other agencies and European institutions engaged in similar approaches.

Since 2009, the Directorate-General for Education and Culture has funded a project entitled *Evidence-Informed Policy in Education in Europe* (EIPEE) in collaboration with the UK Institute of Education and the EPPI-Centre. EIPEE mobilised different European partners to develop networks and mechanisms of knowledge brokerage in the area of education and training to reinforce the links between research, policy and practice and to raise the awareness of policymakers and practitioners with regard to research findings (Gough et al. 2011). Beyond the study of activities, the networking and the development of European centres, this project, which has obtained the support of the Campbell Collaboration, OECD-CERI and the US *Clearinghouse for Educational Research*, aimed to organise data collection and to analyse the capacity of actors to improve the quality of procedures and to inform professionals and policymakers.

The creation of websites and databanks was planned to set up and classify the most relevant activities and research findings and to put the resources and training tools produced during international seminars and disseminated through networks online. Some experts have been mobilised under the leadership of the EPPI-Centre to develop a common understanding of evidence-based policies, while European stakeholders have been associated with putting into place new relations between research and policy in the field of education. An analytical framework was developed.

This framework promoted three logics: the production of evidence, e.g. relevant research findings to be produced, disseminated and made accessible to practitioners; to bring producers and users closer together according to a brokerage function; and the use of evidence or how it directly transforms decision-making or indirectly shapes the knowledge, understanding and attitudes of policymakers. Stakeholders have to be involved in the process (the media, professionals, social partners, civil society organisations, trade unions, employers, etc.). The information system has to assure coordination and effective interventions but also a visibility and a sufficient capacity to produce relevant evidence for policymaking.

Progressively, the European Commission adopted the idea of evidence-based policymaking or EBPM for its lifelong learning strategy, in declaring that EBPM was a good means of gathering and sharing evidence in the understanding of the life conditions, attitudes and values of youths in relation to other areas of public policies.

But the European recommendations for the adoption of the technologies of evidence went far beyond the fields of education and health to be applied to the field of social sciences and humanities. To enhance the communication of evidence-based research, the European Commission recently designed a practical guide for researchers in human and social sciences (The European Commission 2010). It defends the idea that EBPM contributes to stimulating interactions between researchers, policymakers and stakeholders throughout the world and within European institutions. By making research more available and relevant in the support of policies, particularly through new framework programmes, this rhetoric proposes to go beyond the model in which researchers present their research as an 'accomplished fact' to engage them in activities of dissemination and transfer to the most relevant target groups. The guide presents a series of best practices for research data collection, for improving the measurement and evaluation of public policies and for raising awareness of the media and stakeholders.

Before the publication of this practical guide, the European Commission, through its Directorate-General of Research for Humanities and Socio-economical Sciences, produced a synthesis (2008) entitled *The Scientific Evidence for Policymaking* in which it proposed, after several in-depth interviews and questionnaires addressed to policymakers and European scientific advisers, to improve the links between science and policy. The questionnaire positioned on the same level, the knowledge produced by the academic world and the knowledge delivered by think tanks or interest groups. In drawing up the report, experts and policymakers had to identify the obstacles which are preventing the two worlds becoming closer: jargon, legal barriers and gaps in the agendas. Some proposals were formulated to increase the utility of research by framing and better evaluating public policies. The Directorate-General of Research affirmed its will to support the development of EBPM and to play a mediating role in the new framework programmes developed in the European Union.

Conclusion

As has been shown by the European research agenda, social and educational sciences are today being put into competition with other producers of knowledge outside the academic field (international organisations, agencies, think tanks). The pressure coming from policymakers and stakeholders is increasing being associated with the production and use of research findings. Evidence-based policymaking, as a political experimentalism, legitimises new areas of effectiveness and mediation between policy, research and practice as it establishes a hierarchy in the modes of evidence. It therefore challenges the internal scientific division of labour in social and educational sciences while redefining borders between science and expertise. In the field of Eurocracy, policymakers are increasingly asking researchers to produce useful knowledge for Member States while they require them not to make any comment regarding their theoretical doubts and metrological imperfections and also to avoid activist or dogmatic stances (Georgakakis and Rowell 2013).

The mode 2 of production of knowledge and the model of a networking science have become the key principles for some policymakers in international organisations or at the European Commission as they reflect on the reconfiguration of relationships between science and policy in social and educational sciences. The demand for expertise in the design of new instruments of government relates to an assumed policy connecting experts, research units, agencies and think tanks, capable of producing the metrology required for the restructuring of public policies. Creating networks, designing websites and connecting spaces of calculation are all political operations being implemented today by supranational organisations to capitalise, totalise and classify knowledge and tools of measurement which are increasingly independent from the state's power (Latour 1987). In parallel, the democracy of sciences and technics is valued as a legitimate principle for regulating the activities of researchers, their modalities of funding and their evaluation.

Faced with these evolutions, constructivism, in its pragmatist vision, has not succeeded in competing with these capacities of generalisation and synthesis of data led by the new modes of quantification and the return of positivism. Methodologically, its 'accounts' are 'situated' because it aims to understand the local complexity of devices. But, when the state or an international organisation extends and generalises its action, the experiment and its methodological instrumentation are judged to be better adjusted. So, it is expertise which gains from these differential and asymmetrical positions between educational research and the action of statist or supranational organisations. While it provides a modelled representation of the world through its instruments, it modifies the formats which frame and structure social reality by depriving criticism from its exteriority.

The new figures of international expertise, in rehabilitating a positivist vision, tend to legitimate an objectivity far from attachment to the state and its traditional tools of knowledge and action. Criticism has become difficult because devices and agencies of measurement worldwide are distributed between different groups of agents with a low level of explicit coordination. It is therefore problematic for identifying forms of solidarity and complicity between experts for whom activity is always plotted and technically guided while generating global effects in the restructuring of statist structures and cognitive representations. Expertise therefore acts in the earliest stages because it produces knowledge and instruments which directly serve decision-making before the decisions are made public.

If social and educational sciences wish to maintain a certain critical reflexivity, they have to take into account the transformation of their cognitive and metrological environment. In being aware of their relative position among new sciences of government, by taking account of some asymmetrical effects created by the extension of international expertise beyond the academic field, they have to rebuild a survey method capable of simultaneously describing the implementation of evidence-based policy at the European or international level and its normalising effects in different situations, devices and experiences of local social and educational actors.

References

Alkin, M. (Ed.). (2004). *Evaluation roots: Tracing theorists' views and influences.* Thousand Oaks: Sage.

Alton-Lee, A. (2007). The iterative best evidence synthesis programme, New Zealand. In *Evidence in education: Linking research and policy.* Paris: Centre for Educational Research and Innovation, OECD.

Ball, S. J. (2001). 'You've been NERFed!' Dumbing down the academy: National Educational Research Forum: 'A national strategy? Consultation paper': A brief and bilious response. *Journal of Education Policy, 16*(3), 265–268.

Beck, U. (1992). *Risk society: Towards a new modernity.* London: Sage.

Berg, M. (1997). *Rationalizing medical work: Decision support techniques and medical practices.* Cambridge, MA: MIT Press.

Berliner, D. C., & Biddle, B. J. (1995). *The manufactured crisis: Myths, fraud, and the attack on America's public schools.* Reading: Addison-Wesley Publishing Company.

Burns, T., & Schuller, T. (Eds.). (2007). *Evidence in education: Linking research and policy.* Paris: CERI/OECD.

Cabinet Office. (1999). *Modernizing government.* London: The Stationnery Office.

Cabinet Office. (2001a). *Better policy-making.* London: Cabinet Office.

Cabinet Office. (2001b). *Professional policy-making for the twenty-first century.* London: Cabinet Office.

Cambrosio, A., Keating, P., & Bourret, P. (2007). Objectivité régulatoire et systèmes de preuves en médecine: Le cas de la cancérologie. In V. Tournay (Ed.), *La gouvernance des innovations biomédicales* (pp. 155–175). Paris: Presses Universitaires de France.

Campbell, D. T. (1969). Reforms as experiments. *American Psychologist, 24,* 409–429.

Campbell, D. T., & Stanley, J. (1963). *Experimental and quasi-experimental designs for research.* Chicago: Rand McNally.

Clarke, J., & Newman, J. (1997). *The Managerial State; power, politics and ideology in the remaking of social welfare.* London: Sage.

Cribb, A., & Gewirtz, S. (2012). L'éthique du nouvel État-providence et la recomposition des identités morales dans une ère de participation des usagers. *Education et Sociétés, 1*(29), 45–56.

Davies, H. T. O., Nutley, S. M., & Smith, P. C. (2007). *What works? Evidence-based policy and practice in public services.* Bristol: The Policy Press.

Denham, A. (1996). *Think-tanks of the new right.* Aldershot: Dartmouth Publishing Co.

Desrosières, A., & Naish, C. (2002). *The politics of large numbers: A history of statistical reasoning.* Cambridge, MA: Harvard University Press.

European Commission. (2007). *Commission staff working document: Towards more knowledge-based policy and practice in education and training.* Brussels: Directorate-General for Education and Culture.

European Commission. (2008). *Making a difference in policy-making. How to increase the uptake of research results in the socio-economic sciences.* Luxembourg: Publications Office of the European Union.

European Commission. (2010). *Communicating research for evidence-based policy-making: A practical guide for researchers in socio-economic sciences and humanities.* Luxembourg: Publications Office of the European Union.

Georgakakis, D., & Rowell, J. (Eds.). (2013). *The field of eurocracy: Mapping EU actors and professionals.* Basingstoke: Palgrave Macmillan.

German Institute for International Educational Research (DIPF). (2007). *Knowledge for action: Research strategies for an evidence-based education policy.* Frankfurt: Deutsche Institut für Internationale Pädagogische Forschung.

Gibbons, M., Limoges, C., Nowotny, H., Schwartzman, S., Scott, P., & Trow, M. (1994). *The new production of knowledge: The dynamics of science and research in contemporary societies*. London: Sage.

Gough, D., Tripney, J., Kenny, C., & Buk-Berge, E. (2011). *Evidence Informed Policy in Education in Europe: EIPEE final project report*. London: EPPI-Centre, Social Science Research Unit, Institute of Education, University of London.

Hall, D., Gunter, H., & Bragg, J. (2013). Leadership, new public management and the re-modelling and regulation of teacher identities. *International Journal of Leadership in Education, 16*(2), 173–190.

Hammersley, M. (Ed.). (2002). *Educational research, policymaking and practice*. London: Sage.

Hammersley, M. (Ed.). (2007). *Educational research and evidence-based practice*. London: Sage.

Hargreaves, D. H. (1996). *Teaching as a research-based profession: Possibilities and prospects*. London: Teacher Training Agency.

Henry, M., Lingard, B., Rizvi, F., & Taylor, S. (2001). *The OECD, globalization, and education policy*. Oxford: Pergamon-Elsevier.

Hillage, J., Pearson, R., Anderson, A., & Tamkin, P. (1998). *Excellence in research on schools*. London: Department for Education and Employment (DfEE).

Jasanoff, S. (2011). The practices of objectivity in regulatory science. In C. Camic, N. Gross, & M. Lamont (Eds.), *Social knowledge in the making* (pp. 307–337). Chicago: University of Chicago Press.

Jessop, B. (1993). Towards a Schumpeterian workfare state? Preliminary remarks on post-Fordist political economy. *Studies in Political Economy, 40*, 7–39.

Jorland, G., Weisz, G., & Opinel, A. (2005). *Body counts: Medical quantification in historical and sociological perspectives//Perspectives Historiques Et Sociologiques Sur la Quantification Médicale*. Montréal: McGill-Queen's Press-MQUP.

Latour, B. (1987). *Science in action: How to follow scientists and engineers through society*. Cambridge, MA: Harvard University Press.

Lawn, M., & Normand, R. (2014). *Shaping of European education. Interdisciplinary Approaches*. London: Routledge.

Le Galès, P., & Faucher-King, F. (2010). *Tony Blair. (1997–2007), Le bilan des réformes*. Paris: Presses de Sciences-Po.

Levitas, R. (2004). Let's hear it for humpty: Social exclusion, the third way and cultural capital. *Cultural Trends, 13*(2), 41–56.

Lubeck, S., & Garrett, P. (1990). The social construction of the 'at-risk'child. *British Journal of Sociology of Education, 11*(3), 327–340.

MacLure, M. (2005). 'Clarity bordering on stupidity': Where's the quality in systematic review? *Journal of Education Policy, 20*(4), 393–416.

Majone, G. D. (1989). *Evidence argument and persuasion in the policy process*. New Haven: Yale University Press.

Marks, H. (1999). *La médecine des preuves. Histoire et anthropologie des essais cliniques (1900–1990)*. Paris: Les Empêcheurs de penser en rond.

Mosteller, F., & Boruch, R. (Eds.). (2002). *Evidence matters. Randomized trials in education research*. Washington D.C.: Brookings Institution Press.

National Audit Office. (2001). *Modern policy making: Ensuring policies deliver value for money*. London: National Audit Office.

National Audit Office. (2003). *Getting the evidence: Using research in policy making*. London: The Stationnery Office.

Normand, R. (2009). Expert measurement in the government of Lifelong Learning. In: E. Mangenot & J. Rowell (coord), *What Europe constructs: New sociological perspectives in European studies*, Manchester University Press.

Normand, R. (2010). Expertise, networks and indicators: The construction of the European strategy in education. *European Educational Research Journal, 9*(3), 407–421.

Oancea, A. (2005). Criticisms of educational research: Key topics and levels of analysis. *British Educational Research Journal, 31*(2), 157–183.

OECD. (2003). *Knowledge management. New challenges for educational research.* Paris: Publications de l'OCDE.

OECD. (2007). *Evidence in education. Linking research and policy.* Paris: Publications de l'OCDE.

Ozga, J., Dahler-Larsen, P., Segerholm, C., & Simola, H. (Eds.). (2011). *Fabricating quality in education: Data and governance in Europe.* London: Routledge.

Parsons, W. (2002). From muddling through to muddling up: Evidence-based policy making and the modernising of British government. *Public Policy and Administration, 17*(3), 43–60.

Porter, T. M. (1995). *Trust in numbers. The pursuit of objectivity in science and public life.* Princeton: Princeton University Press.

Ricci, D. M. (1993). *The transformation of American politics: The new Washington and the rise of think tanks.* New Haven: Yale University Press.

Riele (te), K. (2006). Youth 'at risk': Further marginalizing the marginalized? *Journal of Education Policy, 21*(2), 129–145.

Sanderson, I. (2002). Making sense of 'what works': Evidence-based policy making as instrumental rationality. *Public Policy and Administration, 17*(3), 61–75.

Sassen, S. (2006). *Territory, authority, rights: From medieval to global assemblages.* Princeton: Princeton University Press.

Smith, J. A. (1991). *The idea brokers: Think tanks and the rise of the new policy elite.* New York: Free Press.

Spring, J. (2005). *Political agendas for education: From the religious right to the Green Party.* Mahwah: L. Erlbaum.

Timmermans, S., & Berg, M. (2003). *The gold standard: The challenge of evidence-based medicine and standardization in health care.* Philadelphia: Temple University Press.

Timmermans, S., & Kolker, E. S. (2004). Evidence-based medicine and the reconfiguration of medical knowledge. *Journal of Health and Social Behavior*, (45), Extra issue: Health and health care in the United States: Origins and dynamics, pp. 177–193.

Tooley, J., & Darby, D. (1998). *Educational research: A critique: A survey of published educational research.* London: Ofsted.

Weiss, C. H. (1979). The many meanings of research utilization. *Public Administration Review, 39*(5), 426–443.

Wells, P. (2007). New labour and evidence based policy making, 1997–2007. *People Place & Policy, 1*(1), 22–29.

Part II
Expertise, Entrepreneurship and Management: The New Spirit of Academic Capitalism

The Multiple Worlds of Expertise

Introduction

As we have seen in the previous chapters, much research has affirmed the role of knowledge in the shaping of education policies and the implement of reforms at national and global scales. The European Commission (EC) has the capacity to mobilise expert networks and groups to address its recommendations to Member States. European technocracy, instead of having a coercive power on states, uses expertise as a form of authority and power (Radaelli 2008). Since the implementation of the Lisbon Strategy, decisions taken by European institutions have been supported by a wide variety of working groups, committees, agencies and think tanks (Gornitzka 2013). The production of knowledge does not just belong to scientists: it is distributed among heterogeneous experts with a central position to give advice and to guide policymakers.

It is a change in the categorisation of power, while in education, as in other public sectors, the technocratic mindset has been disseminated among national and European elites. The search for solutions which has been presented as rational and efficient has overcome the modes of long-term deliberation. Even if issues of justice remain important in the implementation of the European lifelong learning agenda, the need to take quick and short-term decisions and to reduce a strong economic and political complexity has forced European policymakers to arbitrate between multiple pressure and interests to choose a political direction. The European Commission (EC) is at the centre of a network of interactions between Brussels officials, experts and civil servants from Member States who maintain strong acquaintances or even a 'technocratic cronyism' outside of professional relationships (Peters 1995; Majone 1996; Shore 2013; Michel and Robert 2010; Georgakakis and Lasalle 2008). The EC is a political entrepreneur in the sense that it uses a wide variety of resources and expertise while it is opportunistic in persuading its interlocutors (representatives of the Member States and members of the European Parliament) to take decisions and to vote legislative texts.

© Springer International Publishing Switzerland 2016
R. Normand, *The Changing Epistemic Governance of European Education*,
Educational Governance Research 3, DOI 10.1007/978-3-319-31776-2_5

In terms of the production of knowledge and expertise, European policymakers have a regulatory power. Through mechanisms of discussion and negotiation, they try to base their decisions on rational and scientific examinations presented in different instances. The latter are places of compromises of consensuses reducing the direct political fight and open debates (Majone 1996). Meanwhile, the Commission faces a double process of competition and fragmentation: competition with other institutions such as the European Council and Parliament with whom it competes for power, without forgetting the many conflicts in the relationships between directorates-general and units, and fragmentation in the sense that European policy is decomposed into functional areas with its directorates-general, its expert committees, its parliamentary groups and its interest coalitions. It is therefore difficult to grasp the whole coherence while different sectorial arenas are subjected to multiple negotiations and pressures. In the vein of Claudio Radaelli (2008), we shall show in this chapter, by borrowing concepts from political sciences and studies from expert groups, how expertise shapes European policies in the field of education. Policy learning related to expertise and knowledge production will be illustrated (Radaelli and Dunlop 2013).

Each fieldwork is singular. This specificity is both explained by the research approach and the field features. Ideally, and a priori, the development of the inquiry could be conceived as the balance theoretical framework, methodological tools and inquiry plan. But the modalities of the inquiry also depend on a range of opportunities and impossibilities particularly when the inquirer has himself to espouse roles and play the rules of the institution or organisation for which he works. So, he has to seize opportunities and he is an insider through an experience hardly predictable. This situation is partially elated to the field: the international expertise, as well as other social areas, has its own rules and habits. Circles of expertise are difficult to penetrate for social scientists, not only because of the conditions of access but also because of the types of knowledge produced, utilitarian and normative. From the access to the field to the entry in informal relationships, research strategy consists in pragmatically exploit offered possibilities by expert contracts and projects. Constraints are more linked to the understanding of complex worlds, on a cognitive, technical, scientific side, than to the difficulty of accessing to networks which remain quite open. The researcher has also to find a balanced position in maintaining his reflexivity and autonomy of judgement. The insider has to abandon the idea of a fixed methodology to be subjected to contingencies and to adapt the degree of his participation.

In previous research, we analysed a network of experts participating in the design of statistical tools for the Open Method of Coordination in education. By using the actor–network theory, it was possible to identify different types of connections within the European space and to show proximal relationships and leading positions among experts. But this study, which was based on the management of our own databank, was not in depth enough to make an account of the complexity of expertise. We needed to understand the expert at work within the networks we had previously observed. Our perspective is that of the 'insider' or 'embedded' researcher who socialises in different expert groups and produced expertise while maintaining his or her reflexivity, critical distance and categories of judgement as a social scientist. We have not attempted an anthropological study as this has been done by numerous works in the Sociology of Science and Technology (SST) which we described in chapter "The Politics of Standards and Quality". By studying the epistemic dimensions of expertise, our objective is to better comprehend the building of expert knowledge from the inside, to understand its genesis and mechanisms and to complete our previous studies on expert networks and the different epistemic communities (Normand 2010). After presenting the European policy of expertise, we shall introduce four case studies showing different arrangements which can be observed in terms of policy learning when experts seek closer relations with policymakers and to work closer with them. Each of these configurations displays a mode of knowledge production situated outside of the academic sphere. The first case is a think tank whose main aim is to produce 'storytelling' in the media and to help political projects be accepted by public opinion. Then, we shall present expert works led within an epistemic community which promote evidence-based technologies for European policymakers. The third case study focuses on political entrepreneurship by a non-governmental organisation in higher education. Lastly, the fourth case study describes institutional expertise for a directorate-general at the European Commission to help it fine-tune and implement its lifelong learning strategy.

Understanding the Politics of European Expertise

Expertise is a specific activity of knowledge production participating in a process of negotiation and orientation of public policy. This knowledge is technical and comes from professionals working in administrations, international organisations, universities and other higher education institutions, agencies, think tanks or interest groups (Weible 2008). Thousands of expert groups and networks work for the European Commission even if they are not always fully visible (Robert 2003, 2010, 2011; Gornitzka and Sverdrup 2008). They serve to prepare initiatives for the Commission which creates, frames and funds them. Other entities are created by their participation in the Commission's funded programmes in response to calls. Others are created as influence and pressure groups to orientate the European strategy and decision-making. Up to now, there has been little work on the expertise produced in these groups and networks, their activities, their place within knowledge production and decision-making. However, experts have had a determining role in the guidance of European policies, the dialogue with national and international representatives and the political work within the European institutions.

The expert is defined as such as the one that has professional skills in the ownership and exploitation of knowledge and technics. Expertise is not based on ethics but on a scientific legitimacy to tell the 'truth' about issues for which experts are recognised and habilitated by public authorities. However, the expert authority can also be based on experience and social fame acquired for years. Consecrated as expert, researchers, but also professionals or practitioners, can endorse new roles in normative performances and public problem-solving. By difference with the researcher, the expert does not produce new knowledge, and he/she provides expertise limited to his/her specialisation. So, scientific research principles, as they are embedded in academic tradition (ideal of autonomy, axiological neutrality and long-term discovery), appear incompatible with expert activities. However, as we will see, these boundaries become more and more blurred. The expert defines his activity in regard to social demand, and he is commissioned by an institution or its representative who gives him a mandate and requires support in decision-making. Expertise also results from confrontation of uncertainty (or risk) and problematised knowledge in accordance with social and economic stakes. Expertise, because of its utilitarian inclination, is at the intersection between science and policy. The expert can also serve a claiming movement and participate in the public debate in providing critical resources to activists. It is not this type of expertise we consider in this chapter in which we analyse the expert work mainly through its contribution to education policies and reforms.

Experts Within European Politics

Research on European expertise has studied strategies and conflict among experts. It has characterised the technicisation of political discourses through scientific knowledge and the technics used to build standards. Some work has explored the processes of socialisation by analysing individual profiles and careers in order to provide evidence on social properties and the internalisation of norms. It has shown that experts share a same technocratic vision and adhere to a global set of common values outside their national context. They master the same language codes and experience a high level of training (Quaglia et al. 2008). Other researchers have studied the sociopolitical features of these experts by focusing on their identities and interests and the way they contribute to the legitimisation of decision-making through practices of deliberation, communication and argumentation (Majone 1989). Some evidence has been provided on the normative function of expertise and how it depoliticises high stakes and limits debate and conflicts (Checkel 2003; Christiansen et al. 1999). Some studies have highlighted the technical function of knowledge production as a source of power in discussions and negotiations within European Community's meetings (Tallberg 2006; Radaelli 1995).

In previous work, we have studied the place of experts within epistemic communities (Haas 1992) and the way some knowledge and technical skills generate forms of arguments and postures which are considered as legitimate by policymakers, while there are some strong proximities between them in terms of socialisation and peer learning (Normand 2010). Epistemic communities are professional networks with recognised expertise and skills in a particular area related to a public policy. Each community includes individuals sharing the same vision (or *episteme*), e.g. shared beliefs about knowledge which are judged to be rational and valid, a common project for developing this knowledge through experts mobilising their skills and a networking organisation facilitating not just regular meetings but also at-distance work. At the same time, expertise is a set of cognitive and normative tools embedded in instruments and which guides national and European policies (Desrosières 2002; Porter 1996; Lascoumes and Le Galès 2007). Indeed, as we saw in previous chapters, statistical tools and categories, comparative methods and juridical technics contribute to harmonisation and convergence, while expertise inflects the building of public problems at a European scale (Campana et al. 2007).

From these considerations, some links can be established between technocracy, expertise and politicisation (Radaelli 1999a, b). Indeed, European technocrats, as political entrepreneurs, with experts as producers of knowledge, shape interpretations and disseminate information to overcome the traditional obstacles of political negotiation according to reciprocal learning. This articulation depends on the degree of certainty and visibility of the political action. When European decision-making is based on certainty in terms of knowledge and strong public visibility in terms of impact, the bureaucratic process predominates the use of expertise. When uncertainty on information and knowledge is high but public visibility is low, technocracy predominates and expertise becomes endogenous in European institutions. When there are politicised stakes on the public scene and low uncertainty, the use of expertise is quite impossible and the process of politicisation dominates. But when decision-making depends on high uncertainty with regard to available information and knowledge, and visibility is high, the use of epistemic communities and exogenous political entrepreneurs become the key factor. Therefore, the choice of epistemic communities corresponds to an exogenous mobilisation of expertise to confront international political dilemmas. Endogenous and technocratic expertise requires skilled professionals working in the shadows and able to conceive a catalogue of solutions to solve problems by relativising their political implications.

Expertise as Policy Learning

Beyond the distinction between endogenous and exogenous expertise, the role of experts in policy learning has become a subject of investigation for researchers interested in how European policies are built. Policy learning gives rise to multiple definitions, but it also shows the increasing strong intertwinement between expertise and different institutions (governments, networks, think tanks, agencies) and the variety of processes and modes of technical and scientific knowledge. Radaelli defines policy learning as 'a process of updating beliefs about key components of policy (such as problem definition, results achieved at home or abroad, goals, and also actors' strategies and paradigms)' (Radaelli 2009, pp. 1146). Policy learning corresponds to an instrumental approach which transforms policies, programmes and organisations (Bennett and Howlett 1992; Bomberg 2007). It is made up of key actors who, alongside experts, generate processes of knowledge production and cognitive changes and shape new beliefs and ideas and transformations of rationality (May 1992; Radaelli 2009).

In recent studies on European integration (Zito 2013), policy learning has been analysed as a microprocess of judgements based on experience. It implies that actors are engaged in a human interaction and share knowledge and skills. Language, but also intersubjective communication, explains changes in the cognition of experts and policymakers. After Herbert Simon, theories of limited rationality have explained the incompleteness of produced and acquired knowledge by individuals in institutions. Indeed, political changes are explained as social learning, based on experience, as well networking beyond institutional structures. Some researchers, in the continuity of Dolowitz and Marsh (1996, 2000), have shown the importance of voluntary and coercive processes of knowledge dissemination, policy borrowing and transfer in paradigmatic contents or instruments.

Empirical studies, even if there have been few, enable several dimensions of policy learning to be featured (Dunlop and Radaelli 2013). An epistemic dimension was underlined by Haas when he demonstrated that experts can facilitate policy-makers' learning and reduce uncertainty. Furthermore, the autonomy of experts is never completely ensured and learning can be strongly framed by policymakers. Expertise can be delegated along a chain of tasks (production, dissemination, use) or give space to a deliberative assembly, a network or a community of practices. There is a balancing act between deliberative or framing learning, as the social and reflexive dimension of interactions vary according to the type and content of exper-tise. It can lead to loose-coupled relations with policymakers refusing to learn.

Categorisation of the problem is decisive to make it an existing and worthy topic as a moral or political cause. Crossed representations, based on interactions and interlocutions, make the problem real and legitimate. A public problem is an ongo-ing collective activity. It begins with situations experienced by actors who attribute causes and responsibilities, assess damages, identify responsible people, propose solutions, etc. These collective actors share experiences and resources, knowledge and skills that enable them to deploy narratives and build the problem public by mastering a whole set of rhetorical rules which make their narratives acceptable, validated and legitimate on a moral and scientific ground. These actors mobilise toolboxes and discursive repertoires which are subject of discussions and negotia-tions between them, because they correspond to different perspectives, and they can give birth to dissimulation, falsification, trickery, lie, conflict, etc. This is where there is place for expertise to arbitrate between debates and controversies.

To illustrate this case, we consider the example of Joseph Gusfield's famous survey on road safety in the USA during the 1960s–1970s (Gusfield 1984). At that time, the development of cars has led to the multiplication of accidents but nothing had been done to strengthen the drivers' security because of commercial reasons and producers' opposition. More place was given to deviant drivers' control and sanction than to the implementation of security equipment in cars. It has created many reactions and issue of road accidents has become a battle between consumer associations, led by Ralph Nader, automobile manufacturers and public authorities. Two theses were in conflict based on different explanations and claiming strategies. The thesis of 'dangerous driver' considered that accidents were individual and dis-crete events. It claims for solutions minimising the collective dimension of accidents.

The thesis of 'dangerous cars' was interpreting accidents as collective solutions to find an improvement in the production of automobiles.

Science and law were required to provide expertise and answers. Science, at the basis of the dominant thought of the 'drinking driver', is considered by Gusfield as a rhetoric. The experts' claimed objective knowledge takes the form of an argumentation. The scientific presentation of 'drunk driving' is not based on empirical materials but on rhetorical forms forcing consent and reinforcing beliefs. Despite its claims of telling objectively the truth, the production of scientific knowledge aims at gaining support from audiences. Gusfield demonstrates how a partial, fragile and conditional knowledge on 'drunk driving' has been transformed in an established, certain and coherent fact. He also explains how this abstract data have been translated in a dramaturgical register to wake up imaginaries and values which are quite different from scientific knowledge. Gusfield also demonstrates how the law qualifies 'drunk driving' as a crime by accompanying it by a more strict punishment compared to other infractions. On a symbolic level, the juridical field participates in the definition of a normative and moral order which assigns a status of deviant to the drinking driver. The law on alcohol appears as a system of communication instituting a difference between the violations or road safety and the crime of drunk driving, between the small transgressions by a normal citizen (no respect of road lights and stop) and the transgression by the 'drinking driver'. The juridical doctrine and the jurisprudence privilege the person and accentuate the intentional and moral character of the individual act, in making the drinking driver a culprit and not a victim.

From these considerations, we are going now to characterise certain types of encounters which structure the relation between expertise and policymaking. They are interesting events for studying the cognitive modalities of expert work. We will explain, by using the contributions of interactionist sociology, how these encounters participate in a certain definition of expertise in context.

Expertise and Policy Learning in Interactive Contexts

Like an encounter, a process of policy learning brings together actors sharing the same goals and ideas. It can be more or less open to participation, but experts have recognised skills and legitimate authority for valorising recommendations and norms beside policymakers. Encounters are often organised in an international space apart from national and domestic contexts. They are shaped through conferences, seminars and workshops and do not differ from scientific events organised by academics. They are supported by the presentation of papers, discussions, small working groups, syntheses and proceedings distributed to the participants.

As some research in political sciences has shown with regard to the building of Europe, analyses or reports and working documents are not sufficient to characterise expertise. A lot happens during these encounters but they are later occulted in the writing of notes. Furthermore, these meetings are far from being Habermassian spaces of deliberation where all opinions are equivalent: there is a hierarchy between experts according to their degree of legitimacy and skills. Their role can be formal (presidency, contributor, discussant, etc.) or informal (an observer having a direct contact with some convenors of the group or network, or they maintain a technocratic connivance with policymakers) and explicit (they assume a role of expert in front of all) or implicit (they have a power of influence which is not public and is not manifested during the sessions or outside the meetings). The encounter can be considered as a distributed cognition in which experts interact socially and technically between peers through flows of information and communication in order to find relevance from contextualised judgements. These interactions are extended after the encounter by a work at distance through emails, by phone or virtual meetings via Skype.

Erwin Goffman have demonstrated how these ordinary social interactions are developed in concrete encounters (Goffman 1961b). The ideas of 'line' and 'face' are central concepts in his work. 'Line' is the performative strategy the individual has within the interaction. 'Face' is the way each person perceives him/herself and the way he/she perceives others in the interaction process. Maintaining face is challenge of pride and honour, while losing face creates shame and embarrassment. So, people have to do a facework in ordinary social interaction that is taking actions consistent with the face. It is related to what we call in our society tact, savoir-faire, diplomacy and social skills. The image of the self is built through judgement and evidence conveyed by other participants during encounters, and it is confirmed by evidence conveyed and personal agencies in the situation. Social interactions are driven by the conceptions of 'face' and 'line' assumed for the interaction, and lines are largely defined by conventions and scripts. So expectations in encounters are quite prescriptive and they shape previously the type of interactions. From this, Goffman, inspired from Georges Mead's work, develops a double definition of the self. It is shaped by the expressive engagement of the human person in the flows of events and circumstances and at the same time by its play with ritual interactions and expectations in the situation. Against the idea of an authentic self, Goffman considers that the self is also constructed by the social interactions and from moral rules impressed upon him. He makes adjustment to its environment by convincing himself with the influence of others that he is what he wants to be.

Following Goffman, Richard Freeman (2008) shows that a meeting of experts corresponds to different ordinated, sequential and progressive steps: articulation, socialisation, construction and resolution.

Articulation, the first step of the meeting, juxtaposes an introduction and a presentation while giving the different members the opportunity to recognise others and to make acquaintances. Via a game of questions–answers, it constraints experts and policymakers to enter into reciprocal duties. It defines their roles and establishes hierarchies and legitimacies. The meeting often begins by a general presentation from a positioning paper and introductive lectures. It deals with certain issues and disregards others. The general presentation gives objectives and the lines of conduct to be adopted. It defines the scene from which each one is going to play his or her role and narrative.

The *perception* phase begins with the identification of similarities and differences between persons along with the recognition of their respective roles as representative of an institution. A feeling of uneasiness occurs when an individual expert cannot access the cognitive representations of the other experts particularly when he or she is a novice. Listening is important in order to become familiarised with the stakes of the meeting and to be aware of the ideas and visions shared by the spokesmen of a group or a network. Expert knowledge is embedded in action, practice and experience and not all is accessible. Initial meetings and discussions facilitate the exchange of tacit knowledge while allowing the skills of experts to be assessed simultaneously. Confusion often occurs due to the fact that discussions are held in English with cognitive categories of judgement as well as schemes of classification; even if experts master English, there language skills are not always adjusted to the content of the expertise. After a period of unease, the expert familiarises himself or herself with these different contents even if the standardisation of international expert language has greatly facilitated a certain mastery. In summary, when national case studies are presented and discussed, it implies three active modalities of translation: in the first, linguistic, the contributor translates his or her native language into English; in the second, categorical, categories of thought in a native language have to be reformulated into English (the modalities of presentation can change because cultural practices are different), and it is followed by the interpretation by other foreign experts of the contributor's more or less mastered English into their own native language; and in the third, the discourse is adapted into their own national categories of thought. These games of implicit translation do not facilitate communication and mutual understanding. Sometimes, it impedes a deep and critical discussion of concepts.

Socialisation is the third phase. It is made up of formal encounters, for example, in sessions and workshops, in the way people are distributed, and also informal encounters, during coffee breaks, lunch and dinner. The organisers of the meeting, who can be different from the hosts, are busy welcoming and looking after people. Guests interact without any pre-established order shifting between face-to-face recognition and institutional roles. Group pressure is relatively important because participants cohabit closely during several days and there are intensive reflexion and exchanges. The promiscuity brings people closer but it also generates tension and distance. Some people's characters appear, while affinities and reciprocal dislikes emerge. Meals are often an opportunity to espouse less formal roles and to build friendships which are disconnected from the theories and ideas claimed during the sessions. Often, there is a mutual respect and symmetry in exchanges, and there are few attempts to dominate or take over, at least during the duration of the meeting. It is different when strategic orientations have to be discussed by the steering committee.

There then comes the phase of building the content of the expertise through a myriad of interactions and crossed communications. The meeting is progressively built in its own language according to a mutual consultancy which structures exchanges and accumulates evidence and materials to be progressively included in the final report. The variety of discussions and contents in thematic sessions and workshops is reduced to a common, generic and technical language corresponding to the objectives of the expert group or network. It is a kind of mutual cognitive learning, often constrained by time, from which new content is produced by collecting different parts of the individual and collective work. These contents are defined according to an abstract and generic grammar deleting particularities and differences in the points of views expressed during the thematic sessions or workshops. The content of the meeting cannot be reduced to fragmented and incomplete opinions and ambiguous interpretations because experts have to be accountable to policymakers. The message addressed to them has to be clear, understandable and relevant for decision-making. A normative effect is therefore perceptible in the framing of interpretations, thus giving an important place to the most legitimate representative of the expert group or network.

The *resolution* corresponds to the end of the meeting when members of the expert group or network talk about the work to be carried out, the next meetings and progress with regard to the content of expertise. The main summary points are presented and they are used to feed the proceedings and the intermediary or final report. Materials used during the meeting (abstracts, position papers, flyers, briefs, etc.) are gathered to be coherently disseminated on a website. The report connects experts and it opens up other spaces for other types of expertise and policymaking. It provides experts with the same language and vocabulary while offering a state of the art and some development perspectives. It is also a phase of externalisation as the expertise content which can be publicised through recommendations while making the activities of experts more closely visible to policymakers and stakeholders. The report is a key step in the expertise programme and it often feeds its evaluation through a quality assurance process.

The analysis of encounters and interactions between experts and policymakers explains the variety and contingence of the expertise content in a European group or network. Learning is linked to socialisation and the modes of engagement of different actors through games of roles, crossed representations and mutual recognition in terms of hierarchy and legitimacy. Resuming the concepts of the Sociology of Science and Technology, we could say it is a form of agency between human beings, objects and devices shaping interactions and guiding the actors' work towards a final output: the report or recommendations to be transmitted to policymakers. But, as we will see in the following pages, there are also different institutional and epistemic arrangements which define the form and content of policy learning.

By following in the footsteps of Dunlop and Radaelli (2013), we will explore now four main categories of policy learning that we will illustrate networks empirically studied: reflexive learning (a think tank), epistemic community (an evidence-based education network), social interaction (a non-governmental organisation) and learning in the shadow of hierarchy (an institutional policy network).

In *reflexive learning*, power is polycentric and it opens up a space for deliberation. Changes arise through a process of communicational rationality, whereas knowledge is shared a priori by experts and laypeople. What is at stake is to disseminate knowledge in the community or via a network, while learning is supported by a structure of governance facilitating coordination and dissemination. The process of learning relies on an endogenous social interaction which shapes politics. Actors control the means and contents of learning even if objectives can be externally fixed. Reflexivity fails if they do not reach a minimal agreement on common principles.

In the *epistemic community*, experts have a mandate and a certification for participating in collective learning. Policymakers call on expertise to reducing uncertainty in information and knowledge and decision-making. Experts are controlled because it is policymakers who make the decisions regarding the modalities of dissemination and the use of knowledge. Experts have to respect precise specifications defining the modalities of reciprocal learning and knowledge production.

In *social interaction*, the conditions of learning correspond to a political negotiation with a weak separation between experts and policymakers. The negotiation focuses on objectives as procedures and instruments. These 'clever' encounters are achieved under certain conditions and in a loosely structured way.

For *learning in the shadow of the hierarchy*, the relation is less defined by expertise or science than by the content of institutional rules. Actors have to respect certain rules and roles in their interactions but the logic of exploration is relatively free. The first type corresponds to an instrumental learning with some improvements in the tools of governance and instruments of public action. Another mode of learning is the production, dissemination and use of knowledge trough a chain of tasks delegation. A last case is highly constrained learning in its contents and objectives through specific institutional procedures.

Reflexive Learning and Storytelling

Investigating think tanks in the area of expertise is a way of revealing an emergent activity in the production of knowledge, particularly after the Commission's President Mr Barroso had proposed to engage them in the preparation of the annual State of the Union Speech at the European Parliament at the same time as he was mandating the Bureau of European Policy Advisers to be their main interlocutor (Missiroli and Ioannides 2012). However, in Europe, contrary to the USA, they play an important educational and informational role at the national level, particularly with regard to EU policies. They reflect the different national traditions, attitudes and cultures in each country but they also become a link between policymakers and public opinion, especially after the media opened their debates and editorial pages to members of think tanks. Some of these think tanks participate in transnational consortia to facilitate discussion, circulate ideas and carry out academic-level research on European policy issues, via the use of websites to collect views and analyses from different countries. In 1974, a transnational network was established to merge national think tanks with an office in Brussels: TEPSA or Trans-European Policy Studies Association. In the late 1990s, other think tanks were set up such as European Policy Institutes Network (EPIN) and European Network of Economic Policy Research Institutes (ENEPRI), including Brussels-based ones such as Think Global – Act European (TGAE) or the European Forum of Think Tanks. The more traditional ones were founded in the 'golden age' of European integration between the mid-1980s and the late 1990s. They are all generalists but focus on European affairs, while new players from different parts of the world, particularly the USA (the Carnegie Foundation or RAND Corporation), have joined the Brussels scene. Some national think tanks have also opened local offices in Brussels. The French think tank Veritas we studied is considered by the French Ministry of Foreign Affairs as representing French interests in Brussels.

The Veritas think tank, for which we worked as an expert, has different features. It is a reformist and leftist institution producing recommendations in the field of public policies (the economy, welfare, Europe, education, research, justice, etc.). It liaises with other think tanks from the European reformist Left. Veritas includes about a thousand experts coming from national and local government, business and associations. It regularly publishes briefs which have generated significant media interest while regularly organising cycles of conferences for a large audience. Think tanks are mainly funded by major companies. Through their expertise and their claims, they propose concrete solution for policymakers while getting inspiration from the best practices of its European partners and generating public debate.

I was included in this think tank after a meeting with the head of education issues (Mr A). I had been recommended by one of his friends and my expert profile on education policies, and school management was of interest to them. During a lunch, I was introduced to them and I learnt of the project to create a working group on educational governance in addition to the other groups working on education issues. During the meeting, I was offered the position of chair but it was later delegated to a high-ranking, retired civil servant (Mr B) who had occupied leading positions in the administration of education and was well known for his left-wing views and action.

The working group was quickly set up while a first meeting was organised. I was the only academic, and the group included, among the active members, a high-ranking trade unionist, a high-ranking and retired administrative executive and general inspector, a general inspector with close links to the minister's cabinet, two principals, a high-ranking administrator in the training of executives and two inspectors of primary and secondary education. Mr A explained to us that the think tank had to establish a consensus on education beyond the traditional Left and Right divide. The objective was to make midterm proposals that could influence the public debate before the presidential elections, and it was necessary to work in cross-functional ways with other working groups. The work would be carried out at distance, with few meetings, and the objective was to write a 15-/20-page report with precise recommendations.

During the first meeting, a discussion was initiated on the need for a systemic reflection in terms of governance, the preparation of recommendations and the programmatic agenda for the minister and his cabinet, while at the same time we had to communicate the meaning of reforms to the general public. The content of the report could be free but it would not commit the minister who, nevertheless, was persuaded that it was necessary to implement structural reforms in the territorial governance of education. This work was part of a series of reflexions before the state's summit on decentralisation, of which the aim was to go beyond stereotypes and formulate some challenging proposals without forgetting such non-negotiable left-wing values as justice and social mix.

As these initial discussions showed, a working group's tasks within a think tank are similar to shaping narratives to empower a large audience, via the media, but also convincing politicians and policymakers. Some rational arguments regarding the implementation of reforms had to be mixed with ideological ones related to the ideas shared by the members of the think tank, political friends and members of the cabinet. Shaping the contents of discourse is often called 'storytelling', an activity in which think tanks specialise.

At think tank is an autonomous organisation detached from governmental policy or private interests (Stone 1996). It determines its own research agenda to inform decision-making. In order to do so, it builds a body of knowledge and aims to make the results accessible to policymakers and public opinion. A think tank mobilises experienced researchers and experts on social, political and economic issues. Its goal is research, analysis and consultancy, but it can also organise seminars, workshops and conferences to facilitate interactions between policymakers, the media and private sponsors. Brokerage and networking are its two main activities in the dissemination of knowledge.

The expertise work of think tanks is well known (Medvetz 2012; Stone and Denham 2004; Rich 2005). At the European scale, their actions with Member States have been studied for more than a decade (Sherrington 2000; Ullrich 2004). According to Medvetz's classification, experts working for think tanks have various characteristics. Some are academics producing expertise from their research. Others have a role of assistance in participating in the definition of norms and recommendations for policymaking. Experts have the capacity to anticipate emerging political issues from their previous political and administrative experience, as it is the case for Veritas. Others specialise in entrepreneurship and look to place their claims on the market of ideas for policymakers, interest groups, foundations, funders, sponsors and advocacy coalitions. Experts also have an important role in the communication of research findings to different audiences. They strive to have a direct impact on the media and specific targets by adopting a clear, concise and understandable language while using the media devices at their disposal (blogs, Facebook, Twitter, etc.).[1]

---

[1] Shaping narratives begun during the 1970s–1980s when US neoconservatives created their own think tanks to lead the intellectual fight against the principles of political liberalism and the Welfare State (Smith 1991). The development of conservative think tanks is explained by the dissemination of liberal ideas by other think tanks such as the Brookings Institution, the RAND Corporation or the Institute for Policy Studies. The Brookings and RAND Corporation are typical institutions which convey technocratic thought and Keynesian politics of the Johnson and Kennedy administrations (Smith 1991; Ricci 1993). They were favourable to the development of social sciences and funded an important research programme to support the Great Society project and the war against poverty. The Institute for Policy Studies had a key role in the creation of ideas of the New Left with its defence of liberal values and a pluralistic approach to social issues. The conservatives' reaction arose from their fear that the 'establishment' would weaken the ideals of American society and that

The work of US think tanks has been exported to Europe. The proliferation of think tanks has transformed academic tasks and activities while developing links with politicians, pressure groups and business around European institutions. It has led to an increase in the competition of ideas in the public space while strengthening the role of media and reducing the influence of social scientists. In particular, the 'revolving doors' phenomenon, e.g. individuals moving between administrations, universities, think tanks and business, is now a part of the landscape. Think tanks are an interesting career opportunity for young graduates, and they can quickly build a network of influence while they face difficulties entering in the academia.

Veritas is the result of these international and European evolutions even if this think tank has been created recently. As we have seen in chapter "An Epistemic Governance of European Education", France has some specific institutional arrangements in the relationship between research and policy. It is different from the USA or the UK with think tanks that have little influence with regard to public policies. Veritas' structure is also a characteristic of the French context: there is little inter-penetration between academia and the administration. Indeed, there is little academic work on the governance of the education system, and school management is not a developed field of research. Many studies and discourses come from the professional world. This explains the over-representation of executives in the reflection process. But they have different visions of reform based on their personal experience and career, their knowledge and skills, their ideological engagement and their political and professional networks.

Very quickly the papers produced by the experts in the working group appeared extremely heterogeneous even though the work was carried out at distance with rare moments of coordination. Some of them, like the principals, were concerned about the daily experience and problems they faced while they had imaginary representations about the possibilities of making changes which they shared with the Veritas representative. High-ranking civil servants had a technocratic vision inspired by reflections developed in reformist circles but they were also eager to convince members of parliament and bureaucrats to design a bill. These differences are accentuated by the tension between centralisers and decentralisers in the administration as in political parties from top to bottom. Some experts had a political and systemic vision because they had important responsibilities in governance, while others were more focused on devices and rules in context, particularly among the principals. The trade unionists and the Veritas representative had quite an ideological discourse. I, as an academic, tried to deliver a message inspired by some evidence from international research. Papers were therefore compiled without establishing guidelines and it gave the impression of an incoherent and unreadable patchwork.

---

social sciences would disseminate a relativist thought undermining the US people's attachment to tradition. The creation of these institutions was a means of becoming an intellectual force capable of producing solid criticism of political liberalism and its allies. Through the recruitment of researchers, the dissemination of political recommendations and access to politicians, a complex network of think tanks and neoconservative foundations were built to disseminate ideas which became part of the political agenda in education after the publication of the report *A Nation at Risk* (Spring 2005).

This problem of readability alerted Mr A who judged that the report should not adopt a technocratic vision but remain understandable to laypeople attached to reforms. This is why he phoned me because I was, due to my position as an academic and after having read my contribution, able to write a harmonised and consensual report after removing its technocratic vulgate and reformist common sense. He explained that I had to use simple language, which the minister himself could understand, to whom it was necessary to talk as a student parent. During the discussion, some elements of discourse were reflected and they had to be written in the report and transformed into reformist proposals understandable to all. I was then invited to participate in a meeting with the ministry to finalise the report and to better adjust recommendations to the minister's desiderata.

Several weeks later, a meeting was organised at the ministry, in the minister's office, with the head of the think tank and a high-ranking retired civil servant close to the leftist party and highly influent within Veritas. As a general inspector, he had worked in ministerial circles and he supervised all the education working groups in the think tank. The minister welcomed us and proposed that we sit down around his working desk. He was very friendly. He then began his speech about the reform of timetable scheduling and some symbolic violence it was generating (the reform has led to large-scale strikes and protests during the past weeks). The minister did not understand why trade unions, associations and political parties were struggling with this issue. The head of Veritas told him that the Left was more concerned about the family and no longer considered the horizon of equality. It had to focus on the new familial order in relation to the evolutions of the law and social protection. The minister responded that the reform of timetable scheduling had served as a *pro domo* argument for its opponents who refused to recognise that pupils were tired. He believed that the risk was that the school system would become a supermarket in which everyone would choose his or her timetable, his or her curriculum and his or her teachers according to his or her preferences. He also observed a big gap between the claims by parent organisations and what was actually happening at the local level.

Then, Mr A, the representative of our working group in the think tank, presented the key elements of the topic the experts were working on. He argued that the issue of governance has hardly been explored in official guidelines and that it was necessary to reflect on a new share of powers and responsibilities in order to achieve better democratisation and better performances for students. I summarised the arguments we had previously discussed to write the report which focused on a certain number of values which the socialist minister could adhere to: better recognition for the work of teachers, the building of a solidarity between schools in the same catchment area, recognition of the merits of each school according to its pedagogical efforts and development of self-evaluation to improve the conditions of further training. The high-ranking civil servant, seated next to the minister, a counsellor specialising in youth issues, took some notes. The minister listened intently and seemed interested.

The retired high-ranking civil servant, influent in Veritas, took the floor to defend his own ideas about reform. The minister did not seem that interested but he continued his speech. He argued that the ministry should not adopt a technocratic policy but to consider the true meaning of the reform. In his opinion, the diagnosis had been established by research and the general inspectorate's reports. The school system is unequal because of social determinisms that reproduce the elite. That is the real problem. Mr A added comments and explained that there is a process of ghettoisation but that some schools in education priority areas are having success. It is important to take into account teamwork and the psycho-cognitive dimension of pupils. He spoke about his experience as a principal. Then he went back to the topic of the working group. I intervened to say that reform does not work because local actors are not well informed and supported. It would be useful to reflect on an engineering of reforms as has been done in other countries. The retired high-ranking civil servant spoke again and came back to his ideas as he denounced separatism in local education areas. The minister replied that he believed that reducing separatism is desirable but it raises a question of economic efficiency due to budgetary difficulties. There is also a social obstacle. This reflection has to be made when considering the reform of school catchment areas but this evolution will take time. The head of the think tank shared his idea of creating bigger schools to improve social mix and to achieve some economics of scale. The retired civil servant told us about a survey conducted in Paris in which indicators have been built to measure the progress of each school, in a dynamic way, without stigmatising failing schools but by providing examples of good achievement that can be transferred.

The discussion ended because the minister had a dinner with presidents of universities. The meeting was less than 1 h. The contents of expertise from the working group were not really discussed. We agreed that we would keep the minister informed of our progress when writing the report. Outside of the ministry, the Veritas representatives seemed quite disappointed, and they shared their doubts regarding the minister's interest. However, this meeting had collateral effects on the working group of experts. I later learnt that Mr B, the chair of the expert groups, had been recommended by the retired civil servant who had joined the meeting with the minister. They were friends who had been for a long time in the circles of the same political party. The report was revised during the summer. Mr B was helped by another member of the working group, a high-civil servant close to the cabinet. A table of contents was designed and Mr A, the think tank representative, shared the new document and asked everyone to make comments. He said that he was glad that the report had become more coherent but he had revised the introduction by giving it a strong historical orientation. This rewriting suggested that other members of the think tank who were outside the working group had intervened in the writing of the document. Veritas was also advised by an influent academic who played an important role as a counsellor of the former minister of education. Meanwhile other contributions were made by the other members of the working group.

Afterward, a meeting of the working group was organised, while some experts were pushed aside. Mr B, the chair of the working group, began to question the method and considered that a consensus had been reach for writing the report and it should not to be revised. Consequently, he felt that there was no need for a new table of contents but instead it had now become urgent to finish the writing. In an email sent to all the members of the group, he wrote that he could not continue to work without knowing precisely the objective to be reached and that a method had to be defined, a schedule had to be drawn up and tasks had to be allocated between experts. He argued about the necessity of working on writing the report and improving its content.

This crisis in the group of experts can be explained in several ways. The head of the working group learnt about the meeting with the minister, and he felt that his authority had been undermined: it explained his attempt to take power in the writing of the report. But it was also due to tension with the type of management adopted by Mr A, the think tank representative, who sought to inflect the content of the writing by mobilising external allies. There was therefore a game of subtle negotiations in addition to a latent conflict between Mr A and Mr B. A final meeting was organised to resolve the crisis after which some criticism was addressed regarding the report's form and content. It led the head of the expert group having more of a withdrawn position. Meanwhile, political circumstances had changed: the issue of governance was no longer a ministerial priority and other topics had arrived on the political agenda, and the minister of education was replaced. Finally, this report was never published.

This type of expertise characterises a reflexive learning because experts, in developing social interactions, build content and insights while they share knowledge according to an endogenous process linked to politics. However, while they had autonomy, the expert group was externally framed, while members had difficulties agreeing on common objectives. This work gave birth to a dynamic process of reflectivity and common writing. This case also relativises the idea of a direct link between storytelling, think tanks and decision-making. As illustrated by our example, think tanks are subjected to narrative and argumentative constraints so that their arguments can be accepted by policymakers. They are positioned in a highly competitive market of ideas in which individual visions and affinity relationships can undermine a midterm strategy. The pressure of the media and political short-term thinking forces them to anticipate decision-making and to react opportunely with regard to current interests and stakes. In terms of influence, think tanks participate in the framing of the political agenda and are subjected to permanent adjustments regarding politics and the media.

Epistemic Community or Expertise in the Mode 2

My previous work in a research institute led me to familiarise myself with expertise. This institution conducted research programmes and applied research for the ministry, while at the same time it was a reference for foreign institutions interested in education issues in the French context. Proposals from European research projects were often addressed to some colleagues, who, because of their insufficient mastery of English, could not really reply. I had the opportunity to participate in a training programme organised by a knowledge centre specialising in technologies of evidence in education (we give it the KCTEE acronym). My research institute was involved in a European programme coordinated by KCTEE, while I became an expert and participated in several meetings in Europe. The objective was to work with the French Ministry of Education and to professionalise some technicians producing literature reviews in our knowledge centre. This training gave me the opportunity to become familiarised with the new tools of evidence-based research, mainly the protocols of systemic reviews of research literature and the use of databanks. The genesis and development of the project has been already presented in the chapter "'What Works?' The Shaping of the European Politics of Evidence".

We shall assume that experts promoting evidence-based research belong to a transnational epistemic community defining new standards for education. In that sense, they have a high level of expertise: some of them are heads of evidence-based knowledge research centres developing technologies of evidence (systematic reviews, controlled randomised trials, etc.), while others manage evidence-based research programmes. Medicine is the model of reference for evidence-based education. The argument is the following: in education, experiments have an intellectual interest but no practical utility, while their range is limited (Slavin 2002). Educational research helps to reflect about the problems of teachers but they are not a response for policymakers. A more rigorous research demonstrating positive and reproducible effects on students' outcomes will have more chance of being funded. Consequently, these types of experiments can improve the situation of educational research. Once this paradigm of evaluation is adopted, it can be implemented in every educational programme: school knowledge, prevention of violence, use of drugs, dropouts, racial relationships, etc. All these areas of research can contribute to the dissemination of evidence-based scientific knowledge.

Technologies of evidence are particularly appreciated by policymakers as they reduce uncertainty and can give access to knowledge they judge useful for decision-making. Experts and policymakers are not only associated in the production of knowledge but also in its mediation and dissemination, as claimed by the pros of the mode 2 (cf. chapter "An Epistemic Governance of European Education"). However, the production of knowledge is shaped by precise requirements justifying reciprocal learning within an epistemic community.

The European project launched by KCTEE fitted this objective. The aim was to develop a knowledge and exchange platform for technologies of evidence. The project brought together various actors: individual experts, policymakers from ministries, knowledge centres, agencies, universities, specialists of media tools and digital platforms. According to Haas' definition (1992), KCTEE is an epistemic community. It shares some normative principles and beliefs on rationality which serve the action of its members. The experts involved in the European project were persuaded that technologies of evidence are a means of improving the quality and effectiveness of educational research to better serve decision-making. They were searching to elucidate the multiple links between political actions and the desired results by analysing series of practices and problems related to the contribution of research and teaching to the improvement of student scores. They had intersubjective criteria which validated knowledge in the area of expertise, in an endogenous way when they claimed a positivist epistemology and in an exogenous way when it aimed to define the criteria of validity for other scientific knowledge. It supported a political enterprise, while their common practices and skills were destined to improve well-being in education. They also worked in conditions of uncertainty and technical complexity which have a high level of legitimacy to their expertise.

Haas gives us a clear definition of the learning process in this type of epistemic community. It is an information process for policymakers' beliefs when confronted with uncertainty. Experts control the production of knowledge, thus substantively influencing political arrangements and the states' interests. Two types of epistemic community are generally distinguished (Dunlop 2009): in the first type, experts regulate themselves and they are called upon by policymakers for advice, and the second type corresponds to experts deliberately selected by policymakers to justify a determined political decision or to depoliticise a disputed issue. We could consider that KCTEE belongs to the second type.

The KCTEE project is also related to the mode 2 of knowledge production. In addition to gathering a vast range of European actors from many countries, it establishes a balance between experts, policymakers, stakeholders and professionals who are invited to produce new knowledge. It presents itself as a triangulation between the production of evidence, its mediation and use in context. In the formulation of the project, it is considered as an imperative to create incentives encouraging researchers and policymakers to change their attitudes and behaviour in the production, communication and use of scientific knowledge. Everything is done to exert a social influence and to facilitate the availability of evidence-based technologies for policymakers and practitioners. A website was created to mutualise knowledge between experts and to facilitate the sharing of knowledge via different meetings in Europe. The objective is to set up infrastructures able to strengthen the links between research, policy and practice in the field of European education.

Within this context, expertise is not autonomous but subjected to a previous framing through a set of 'work packages' (networking, accessing research, mediation, research products and use, stakeholder engagement, sustainability) with different roles and responsibilities defined and shared between the network's experts. The aim is to develop and extend the transnational European network via the website, to improve evidence-based research both in person and at distance and to encourage the development of innovative projects and experiments, but also to create indicators, to conceive a support service for professionals, to encourage the participation of stakeholders and to ensure the sustainability of the network beyond the European project by the development of other projects and publications.

Meetings conformed to the sequential order described by Freedman (see above). We shall specifically focus here on the configuration of the device. Expertise depends on the content of exchanges and modes of socialisation among experts. But, beyond this cognitive dimension, the arrangements between people and objects contribute to define the space of discourses and the legitimacy of spokesmen while justifying a division of labour which, even if it defines operational tasks and activities, circumscribes the eventual incidents, disciplines the members of networks and canalises criticism. We can take network's second meeting as an example. The morning started, after the welcome, by a presentation of the work packages, reminding the experts of the framework from which they had to deliver their expertise. They were then sent to parallel workshops corresponding to each work package, with a head in charge of presenting their findings to the plenary assembly to be held at the end of the morning. The shaping of topics was doubled by another framing from the representative in charge of controlling and orientating the discussions between groups of experts but also the reinterpretation of these exchanges in light of the project's general philosophy. Some divergent points of view between individual experts emerged in the workshops, but they disappeared on behalf of a consensual content expressed by the group's spokesperson, which was then later combined with the other consensual content expressed by the other groups, in a generalisation preventing any contradictory stance. Anyway, criticism can be only listened to in reference to an implicit epistemology shared by the members of the network: an entirely external criticism challenging this epistemic foundation of the expertise would not be really understood.

The day's session was followed by an official dinner in a restaurant of the city. It was a convivial moment in which experts talked not so much about the content of the expertise but exchanged about real life, cultural episodes, their institutions, etc. These moments are very important for developing acquaintances and affinities between experts but also in building the group's identity. The people who are the most dogmatic in their expertise are not always those who are the most unfriendly in face-to-face relationships. One can be a fervent positivist, defending experimental method and quality standards, and at the same time have a lot of charm, humour and a reflexive distance in exchanges with his or her fellows. These moments of conviviality were increased by the many coffee breaks during the meeting: this is an informal arena for exchanging business cards and an opportunity to extend personal networks by creating new links.

The second day of the meeting was mainly based around plenary sessions. There were some discussions about the possibilities of extending the network to policy-makers and stakeholders. The European Commission is particularly keen on entrepreneurship as it wishes that these activities be extended to a large number of people to promote evidence-based research across the European space. But it is also in the interest of the project to have mobilised experts participating in its activities, particularly in feeding the website. Other conferences were already scheduled with two European ministers of education. I later discovered that these hosts had not been randomly chosen. The aim was to locally empower national policymakers.

Progressively, encounters were enriched by a certain number of European policymakers and experts, invited by the leaders of the network for conferences. Throughout the project, the website is updated by the productions of experts, the findings of conferences, the reports of workshops corresponding to work packages and the tools and resources specifically produced outside the network by institutions, knowledge centres and agencies pursuing their own development programmes on evidence-based education. During the second phase of the project, the epistemic community became more and more visible in its ramifications and activities, while the number of participating policymakers and stakeholders increased. A final report ended the project and recommendations were addressed to European policymakers, and a second project has been planned in order to continue the network's activities. It has been agreed that the network of experts will be divided into special interest groups (SIGs) and task groups (TGs) to develop other issues and to extend collaboration with other European partners.

This apparent unity in the coordination and rhetoric of the project must not hide some extremely heterogeneous realities and implementations in each country. It is the interest of the European project's leader to claim for a relative harmony and coherence with the Commission who funds and regularly evaluates the activities. This facade can dissimulate strong disagreements with the board in charge of the coordination but it is often unknown by the other experts. Participation in a project varies according to the understanding and interest of policymakers and stakeholders for evidence-based education. For example, the categories used in the English language do not penetrate easily into the cognitive world of participants from the South of Europe.

On the French side, the project received a mixed reception. While my institute and the ministry of education were officially involved, and a working group had been set up, the institutional and political structure was not adjusted to welcome a project of this scope. The members of the small knowledge centre in my institute quickly judged that technologies of evidence could threaten their professional identity, while they were not skilled enough to move from documentary reviewing to systematic reviews of research literature. The adoption of protocols was a constraint on their work and they did not want the research community to overview and supervise on their work. They were therefore pretty hostile to this evolution. The head of the European network had the opportunity to present the objectives and contents of evidence-based education as a guest speaker at the institute in front of practitioners and researchers. But he was not warmly received and often misunderstood because of the existing gap this epistemology has developed at the international level and which French educational sciences largely introverted within the French-speaking area and globally hostile to the import of Anglo-Saxon influences.

The ministry itself, albeit interested by a reflection on the conditions for transferring and disseminating research findings, did not have sufficient internal means to build an infrastructure fitting the criteria of evidence-based education. In addition, this operation would have required a significant effort of translation for national policymakers. The solution was to delegate to the institute the design of a mapping of French research and the building of a databank, while some metrics were developed to monitor general trends and to provide information to policymakers. Another development was the organisation of consensus-based conferences with a national agency of school evaluation to raise awareness among national policymakers and stakeholders regarding key evidence-based international research findings. But these initiatives, limited and poorly interconnected, remained loosely coupled with European policy.

Social Interactions and Instrumental Politics

As we have seen in the previous chapters, benchmarking uses standards to measure, compare and judge the quality of objects or actions in order to promote and disseminate best practices. This technology took over US higher education during the 1990s to improve organisational productivity and quality. In 1996, the Houston-based American Productivity and Quality Center (APQC) developed studies on benchmarking with State Higher Education Executive Officers (SHEEO) and other organisations (Levy and Ronco 2012). Since then, technics of benchmarking have penetrated US higher education, and they were extended to other countries up to the Bologna process (Farquhar 1998; Lund 1998; Lund and Jackson 2000; Massaro 1998; Schreiterer 1998). Endorsing the Lisbon Strategy, heads of states and governments legitimated the practice of benchmarking as a technology of intergovernmental coordination.

The objective of the European Commission is to build a European space research and higher education supported by statistical technics and performance-based measurements to promote competition between national systems in order to generate innovation and to support higher education systems contributing to growth and economic competitiveness (Ritzen 2010; Aghion et al. 2010; Hazelkorn 2007, 2008, 2011). In creating a European market and strengthening emulation and competition, European policymakers' intent was to rationalise training provision and research by avoiding the fragmentation of activities, segmentation between the public and the private and dispersion of funding. The objective was also to confront international competition from North America and Asia. Benchmarking is therefore a statistical tool which enables the adoption of a common language for European policymakers and creates a platform of coherence for national policies so that a dynamic European territory can be progressively built and one which is open and attractive in the international rankings landscape (Bruno et al. 2006; Pusser and Marginson 2013).

The group of experts we were involved with had the task of building benchmarks for higher education policies in Europe. This work followed an initiative initiated by three former European important policymakers in education when they launched a common call urging universities to use their potential of innovation and to transform their modes of governance in order to improve their attractiveness and rank in global competition. This manifesto invited universities to be more autonomous under a more performant leadership and management capable of better preparing young people to enter the global labour market. The call also proposed to reflect on guidelines to better evaluate the performance of European Member States in the implementation of the new higher education policy. The leader of the call had been a high-ranking manager in international organisations and had diplomas from famous US universities. The second one, after a high-ranking academic career, had an active role in reformist circles and the think tanks of his country with influence in parliament and was an adviser to different ministerial cabinets. The third one was very active in the Bologna process and in some agencies and national councils for the development of research and innovation. The call was quickly followed by the creation of a non-governmental organisation with a 'task force' which included young European graduates in law, political sciences and economics.

These policymakers, high-ranking experts from the European reformist Left, characterised a different kind of expertise from that which we have mentioned above: they are political entrepreneurs. They search to promote change in higher education policies in Europe by participating in the definition of public problems. They use opportunity windows to promote their arguments. In this way, they attempt to justify the idea of a crisis or major dysfunctions in European higher education thus making decision-making more urgent. To assert their rhetoric, these experts use their political networks but also expert networks with different knowledge and skills to amplify their message while at the same time benefiting from certified knowledge. The mobilisation or empowerment of experts and policymakers remain fundamental for the success of the enterprise. These political entrepreneurs also have to prove the realism of political proposals formulated in a conceptual framework or programme which has to produce results and show the example to follow.

As Charles Lindblom (1968) has argued, proximity between policymakers is a key success factor (Mintrom and Norman 2009). When policymakers are close to each other, they tend to influence each other, while these types of acquaintances help them to make political choices. They find interlocutors more easily in the high administrative and political spheres, particularly at the European Commission, because they share the same codes and values. They are also aware of the best political timing to advance their cause. The work of European political entrepreneurs is close to that of the advocacy coalitions studied by Paul A. Sabatier (1988, Sabatier and Jenkins-Smith 1993, and Weible et al. 2011). In the sense that they share values, causal imputations and even the same perception of problems, their size as an expert group and the scope of their mobilisation are less. It is a policy learning in terms of social interaction, to resume Radaelli's classification, with a weak divide between experts and policymakers but also some possibilities of more important informal encounters.

The task force was quickly active in organising a first meeting in a small European city bringing together a group of experts. At the beginning, the objective was set by the three policymakers: improving the positions of universities to foster economic growth and competitiveness in Europe while emphasising innovation. The drafting of a review of higher education was scheduled for the European Commission. In order to do so, the task force had designed a set of indicators linking policy, performance and growth and using methods of regression and European databanks. These indicators were grouped into different topics (policy, performance, economic output) to assess national higher education systems. The discussion between experts was essentially focused on technical problems regarding data collection and their adaptation to national realities, without challenging the global approach. Two-hour workshop sessions were divided by group of countries to present a quick, descriptive and quasi-institutional review higher education in each country, followed by a discussion about the degree of reliability and validity of the collected data. Recommendations were then made to improve the data collection by taking into account additional indicators and improving the first version of the report for the

Commission. These workshop sessions were followed by mini-lectures by experts on the problems posed by higher education in Europe and the political solutions to be implemented to remedy the crisis. Discussions were again supported by official reports or international organisations and recurrent topics such as new mobility, the brain drain, innovation, patents, public costs and expenditure, internationalisation and the recruitment of foreign students. In conclusion, it was affirmed that European universities' autonomy and attractiveness needed strengthening.

During the following months, experts were invited to work at distance before the next meetings to compare the evolution of higher education policies from indicators provided by the task force. Each topic was decomposed into indicators (autonomy, research, access, fund mix, productivity, attractiveness, competitiveness, innovation), from which countries were ranked in a two-column table. A set of colours (green, orange, red) was used to indicate the positive or negative evolution of each country with regard to the benchmarks formalised by the task force, while each indicator was graphically represented. This data was accompanied by comments on each country: each national expert, based on his or her review of the situation of higher education, had to confirm or infirm the proposed analysis. A technical document was designed to explain the complexity of statistical calculations and regressions used to frame different benchmarks.

Some members of the networks organised other meetings in Europe, while the benchmarks and report were updated after collecting advice from experts. Opportunity was given to reflect on a common programme responding to a European call from the European Commission to lead a project on best practices in the governance of higher education. Meanwhile, the representative of the expert group participated in high-level meetings with European policymakers, from the European Commission, in charge of education, research and innovation, as representatives of the Academic Cooperation Association Conference. Recommendations from the expert group served to justify the development of policies focusing on innovation, autonomy and the quality of higher education, while the idea of a long-term strategic plan was put forward. One of these meetings was organised under the auspices of the European Investment Bank along with the European commissioner for research, science and innovation and with the three policymakers at the origin of the benchmarking project.

Learning in the Shadow of Hierarchy

We shall now describe endogenous expertise at the European Commission characterising policy learning in the shadow of hierarchy, in the sense that a network of experts produces knowledge for the units of the Directorate-General for Education and Culture (DG EAC) to help it with its proposals and recommendations in the field of lifelong learning policy. This network, entitled NEXUS, was created by the DG EAC and was subjected to a narrow frame to deliver its expertise and was supervised by a technocrat, or policy officer, in charge of transmitting the directives of his hierarchy to the head of the expert group. NEXUS's aim is to produce expertise content, supported by international research findings in education, to guide European decision-making and to facilitate DG EAC's negotiations with other directorates-general, the Commission itself and other European institutions.

The network's first task was to carry out a mapping of research fields in education and training and to identify some issues related to the Commission's political agenda. In parallel, a website was launched to facilitate the activities of transferring and disseminating information to stakeholders but also European technocrats. DG EAC had explicitly formalised contract scheduling seminars with European high-ranking civil servants. The expert network also had to formulate analyses and proposals to become directly operational in the implement of policy and to organise meetings at the European level with other experts, policymakers and stakeholders.

Experts, mostly academics, were extremely reluctant to accept this approach of expertise which they considered utilitarian and instrumental, and this created problems later. The first meeting held in Brussels with the head of one of the DG EAC units, in charge of the expertise programme, was a shock for most of them. The policymaker explained that the expertise of his unit was limited but it had a lot of relations with a wide variety of ministries, research and expert communities, practitioners and stakeholders at the European level. He described the functioning of another group of experts as a good example and explained that it was DG EAC's ambition to better link policy, research and evidence, while a report was being prepared on the efficiency and effectiveness of education systems. It was also argued that a lot of work had already been carried out and the European Council was ready to promote evidence-based policy and to mobilise stakeholders.

The objective of the meeting was to clarify the work of the NEXUS network, its methods with regard to contractual individual and collective arrangements varied according to national contexts. DG EAC's policymaker wanted the expert group to quickly prepare the next communication on the topic of evidence-based policy. He then recalled the objectives of the Open Method of Coordination, its indicators and benchmarks and the need to exchange on best practices and to develop peer learning between policymakers, to find effective methods for the development of education policies in relation to PISA scores. The objective was also to strengthen DG EAC's credibility and to work with the Commission alongside Member States in producing political documents and effective recommendations. The idea was not to provoke resistance but to have a real impact on the transformation of education systems. This is why the expert network had to be selective in its messages and to work on evidence-based issues to avoid problems with the OECD and European governments.

He then presented the European policy for lifelong learning, with its different programmes and clusters launched by the Commission to develop exchanges of best practices and peer learning between policymakers: modernisation of higher education, teacher training, better use of resources, mathematics, sciences and technology, social access and inclusion, key competencies, ICTs and recognition of learning outcomes. Policymakers explained that there were numerous working groups and efforts had been made to bring policymakers, experts and stakeholders closer together but also to work with the OECD. In his opinion, the DG EAC was producing a lot of recommendations in its reports in order to provoke a debate between Member States, but he was now interested in specific expertise in terms of analysis and comparison of education systems and policies. The objective was not to inventory the contribution of individual researchers nor to reflect on debates within the scientific community, nor to work out different disciplinary topics. It was to produce knowledge which has a direct impact on policy and practice and contributes to the professional development of DG EAC's technocrats.

During the second part of the meeting, we listened to the communication of the head of the other European network, with whom we had to work with in the preparation of a future communication related to the evidence-based policy. He explained that new indicators and data had been produced to ensure progress in the implementation of the Lisbon Strategy but these indicators and benchmarks now had to be extended to an evidence-based approach for improving current tools. We were solicited as a group of experts to propose constructive solutions to improve these tools and make them politically acceptable, with the aim of obtaining a large consensus between the research community and the Member States. A culture of evaluation, conforming to the triangle of production, mediation and use of knowledge, had to be implemented. Then, the general director of DG EAC came and told us that we were facing major challenges in European education and that our network of experts would support reforms at different scales by contributing to economic growth and the maintenance of social cohesion. DG EAC needed 'good research' complying with policymakers' practical needs and distant from academic discourse and jargon. The issue of evidence-based policy was controversial, and DG EAC wished to have constructive proposals and advice based on a compilation of knowledge useful for the shaping of European policies.

Quickly, an agenda was fixed to the NEXUS network with precise tasks defining the participation of some experts in seminars and conferences organised by DG EAC in different parts of Europe. Experts had to regularly provide advice on drafts DG EAC wanted to make public, on the initial elements of the mapping assigned to my institute and on the development of the website. Later on, the network of experts received 'ad hoc questions' sent by DG EAC's services and two- to three-page documents summarising the European Commission's publications on a topic and formulating three key questions about policymaking or decision-making to which experts had to respond within a limited period of time (15 days to 1 month). These ad hoc questions, highly precise or on the contrary very broad, corresponded to the concerns of Brussels' technocrats who were incapable of finding a response by exploring internal reports and studies or existing databanks. Or sometimes the research in this field did not exist or the question was so broad that it would have required a vast and selective review of international research findings.

The rhythm imposed by DG EAC, based on a quality insurance procedure and control, and the reluctance of some experts to respond to such complex questions, often outside of their disciplinary area, and the highly bureaucratic and inexperienced management of our institute in the design of the mapping and the Internet website quickly led to an institutional crisis. DG EAC, through its policy officer, convoked an urgency meeting to specify the European Commission's expectations, to remind the experts of the framework and their duties. They were required to contribute better and more to the formulation of recommendations but also to step outside of their scientific expertise area to provide information to the network and to be more available. As for DG EAC, it had to make an effort to reduce timeframes and the number of ad hoc questions and to set up a new schedule for achieving tasks. In fact, these tensions were the expressions of a larger misunderstanding between DG EAC's representatives and those of the expert group.

Indeed, technocrats are used to manipulating instrumental and positivist scientific knowledge, and they do not understand that some issues could lead to tergiversations in the responses of experts who have more mobilised, more reflexive, critical and pluralist knowledge. Furthermore, they wanted to closely control the production of expertise and believed that setting up a quality insurance procedure and tasks schedule would be sufficient to frame the work of experts. Experts, who were mostly all academics, and unfamiliar with the requirements of international expertise, they were not disposed to abandon their academic freedom and apply norms and conceptions they did not agree with. They were also busy with other tasks for their research community and they did not have always the time to respond, while other broader questions or those which were too narrowly focused would have required the development of new research projects or an extended review of research literature which would have taken months or years. A perverse effect of this pressure on expertise was that some academics were resuming the contents of the European Commission's documents or already-produced expertise to provide a quick review and to finish tasks within the network. Disagreements grew between DG EAC and the group of experts regarding the evaluation of quality and the relevance of deliverables as well as the content of expertise.

I had the opportunity to test the quality approach of the European expertise. When an expert responded to an ad hoc question, I publicly protested that it was a partial and irrelevant account for DG EAC's policymakers. This incident showed that experts do not necessarily have a homogenous epistemological and methodological approach when delivering expertise, and this added to the incoherence and confusion felt by the Commission's technocrats. I wrote to the policy officer, copying the message to the head of the expert group, to share my doubts and uncertainties about the produced knowledge which I found partial and misguided. The reaction of DG EAC's members demonstrates the extreme pressure they face to deliver real-time recommendations but also the representations they have regarding the control of knowledge produced by expert groups. An official letter was sent from the Commission to protest against the poor quality of the coordination of the experts and to recall that the protocol and standards by which an expert note had to be supervised beforehand by the head of the network. Beyond the anecdote, this experience indicated that the DG EAC units are often incapable of being the last evaluator and they expect certitude from expertise and not the introduction of complexities or relative ideas they will not be able to manage in time for decision-making.

As it has been demonstrated by this case study, the cognitive world of Brussels' technocrats is relatively constrained. Urged to find responses to questions and to deliver notes, reports and recommendations within tight deadlines, they do not have time to take into account the problems of interpretation and reflexivity induced by the exploration of international research literature. They also cannot penetrate epistemic and methodological debates. They have to produce a normative discourse embedded in previous programmes and actions while claiming a continuity and coherence of European policy. Taking a step back is impossible because it would challenge the assumptions and foundations of an acquired expertise already accepted and officialised by Member States.

To guarantee this continuity and to discipline expertise and experts, DG EAC forces them to work in a restricted framework and protocol and uses quality standards and financial penalties to ensure deadlines are respected and the works fit the normative requirements of technocrats. Experts, forced to produce expertise in a very short time, have no real possibility to explore the entire extent of research literature required to respond to complex, technocratic, and wide-ranging questions far from scientific questioning. In order to do so, it is necessary to translate and reformulate technocratic statements to make them acceptable with regard to scientific content. Because of lack of time, experts have a tendency to 'cut and paste' elements of expertise close to their work; to quickly select papers, reports and other documents; and to privilege existing syntheses produced by the Commission itself. These experts maintain a kind of hermeneutic circle through which technocrats learn some expert content that they themselves contributed to develop in other expert networks or other epistemic communities, without gaining any exteriority and reflexivity from an endogenous and self-perpetuating 'technocratic doxa'.

Conclusion

As we have shown in the previous pages, expertise has led to different policy learning processes which link experts and policymakers. Scenes and arenas defining the work and the content of expertise are multiple and entail different types of mobilisation and interaction. The transmission of expertise is not homogenous and linear and it is not always successful. Various interpretations and categorisations, but also heterogeneous and uncertain assemblages, have paved the way for knowledge from the field of expertise to that of decision-making. The worlds of expertise are plural and they have their own logic of action which, contrary to what the technocrats think, cannot be prescribed in advance through quality frameworks and protocols.

In departing from an analysis of paths and careers of experts, and from a critical stance aiming to denounce the interests and power games which characterise depoliticisation by expertise, we have explored the cognitive dimension of the experts' work by showing how interactions and relationships are shaped in formal or informal ways. In doing so, we have emphasised the exploratory and incomplete dimension of expertise in action while demonstrating that experts are also subjected to contingency, doubt, misunderstandings and limited rationality and that they are not always able to give meaning to their action. As a process of socialisation, expertise is made up of multiple attachments and dependences both at proximity and at distance and which participate in a distributed cognition and learning similar to certain conditions found in academic work.

Albeit that content in the production of knowledge is different, the two activities share similarities: regulating and self-control by peers, a sense of legitimacy and hierarchy, competition, sharing implicit knowledge and networking. Evidently, there are differences in expertise: lack of time dedicated to the production of knowledge, the normativity of content which puts reflexivity and criticism at a distance (and this is a problem for social and educational sciences), the lack of clear divide between analysis of facts and values generating and maintaining a certain 'doxa' and/or satisficing to 'discursive fashions', a lack of historical perspective regarding several issues and a mono-epistemic dimension recusing interpretative pluralism. Some researchers have not taken into account these differences in reducing the gap between science and expertise and producing sciences of government. For others, the two perspectives cannot really be conciliated but these researchers have been relegated to the periphery of expert networks criss-crossing the traditional boundaries between policy, research and practice.

References

Aghion, P., Dewatripont, M., Hoxby, C., Mas-Colell, A., & Sapir, A. (2010). The governance and performance of universities: Evidence from Europe and the US. *Economic Policy, 25*(61), 7–59.

Bennett, C. J., & Howlett, M. (1992). The lessons of learning: Reconciling theories of policy learning and policy change. *Policy Sciences, 25*(3), 275–294.

Bomberg, E. (2007). Policy learning in an enlarged European Union: Environmental NGOs and newpolicy instruments. *Journal of European Public Policy, 14*(2), 248–268.

Bruno, I., Jacquot, S., & Mandin, L. (2006). Europeanization through its instrumentation: Benchmarking, mainstreaming and the open method of co-ordination… toolbox or Pandora's box? *Journal of European Public Policy, 13*(4), 519–536.

Campana, A., Henry, E., & Rowell, J. (2007). *La construction des problèmes publics en Europe. Emergence, formulation et mise en instrument.* Strasbourg: Presses universitaires de Strasbourg.

Checkel, J. (2003). Going native in Europe? Theorizing social interaction in European institutions. *Comparative Political Studies, 36*(1/2), 209–231.

Christiansen, T., Jorgensen, K., & Wiener, A. (1999). The social construction of Europe. *Journal of European Public Policy, 6*(4), 528–544.

Desrosières, A. (2002). *The politics of large numbers: A history of statistical reasoning.* Cambridge, MA: Harvard University Press.

Dolowitz, D. P., & Marsh, D. (1996). Who learns what from whom: A review of the policy transfer literature. *Political Studies, 44*(2), 343–357.

Dolowitz, D. P., & Marsh, D. (2000). Learning from abroad: The role of policy transfer in contemporary policy-making. *Governance, 13*(1), 5–23.

Dunlop, C. A. (2009). Policy transfer as learning: Capturing variation in what decision-makers learn from epistemic communities. *Policy Studies, 30*(3), 289–311.

Dunlop, C. A., & Radaelli, C. M. (2013). Systematising policy learning: From monolith to dimensions. *Political Studies, 61*(3), 599–619.

Farquhar, R. (1998). Higher education benchmarking in Canada and the United States of America. In A. Schofield (Ed.), *Benchmarking in higher education: An international review.* London: CHEMS; Paris: United Nations Educational, Scientific and Cultural Organization.

Freeman, R. (2008). Learning by meeting. *Critical Policy Analysis, 2*(1), 1–24.

Georgakakis, D., & De Lasalle, M. (2008). *La nouvelle gouvernance européenne: Genèses et usages politiques d'un livre blanc.* Strasbourg: Presses universitaires de Strasbourg.

Goffman, E. (1961). *Encounters: Two studies in the sociology of interaction.* Indianapolis: Bobbs–Merrill.

Gornitzka, Å. (2013). The interface between research and policy – A note with potential relevance for higher education. *European Journal of Higher Education, 3*(3), 255–264.

Gornitzka, Å., & Sverdrup, U. (2008). Who consults? The configuration of expert groups in the European Union. *West European Politics, 31*(4), 725–750.

Gusfield, J. R. (1984). *The culture of public problems: Drinking-driving and the symbolic order.* Chicago: University of Chicago Press.

Haas, P. (1992). Introduction: Epistemic communities and international policy co-ordination. *International Organization, 46*(1), 1–35.

Hazelkorn, E. (2007). The impact of league tables and ranking systems on higher education decision making. *Higher Education Management and Policy, 19*(2), 1–24.

Hazelkorn, E. (2008). Learning to live with league tables and ranking: The experience of institutional leaders. *Higher Education Policy, 21*(2), 193–215.

Hazelkorn, E. (2011). *Rankings and the reshaping of higher education: The battle for world-class excellence.* Basingstoke: Palgrave Macmillan.

Lascoumes, P., & Le Galès, P. (2007). Introduction: understanding public policy through its instruments—From the nature of instruments to the sociology of public policy instrumentation. *Governance, 20*(1), 1–21.

Levy, G. D., & Ronco, S. L. (2012). How benchmarking and higher education came together. *New Directions for Institutional Research, 2012*(156), 5–13.

Lindblom, C. E. (1968). *The policymaking process.* Englewood Cliffs: Prentice-Hall.

Lund, H. (1998). Benchmarking in UK higher education. In A. Schofield (Ed.), *Benchmarking in higher education: An international review.* London: CHEMS; Paris: United Nations Educational, Scientific and Cultural Organization.

Lund, H., & Jackson, N. (2000). Benchmarking in other HE systems. In N. Jackson & H. Lund (Eds.), *Benchmarking in higher education.* Buckingham: Open University Press.

Majone, G. D. (1989). *Evidence, argument, and persuasion in the policy process.* New Haven: Yale University Press.

Majone, G. D. (1996). *Regulating Europe.* London: Routledge.

Massaro, V. (1998). Benchmarking in Australian higher education. In A. Schofield (Ed.), *Benchmarking in higher education.* London: CHEMS; Paris: United Nations Educational, Scientific and Cultural Organization.

May, P. J. (1992). Policy learning and failure. *Journal of Public Policy, 12*(4), 331–354.

Medvetz, T. (2012). *Think tanks in America.* Chicago: University of Chicago Press.

Michel, H., & Robert, C. (2010). *La fabrique des "Européens". Processus de socialisation et construction européenne,* PU de Strasbourg, Coll. 'Sociologie politique européenne'.

Mintrom, M., & Norman, P. (2009). Policy entrepreneurship and policy change. *Policy Studies Journal, 37*(4), 649–667.

Missiroli, A., & Ioannides, I. (2012, September). *European think tanks and the EU.* Berlaymont paper, (2). Brussels: Bureau of European Policy Advisers (BEPA), European Commission.

Normand, R. (2010). Expertise, networks and indicators: The construction of the European strategy in Education. *European Educational Research Journal, 9*(3), 407–421.

Peters, G. B. (1995). *The politics of bureaucracy.* New York: Longman Publishers.

Porter, T. M. (1996). *Trust in numbers: The pursuit of objectivity in science and public life.* Princeton: Princeton University Press.

Pusser, B., & Marginson, S. (2013). University rankings in critical perspective. *The Journal of Higher Education, 84*(4), 544–568.

Quaglia, L., De Francesco, F., & Radaelli, C. M. (2008). Committee governance and socialisation in the EU: The state of the art. *Journal of European Public Policy, 15*(1), 1–12.

Radaelli, C. M. (1995). The role of knowledge in the policy process. *Journal of European Public Policy, 2*(2), 159–183.

Radaelli, C. M. (1999a). The public policy of the European Union: Whither politics of expertise? *Journal of European Public Policy, 6*(5), 757–774.

Radaelli, C. M. (1999b). *Technocracy in the European Union.* New York: Addison Wesley Longman.

Radaelli, C. M. (2008). Europeanization, policy learning, and new modes of governance. *Journal of Comparative Policy Analysis, 10*(3), 239–254.

Radaelli, C. M. (2009). Measuring policy learning: Regulatory impact assessment in Europe. *Journal of European Public Policy, 16*(8), 1145–1164.

Radaelli, C. M., & Dunlop, C. A. (2013). Learning in the European Union: Theoretical lenses and meta-theory. *Journal of European Public Policy, 20*(6), 923–940.

Ricci, D. M. (1993). *The transformation of American politics: The new Washington and the rise of think tanks.* New Haven: Yale University Press.

Rich, A. (2005). *Think tanks, public policy, and the politics of expertise.* Cambridge, MA: Cambridge University Press.

Ritzen, J. M. M. (2010). *A chance for European Universities: Or, avoiding the Looming University crisis in Europe.* Amsterdam: Amsterdam University Press.

Robert, C. (2003). L'expertise comme mode d'administration communautaire: entre logiques technocratiques et stratégies d'alliance. *Politique Européenne, 11*(3), 57–78.

Robert, C. (2010). Who are the European experts; profiles, trajectories and expert 'careers' of the European Commission. *French Politics, 8*(3), 248–274.

Robert, C. (2011). Les groupes d'experts dans le gouvernement de l'Union européenne. *Politiques Européennes, 32*(3), 7–38. L'Harmattan.

Sabatier, P. A. (1988). An advocacy coalition framework of policy change and the role of policy-oriented learning therein. *Policy Sciences, 21*(2–3), 129–168.

Sabatier, P. A., & Jenkins-Smith Hank, C. (1993). *Policy change and learning: An advocacy coalition approach.* Boulder: Westview Press.

Schreiterer. U. (1998). Benchmarking in European higher education. In A. Schofield (Ed.), *Benchmarking in Higher Education: An International Review.* London: CHEMS; Paris: United Nations Educational, Scientific and Cultural Organization.

Sherrington, P. (2000). Shaping the policy agenda: Think tank activity in the European Union. *Global Society, 14*(2), 173–189.

Shore, C. (2013). *Building Europe: The cultural politics of European integration.* London: Routledge.

Slavin, R. E. (2002). Evidence-based education policies: Transforming educational practice and research. *Educational Researcher, 31,* 15–21.

Smith, J. A. (1991). *The idea brokers: Think tanks and the rise of the new policy elite.* New York: Free Press.

Spring, J. (2005). *Political agendas for education: From the religious right to the Green Party.* Mahwah: L. Erlbaum.

Stone, D. (1996). *Capturing the political imagination: Think tanks and the policy process.* London/ Routledge: Psychology Press.

Stone, D., & Denham, A. (Eds.). (2004). *Think tank traditions: Policy research and the politics of ideas.* Manchester: Manchester University Press.

Tallberg, J. (2006). *Leadership and negotiation in the European Union.* Cambridge: Cambridge University Press.

Ullrich, H. (2004). *EU think tanks: Generating ideas, analysis and debate.* Manchester: Manchester University Press.

Weible, C. M. (2008). Expert-based information and policy subsystems: A review and synthesis. *Policy Studies Journal, 36*(4), 615–635.

Weible, C. M., Sabatier, P. A., Jenkins-Smith, H. C., Nohrstedt, D., Henry, A. D., & Deleon, P. (2011). A quarter century of the advocacy coalition framework: An introduction to the special issue. *Policy Studies Journal, 39*(3), 349–360.

Zito, A. R. (Ed.). (2013). *Learning and governance in the EU policy making process.* Abingdon: Routledge.

The New Spirit of Managerialism

Introduction

By analysing the politics of quality and evidence-based standards, we can capture the extent of the Europeanisation process, which by developing measurements and governing by numbers has diminished the importance of the state in favour of transnational actors and organisations. We then showed how expertise was built among international networks beyond the borders of the academic world to institutionalise new forms of knowledge production and their transfer/translation to policymakers and stakeholders. The two pillars of academic work, teaching and research, characterised by a disciplinary background and belonging to a national scientific community, have been challenged by the new configurations valuing interdisciplinary knowledge and its mediatisation through worldwide connections. We have qualify this change of state as 'new spirit of academic capitalism' in relation to Luc Boltanski and Eve Chiapello's work which has shown how capitalism has, via managerial technologies, recovered and shifted by avoiding the recurrent criticism it has faced (Boltanski and Chiapello 2005; Weber 2002). By transposing this analysis into higher education, it is possible to characterise a new managerial regime which shifts instituted trials of academic tradition, deconstructs its values and traditional modes of attachment to the Enlightenment and subverts its sense of creativity and its epistemology in the production of knowledge. Thus, without praising a golden age and adopting a nostalgic outlook, we have highlighted through ideal types the new configurations of academic work emerging in the international and European space in which mobility and networking have become the components of a new relationship between academics and their institutions and colleagues.

We shall begin by outlining the main features of global academic capitalism which, even if it is not limited to marketisation, has strengthened competition between higher education institutions and given increasing legitimacy to entrepreneurship. However, the sense of entrepreneurship and its linked values must be viewed with regard to the loss of legitimacy of the academic profession which is

© Springer International Publishing Switzerland 2016   161
R. Normand, *The Changing Epistemic Governance of European Education*,
Educational Governance Research 3, DOI 10.1007/978-3-319-31776-2_6

facing increasing criticism but also to New Public Management's studies with the different variations between countries. We shall then demonstrate how this entrepreneurial role, alongside that of the expert which we described in the previous chapter, is embedded in a new conception of professionalism and conventions of academic work while it is shifting the instituted trials initiated by tradition.

The New Spirit of Global Academic Capitalism

Slaughter and Leslie, in their book *Academic Capitalism*, wrote a precursory work by analysing the transformations of the working conditions of academics in English-speaking countries (Slaughter and Leslie 1997). They showed how academics now have to find resources outside of the university by developing applied research thus making them dependent on business. Consequently, competition for access to resources, whether it concerns funds or students, is increasing while research has taking an entrepreneurial turn. Values from the private sector are invading the academic world and tensions related to globalisation are being felt in the relationships between academics in universities. The new spirit of academic capitalism, while it extents the market, has forced the state to deregulate which has led to the private sector penetrating universities. Academic capitalism therefore refers to a wide variety of market (e.g. patents, spin-off companies, etc.) and market-like (e.g. grants, university–industry partnerships and tuition fees) activities and institutions that are used by faculties and institutions to secure external funding due to reduced public funding. While multinational firms have increased their R&D efforts in new technologies, academics are adopting opportunistic behaviour in a more competitive environment by seeking private funds and producing licences or patents to fund their future research projects. Academics, by developing applied research even though they continue to be mainly funded by the state, are subverting the public interest mission of research.

Academic Capitalism Beyond the Market

However, academic capitalism cannot be reduced to marketisation. It is a complex process involving diverse international and transnational activities regarding the content of curriculum, the mobility of scholars and students and the establishment of branch campuses, technical assistance and cooperation (Kauppinen 2012). This is achieved through a combination of locally, nationally and or transnationally organised practices, networks, intermediating and interstitial organisations, new circuits of knowledge, funding mechanisms and policies that are blurring the boundaries between higher education, states and the private sector at a transnational scale. Even at the European level, this form of academic capitalism is being developed through the Higher Education-Business Forum, the Association of European

Science and Technology Transfer Professionals or the European Commission's Research Framework Programmes (Slaughter and Cantwell 2011). The European Research Area is encouraging the involvement of corporations by developing and promoting innovation, by bringing research institutions and business closer together, for example, the European Round Table of Industrialists, and opening a free space for transnational synergies and complementarities for knowledge and technologies (EC 2010).

Furthermore, as we saw in chapter "An Epistemic Governance of European Education", academic capitalism is related to other aspects of universities and the changing relations between universities and knowledge. In this global competition, the universities' external revenue depends on the knowledge and intellectual property rights provided by R&D and innovation (Communication from the European Commission 2003). Academic capitalism components include knowledge regimes and networks that intermediate between the public and private sectors and integrate various investments and groups in the links between universities and the global new economy (Slaughter and Rhoades 2004). Globalisation enhances economic competition between universities and academics for high-technology and knowledge-intensive products.

Among discourses defending the new spirit of academic capitalism, the assumptions of Burton Clark, in his analysis of the transformations of academic work, have accredited and disseminated the idea of an entrepreneurial university (Clark 1998, 2004). The concept of an 'entrepreneurial university' was highlighted in his first book *Creating Entrepreneurial Universities* and has since been the theme of many publications across the world. The UNESCO-CEPES Institute devoted a special issue of its journal *Higher Education in Europe* to this theme (2004), and the OECD journal *Higher Education Management and Policy* published a special issue on entrepreneurship from papers issued from this project in 2005. Clark's ideas have been widely supported and promoted during several conferences organised by the European Higher Education Society and the Consortium for Higher Education Researchers, while the Mellon and Spencer foundations also provided specific funds to disseminate his ideas (Shattock 2010). This rhetoric criticises European higher education systems enclosed in their Napoleonic or Humboldtian models which give too much importance to the state to the detriment of management which is considered to be more effective. According to Clark's entrepreneurial conception, the transformations of higher education and the pressure on European universities have forced them to become more flexible; autonomous and managerial power has been devolved the presidency. The implementation of contracts, the increase in self-funding and the adoption of leadership practices must allow changes which are often considered as strategic and necessary.

All these discourses, published in papers and books, have had an impact on policymakers (Bleiklie 2005). Firstly, in the UK after a long period of austerity in higher education, the idea that universities had to rely on themselves and not on state intervention was widely shared (Deem et al. 2007). The OECD itself, in its higher education programme, has adopted Clark's entrepreneurialism. The European Commission summarised many of his ideas in the following communications: *The Role of the Universities in the Europe of Knowledge* (CEC 2003), *Mobilising the Brainpower of Europe* (CEC 2005) and *Delivering the Modernisation Agenda for Universities*: *Education, Research and Innovation* (CEC 2006). These communications invoked the challenges facing European universities: internationalisation, relations with industry, the reorganisation of knowledge, etc.

Global Networks and Local Agencies

Slaughter and Leslie's analyses, like those of Clark, characterise the two extremes in the debate between the pros and cons of academic capitalism. The transformations of higher education are seen through a structural opposition between the state and the market while the comparison is limited to nation-states. As Simon Marginson (2006) writes, these theories have not taken into account a reflexion on agencies and the processes which participate in transnational and local changes in academic institutions and activities. The metaphor of academic capitalism reveals a powerful global trend but ignores the power of national traditions, agencies and agents in shaping the work of higher education, as well as local agencies exercised by students, the faculty, nonfaculty professionals and administrators, pursuing prestige, knowledge, social critique and social justice (Marginson and Considine 2000; Rhoades 1998). This is why Marginson and Rhoades suggested considering the 'glonacal agency' to capture the global, national and local transformations of the new spirit of academic capitalism (Marginson and Rhoades 2002). International organisations, states and professional groups interact at different scales and beyond national borders to frame policies and practices in higher education. The analysis of these global flows and agencies reveals interconnections between institutions, and politico-economical resources have significantly restructured higher education policies, created new equivalences between programmes driven by international organisations and adapted to national/local governance and management.

Reasoning in terms of 'glonacal agency' makes it possible to highlight adjustments and resistance to the globalisation of higher education and to take into account national and local specificities. For example, the World Bank is very influential in developing countries through its funding mechanisms, while the OECD and the European Commission mainly have a structuring effect on Western countries in terms of standards and best practices. Indeed, professional associations and networks, such as foundations, think tanks and agencies, participating in the definition of standards and the circulation of expertise, are configured differently from one continent to another. It is the same for the collecting and management of data which legitimise expertise and justify government by numbers in higher education.

These arguments are shared by Stephen Ball. He sees neo-liberalism in education as a complex, incoherent, unstable and often contradictory set of practices and projects organised around the imaginary of the market and its extension into social relationships (Ball 2008, 2012). This economisation of social life fabricates self-governing entrepreneurial individuals. Neo-liberalism, by reconfiguring relationships between knowledge and power according to a complex game of interactions between instruments, networks and interests, shapes behaviour and brainpower to serve an intellectual project previously advocated by economists such as Friedrich Hayek and Milton Friedman. Indeed, by participating in new regulative institutions and governing modes, the new spirit of academic capitalism is embedded in a global circulation of ideas which transcend states borders and legitimate transnational networks thus bringing the interests of policymakers and edu-business closer together. These politico-economical networks, by including supranational organisations (OECD, the World Bank), transnational agencies and companies (Educational Testing Service, McKinsey, Microsoft), non-governmental organisations (think tanks and foundations) and global professional associations, and by promoting new managerial and entrepreneurial forms, have shifted traditional hierarchies and have influenced political decision-making by proposing to repair the state's failure. As new political assemblages, they transcend the classical forms of political representation and traditional spaces of negotiation between national actors. It is therefore a mix of bureaucracy (or technocracy), markets and networks which have contributed to meta-governance in the shadow of the state's hierarchy while generating a global flow of ideas and instruments summarised and transferred into national reforms. This policy entrepreneurship adds up to policy transfer mechanisms by strengthening the convergence process between states and the adoption of international standards.

In fact, the new spirit of academic capitalism has strengthened competition between higher education institutions. The most prestigious universities valorise their tradition and prestige to attract the best candidates among academics and students. They profit from global competition through high fees guaranteeing good operating conditions for their faculties and research centres. The other higher education institutions struggle to attract students who mainly chose Anglo-Saxon universities according to their global rankings. This mobility is supported in Europe by the convergence of European diplomas under the Bologna process and by programmes such as Erasmus which support student mobility in the European space of higher education. In addition to the brain drain created by international competition, particularly for developing countries which are struggling to maintain their national elite, the segmentation and ranking of higher education systems is increasing at global and national scales as it positions universities in an unfair and unequal competition because of the asymmetry of resources and the initial starting point. The reduction of public budgets has reinforced this margin squeeze as universities cannot be attractive and be included in the global market of higher education. Marketisation is extended to the delivery of higher education services and the implementation of universities of higher education platforms abroad which directly compete with the local provision.

Rankings and Global Competition

In this global environment, rankings have accelerated global competition during the last decade. A ranking regime suggests an interrelatedness of various kinds of organisations (e.g. government accountability, accreditation, commercial rankings), which work together to define what is excellent higher education, valuable knowledge or, at the grandest level, what are 'world-class universities' (Gonzales and Núñez 2014). In this manner, commercial rankings, governmental accountability bodies and similar evaluative entities claim to measure excellence, value and/or quality in order to develop hierarchies of higher education institutions. The daily life of faculty members and the content of the curriculum are steadily being transformed by audit cultures, the production of evidence and entrepreneurial behaviour (Power 1994, 1997; Shore and Wright 1999; Strathern 2000). Such rankings influence investment in specific programmes to identify 'world-class' universities or 'global research universities'. This competition hinges on research, knowledge production and knowledge dissemination, which are measured with impact rates or the number of prestigious appointments. The ranking regime has influenced the evaluation of faculty work, especially knowledge production, through the perpetuation of the following values or practices: (a) individualism, (b) standardisation, (c) commodification and (d) homogenisation.

The ranking regime is structured and monitored in ways that encourage individual achievement. Individualism means that faculty work is oversimplified into singular products or processes and represented by singular activities which enable standardisation. It takes form in evaluative exercises and records of publications that faculty members have to document carefully and report in order to receive awards and recognition. Standardisation simplifies and decontextualises faculty work and knowledge production so that they become comparable. The ranking regime calls for standardised approaches to measure faculty and institutional characteristics and activities. As we have seen in chapter "The Politics of Standards and Quality", standardisation enables comparisons of wildly different settings and contexts in order to gauge universities by single definitions of quality or excellence. Comparison, with the implication of competition, implies the commodification of one's work as a product with exchange value. While grant-getting is a key strategy in the commodification of knowledge, a faculty might prioritise research and/or grant-writing, as it is important for the university's desire to earn a higher ranking. Finally, the ranking regime emphasises or assigns more value to certain types of faculty contributions, thus facilitating homogenisation as it relates to the production and dissemination of knowledge.

If academic capitalism is an ideological fabrication and a transformation of academic work, it is also based on the economic belief that the production of knowledge in higher education increases the investment in human capital and economic competitiveness. Based on a utilitarian calculation instituted in the design of measurement tools such as rankings, increase of profitability and the decrease of costs through privatisation and marketisation of services, the search for effectiveness and efficiency through New Public Management has been justified by those who wish to diminish the importance of the state and academics in regulating academic activities. We shall see later how the new spirit of academic capitalism is defining new stances among academics. Beforehand, we will analyse the way in which the academic profession has been subjected to a certain number of critiques which have contributed to its decline and loss of legitimacy while a new managerial configuration is emerging at the global level.

The Criticism and Trials Against the Academic Profession

To understand the loss of the academic profession's legitimacy, its subversion by the new spirit of capitalism and the increasing challenges it faces, it is necessary to map out the range of critiques it has been confronted with. The broad access to higher education, the devaluation of academic diplomas and the slowdown in economic growth have diminished opportunities of inclusion for young graduates, increased distrust towards a community accused of maintaining its privileges and disregarding the utility of its teaching and research. Our aim is not to discriminate the right and the wrong of these critiques but to put these discourses in perspective and to reflect on the arguments deconsecrating or delegitimising the profession in the eyes of policymakers and a larger audience.

A first type of argument can be found among sociologists themselves. The accomplished work of Pierre Bourdieu *Homo Academicus* can been considered as a *pro domo* accusation against academic institutions (Bourdieu 1988). By showing the crisis in the academic world during the 1960s, Bourdieu underlined the game of power relationships conditioning individual paths and careers through disciplinary wars relativising the universalistic claim of knowledge produced by the academia. Thus, he explains that academic power is based, on the one hand, on the capacity of acting upon hopes (themselves based on the disposition to play and invest the game) and the objective uncertainty of the game, and on the other hand, on objective probabilities, particularly in delimitating the universe of possible competitors. Indeed, relations of dependence depend on the strategies of 'bosses' and 'clients' according to the tensions on the market of positions in such a discipline. This power of the mechanisms of reproduction on the academic profession is based on control, co-optation for access to academic bodies and mastery of institutional positions of power (juries, councils, etc.). By disclosing the logics of interest and underlying strategies which divide disciplines, Bourdieu contributed to showing the position of corporatism and conservatism while challenging established hierarchies and academic orders. This criticism of the state's nobility, developed in his other book, accredited the idea that the functioning of universities had to be revised and that it has resumed by intellectuals and policymakers to justify reforms.

While the 1950s–1960s were announced as being the end of ideologies, in particular by Daniel Bell (1960), the 1980s were marked by the return of a reactionary rhetoric hostile to academics and academia denounced for their proximity to the

Marxist and reformist Left and their contribution to the decline of standards and intellectual tradition (Chitty 1989). Against Marxist thought on the one hand and the Social Democrat thought on the other hand, new intellectuals close to political power and the media, or researchers supported by think tanks, disseminated new ideas against academism, while business representatives criticised the lack of economic effectiveness of higher education and claimed that training needed to be adapted to the provision of professional skills. This criticism was increased twofold by accusations of corporatism against a profession considered as an establishment defending its narrow interests and maintaining its advantages while the rest of the society had to make sacrifices during economic crises. While the working class and social movements against capitalism in Europe had collapsed, the principles at the foundation of a compromise between trade unionist representation and self-regulation by peers were recused on behalf of the need to restructure academic activities and to introduce evaluation. The managerial rationale penetrated universities and significantly diminished collegiality and 'esprit de corps' by differencing tasks and responsibilities within faculties. If certain academics are still resisting this managerialism, others have adopted these new norms, in a more or less strategic way, to profit from advantages, to conquer new positions of power, or just simply because they agree with the current transformations. Academics have also been the victims of a more general criticism addressed against academic institution accused of having a bureaucratic order which is not adjusted to changes in its environment and to the challenges of globalisation.

As Hirschman demonstrates, the reactionary rhetoric had several arguments in the fight against progressive ideas by accrediting theses with perversity, futility and jeopardising public action (Hirschman 1991). Applied to higher education policies, this rhetoric has shorn up the accusation against the academic world and the democratisation of higher education systems. Under the rule of perverse effect, the quality objective has generated increasing bureaucracy and a decline in standards. Higher education systems, by consecrating democratisation transformed into mass expansion, have increased the number of academics and civil servants in charge of students and have impacted costs and public expenditure. Furthermore, the increase in student enrolments has devaluated diplomas and diminished standards in curricula. Under the rule of futility (or inanity), higher education policies have not raised deprived students' achievement rates despite the rise in public expenditure. This rhetoric argues against the failure of students, the increase in the dropout rate and the low rate of professional inclusion among graduates. Finally, the thesis of jeopardising public action argues that the equalisation of teaching conditions is threatening freedom of choice and traditional values. Fearing a loss of distinction, some higher education institutions have reacted under the pressure from interest groups and have increased the selectivity of their recruitment by providing options and diverse curricula to the most gifted (or deserving) students and in organising mobility and equivalences between foreign diplomas to maintain a differentiated choice. The most popular and prestigious institutions have sought to maintain their comparative advantages while the competition between students has increased worldwide.

Another recurrent criticism, in the rhetoric used during the past few decades, is the denunciation of academics enclosed in their ivory tower (Soley 1995). At the same time, it raises the idea of an entrepreneurial university focused on innovation and new technologies. The 'third mission' of the university, beyond teaching and research, is to engage academics in entrepreneurship and to promote new relationships with business and industry. Beyond the commercialisation of research findings into patents and licences, which is ignored when academics are accused of not contributing to the economy, it is expected that they are involved in different services for the community, the well-being and inclusion of students. The promotion of the mode 2 of knowledge production, or the triple helix, has maintained the idea that the enclosure of the academic in his or her discipline and scientific community, without transdisciplinary openness and an interest in the impact on the society and the economy, is a gesture of egoism, conservatism and scientific ineffectiveness. Though this stance varies from one academic discipline to another, and from institution to another, new managerial norms imposed on research programmes and units are driving an increasing number of academics to adhere to a collective project and to spend time for the institution beyond their teaching and research interests.

In parallel to this criticism, it is possible to trace a clear pedagogical rhetoric inspired by the developments of psychology and one which denounces the lack of consideration for student learning in academic teaching (Newble and Cannon 2013). By reflecting on the curriculum and the formalisation of skills, and eager to inscribe its epistemology into behavioural sciences and within the scope of a quest for effectiveness, this science, at the crossroads of expertise and training, has widely defended the idea that the design of technologies, devices and methods can improve the link between teaching and learning and that it is necessary to identify key success and failure factors among students. It has since become part of the development of an expert and scientific nebula, a specialist of information-based technologies, which proposes to reverse the established order and to revolutionise training particularly through e-learning and MOOCs. It coexists, as we shall see later, with knowledge management, and legitimates a bridge between pedagogical issues and the recent theories of cognition and neurosciences. This rhetoric has largely penetrated the field of political decision-making and gives additional arguments to those who wish to liberate the university from the conception of magisterium which is considered to be outdated and one which produces inequalities.

Critical work borrows its discursive forms from a progressive or conservative rhetoric and delegitimises the academic profession for its assigned role in the democratisation of access and knowledge in higher education. The academic tradition is denounced for its lack of creativity and innovation while it is presented as being enclosed in its institutional routines and mandarin positions which are out of synch with the dynamics of change. Instead of the inherited rules of academic culture, claims are now being made for the originality of new modes of knowledge production. The weight of relationships of dependency and patronage is perceived as an obstacle to entrepreneurial freedom. Paternalism and the cult of secrecy are criticised on behalf of transparency and democratic access to knowledge that has to be discussed, negotiated and shared between academics, policymakers, stakeholders and practitioners. Hierarchical relationships are recused for more horizontal and networking coordination. The modalities of trade unionist and collegial representation are considered as a democratic deficit based on power relationships and influence, while the new governance of universities needs to overcome local stakes and corporatist divides to take into consideration the challenges of globalisation and the internationalisation of activities. The extent of market forces and competition between higher education institutions has led to an erosion of the local and a mindset of satisfying students and partners' needs. At the very least, the university has to be more effective and profitable by better recognising skills and developing assessment and a management capable of rationalising the provision of training and research programmes.

As Luc Boltanski and Eve Chiapello (2005) explain, criticism uses different principles of legitimation to make a claim for justice and the common good. It aims to challenge the instituted trials which define the rules at the university by advocating reformist proposals. This criticism has a corrective orientation when it aims to make things fairer by producing different norms and recommendations. It claims a certain legitimacy and has to be embedded in an acceptable order of justification for the many. On the contrary, radical criticism does not aim to make trials fairer but to replace them by others, e.g. to transform living conditions for institutions and individuals. In that sense, the advocates of the new spirit of capitalism intend to radically transform the academic world by instituting multiple but non-visible shifts via the institutionalisation and codification of new trials disqualifying the old ones. This transformation role has been partially delegated to New Public Management. We shall now present its different trajectories in the European Space of Higher Education.

Trajectories and Trends of New Public Management in Higher Education

During the 1980s, the first wave of reforms of public administration was to improve the efficiency of public services and to end with bureaucratic planning and decision-making (Bleiklie and Michelsen 2013). The implementation of decentralised management with cost control has shaped a neo-Taylorian state. Policymakers wanted mainly to transfer managerial practices from the private sector into administration to guarantee performance and productivity in accordance with a decentralised accountancy of rarefied resources. The second wave, during the 1990s, introduced a market-oriented regulation, particularly privatisation and contracts for a certain number of services and administrative units. The development of partnerships and the externalisation of certain resources have blurred the boundaries between the public and the private sectors. Progressively, New Public Management was imposed and it has broken existing conventions within the state administration. Contrary to the former period, the aim has been to set up 'best practices' and to restructure public services through semi-autonomous agencies able to govern themselves by respecting a framework defined by the state. This transformation was made according to the following principles (Clarke et al. 2000):

- A reconfiguration of public budgets to be more transparent and accountable, with costs directly linked to outputs (or results) and no more inputs (or resources), and results measured by quantitative performance indicators
- A new vision of organisations according to a chain of principal/agent relationships in which low costs are sought and a network of contracts linked strongly incentives and performance
- A disaggregation of administrative functions according to quasi-contractual or quasi-market forms by the introduction of a distinction between sellers and buyers, the removal of classical structures of service supply and planning
- The openness to other service providers to create competition between public agencies or between public agencies and private companies
- A devolution process with smaller size agencies to enable users to easily change of services and to limit claiming procedures and trials in courts

However, the restructuring of the state has not been limited to giving predominance to market regulation over classical mechanisms of redistribution or event to implementing new management to gain productivity and reduce public expenditures. This 'reinvention' of government has been supported by a technical and organisational instrumentation aiming to reduce costs and to improve effectiveness in the administration criticised of its excessive bureaucracy. But it has also been relayed by a rhetoric of change aiming to transform the culture of the organisation itself. The objective was insufflating 'entrepreneurial spirit' in public services. This rhetoric took different forms, but it has been strongly held in managerial texts, official documents, political discourses and strategic programmes (Clarke and Newman 1997).

The Principles of New Public Management

As John Clarke and Janet Newman wrote, this rhetoric is based on diverse principles of justification. A first narrative of this managerial theory has praised the natural character of change in accordance with the organicist and evolutionist metaphor asking for the adaptation of administration to its new environmental conditions. The development of the administrative organisation, for its health improvement, required a strategic plan more external than internal centred. Another justification considered the administration exposed to dangers and hostile forces that forced the public service to defend itself by forging alliances and elaborating adjusted answers for its survival. Some more progressive arguments claimed that a 'reinvention' or a 'new vision' was necessary to break with the ossified and bureaucratic order. Administration had to be improved by becoming more innovative and entrepreneurial. Other discourses were using metaphors of discontinuity, instability, fluidity and even chaos, to demonstrate that public services entered in a new wave of turbulence and were called to an ineluctable revolution. Finally, a whole series of arguments insisted on an imperative and complete restructuring based on managerial principles to improve the performance of public agents. All these narratives were narrowly complementary and linked in official documents and papers claiming for reforms.

Three topics were particularly at stake: the focus on consumers, the suppression or bureaucracy and the dynamic of change. The focus on consumers was a good means to challenge the monopoly of public services' supply. Compared to the private management, bureaucracy was considered as the worst example of ossification privileging stability over adaptation, repetition over innovation, rules over responsibilities, hierarchy over performance and statutes over users. Change sustained by 'entrepreneurship' would be a good mean to extend 'leadership' and to institute an 'entrepreneurial governance' able to meet the challenges of modernisation and to fight against the decline of competitiveness.

However, there were different configurations in the advancement of New Public Management worldwide. As Pollitt and Bouckaert wrote (2004), two differentiated groups emerged in NPM trajectories: the 'modernisers' which believe in the role of the state but recognise the need for important changes in the way administrative systems are organised. These changes imply budgetary reforms focused on the measurement of results and performance, the easing of statutory rigidities in public services, increased decentralisation and devolution from ministries to agencies and local authorities, increased quality of public services for citizens and the development of digital technologies (Dunleavy and Hood 1994; Hood and Margetts 2007). Within this group of modernisers, some countries, like France, give more importance to managerial modernisation (in other words, focusing on systems, tools and techniques) in a hierarchical and technocratic framework, while others, like the Scandinavian countries, focus more on a participative modernisation (giving more weight to local governments and the mobilisation of citizens). The move towards privatisation of statist organisations is a selective and graduated one, giving priority to intermediary entities between the public and the private sectors.

The other group, the 'competitors', which includes the UK and New Zealand, gives importance to competition in the public sector and facilitating quasi-markets as large-scale contracts, contract-based appointments and performance pay for civil servants, reducing the gap between the public and the private sectors. They are fervent advocates of importing managerial techniques from business, as quality insurance and benchmarking. However, most of these countries have distanced themselves from the conception of minimum state intervention and the aim of strongly reducing public services via privatisation, as it was the case during the Thatcher period in the UK in the beginning of the 1980s and during the government of the National Party in New Zealand in the beginning of the 1990s. Only the USA has truly been driven by the market and private regulations.

New Public Management in Higher Education

Different explanations have been advanced to characterise the introduction of New Public Management in the higher education systems. According to Clark (1983), advanced industrial countries have developed different forms of 'coordination' of higher education which are located on three axes: a more market-like coordination (e.g. the USA), a more state-induced coordination (e.g. the USSR and Sweden) and a form of coordination which is above all based on the ruling of an academic oligarchy (e.g. Italy, France and the UK). Van Vught reduced Clark's three-dimensional space of governance to a two-dimensional one and suggested that a state control model and a state supervising model should be differentiated (Van Vught 1989; Van Vught and Westerheijden 1994). The state control model is present in many European states. It is characterised by the strong authority of state bureaucracy, on the one hand, and the relatively strong position of the academic oligarchy within universities on the other hand. The state interferes in order to regulate access conditions, the curriculum, degree requirements, the examination systems and the appointment and remuneration of academic staff. The academic community maintains considerable authority in the regulation of internal university affairs in particular concerning education and research content. The state supervising model is to be found in countries with an Anglo-Saxon tradition and is characterised by a weaker authority of state bureaucracy. In this case authority is divided between a strong academic community and the internal administration of universities.

Ferlie et al. (2008) identified five main NPM reforms in higher education that have been commonly implemented in Europe. Firstly, market-based reforms have flourished. This first of these concerns reforms aimed at increasing the level of competition among institutions, staff, students and territories. In many cases, increasing competition comes with economic evaluation and exchanges of goods and services that were previously not considered to be of economic value, thus leading to the constitution of markets or quasi-markets (Paradeise et al. 2009). Secondly, budgetary constraints have been tightened through reduced funding or by the introduction of new budgetary instruments based on indicators and output rather than on inputs. Thirdly, budgetary reforms often implied a stronger emphasis on performance and explicit performance measurement, assessment and monitoring of research and teaching. Furthermore, there has been a concentration of funds in the best performing higher education institutions and a broader vertical differentiation among higher education institutions. Finally, institutional governance has become a crucial issue. University leaders are expected to play managerial roles. Executive leadership has been strengthened at the expense of collegial power in deliberative, representative bodies, while the academic community has been transformed into staff and submitted to human resource-based management.

Other work has demonstrated that the pace, methods and extent of reform and policy change vary across countries (Bleiklie and Lange 2010; Bleiklie et al. 2011; Paradeise et al. 2009). Reforms and instruments have been largely contained within national higher education traditions, and the new levers of action were in fact digested by the environment they were supposed to impact. Implementation processes have tended to follow incremental rather than radical trajectories. But a tendency towards systematic reform has become more perceptible since the turn of the century, and more powerful funding, evaluation and governance instruments have been introduced in countries like France, Norway, Germany and Switzerland. However, some other ideas influenced HE reforms over the same period of time, and the vertical form of steering inspired by NPM has been complemented by forms of network governance (Bleiklie et al. 2011). Firstly, some policies encouraged the inclusion of stakeholders in academic affairs, on institutional boards and in the decision-making process on research funding, thus widening the networks of actors involved in decision-making and opening up the introduction of nonacademic criteria, principles and preferences in such processes. Secondly, centralised ways of steering have been challenged by the participation of inter- and supranational actors in HE. As a result, most teaching or research projects now mobilise a combination of resources from different sources and rely on multiple levels and actors. Finally, academic autonomy is often explicitly promoted and has come to mean institutional autonomy, while it is increasingly perceived as the competency given to institutional leaders to make strategic decisions on behalf of their institutions. Thus, budgetary reforms imply less detailed regulation and more leeway for institutional leaders to allocate funding as they wish. However increased autonomy also tends to be circumscribed by increasing standardisation in terms of procedures and performance criteria that may severely limit the space for strategic decision-making.

Some common trends can also be identified in the new relationships between academics and higher education institutions. Universities are increasingly empowered as institutional actors, and they exercise more control over academic activities and academic careers, despite persisting variations and national specificities (Musselin 2013). Firstly, many competences and decisions previously managed by national or regional public authorities have been partially or completely transferred to higher education and research institutions. This impacts the academic profession, while the supervision of staff and human resource management and academic careers has been delegated to universities. They have become responsible for opening and redistributing job positions and transforming them into casual posts and contractual arrangements. New professors are no longer civil servants and less and less of them are recruited on tenure positions. Furthermore, university leaders are introducing merit-based salaries, contracts by objectives, advancement rules and are increasing their influence over decisions pertaining to the development of academic careers, their level of income and the reward system.

The shift in the management of careers can be characterised by an increase in formalisation and rationalisation. Requirements to get access to the academic profession are more standardised than they were some years ago. When one looks at a job announcement, it is clear that the compulsory requirements as well as the information to be included in the application files are expanding and becoming more precise. The very informal, sometimes very interpersonal and local arrangements that might have prevailed before are now criticised and replaced by more formalised, more (apparently) transparent and more intensive processes. The types of candidates have also evolved; recruiting international staff and hiring outside of traditional circles are considered as an evidence for performance, reputation and quality (if not excellence). Regular appraisals of the tasks carried out by academics once they have been recruited have also been introduced. In many countries, regular assessment of teaching has been developed, and it has led to more managerial control over academics and evaluations, with promotions and rewards being more closely linked. While the differentiation between academics has been accentuated, some universities have introduced bonuses and abandoned national salary scales for an individual management of academic careers. In parallel to the traditional definition of academic activities and positions, there is also a trend towards the emergence of new functions held by new professionals with an academic background and achieving tasks at the frontier between administrative and scientific activities: rewriting research projects, working on technological platforms or providing support in technology transfer offices. The classical divide between academia and administration has thus become blurred, and new professional groups are developing and transforming universities into multi-professional organisations.

The Trials of Managerialism and Professionalism

New managerialism is a concept used to refer to ideas about changes in the way that publicly funded institutions are managed, following the widespread restructuring of welfare services in Western societies (Deem 1998, 2001). The concept refers both to ideologies about the application of techniques, values and practices of NPM derived from the private sector to the management of organisations concerned with the provision of public services, and to the actual use of these techniques and practices in publicly funded organisations (Ferlie et al. 2008; Clarke and Newman 1997; Hood 1991). Those promoting new managerialist discourses claim that the ideas of new managerialism are based purely on an objective search for efficiency, effectiveness and excellence, with assumptions about the continuous improvement of organisations often a further underlying theme. The search for new sources of finance to replace declining government funding of higher education has provide justifications for adopting new managerialism in higher education. New organisational and management practices have been imposed to academic departments, while new forms of evaluation and audits of teaching and learning have been introduced. In the UK, universities have been exhorted to raise the standards of educational provision, and the quality of their teaching, learning and research outcomes, while prevailing government and funding policies also require annual 'efficiency gains' to be made, resulting in a declining unit of resource per student taught, less money for equipment and a decrease in research resourcing (Deem and Brehony 2005).

The Dissolution of an Institutional Compromise

Managerialism includes attempts to change the regimes and cultures of organisations and to alter the values of public sector employees so that they more closely resemble those found in the private 'for profit' sector (MacLaughin et al. 2002). Clarke and Newman (1997) suggest that 'new managerialism' can be detected in the organisational forms, cultures and narratives and management technologies of organisations. Historically, the building of the state was structured through two modes of coordination: bureaucratic administration and professionalism. The public service defines a compromise between the two, and a set of values, codes and practices then become institutionalised. It is distinguishable from the second mode of coordination: managerialism. The first mode of coordination is embedded in the centre of the state through its bureaucratic administration. The development of public administrations in Europe consisted of transforming complex tasks of evaluation and calculation into stable and predictable forms supported by rules and regular controls. In higher education, the administration promises that each student will be treated fairly in accordance with rules and current administrative procedures. Equitable treatment is also a specific feature because the public service is assumed to be socially and politically neutral. Despite the criticism of bureaucracy, the latter was an alternative to the patronage, corruption and nepotism which existed before its inception. The administration proposed a system of government treating everybody impartially without consideration of his or social status, wealth and influence. The principles of bureaucracy guaranteed the isolation of politics from personal rumours, passions and circumstances. What is often described as the 'depersonalisation' of relationships in a bureaucratic order was in fact the result of the separation between the public and the private.

But the public administration was not sufficient to guarantee the state's prerogatives. It has to be supported by an expertise capable of solving social and political problems beyond bureaucratic skills. The second mode of coordination, professionalism, is a legacy from the expansion of education systems. In difference to bureaucratic administration, this expertise is based on a relative autonomy and embodied by a person. Professionals, like academics, particularly during the moments of post-war reconstruction, were called upon to serve the common good and public interest and in higher education to work on democratisation. Their expertise and knowledge were considered as means to support economic development and investment in human capital. The neutrality of academics parallelises bureaucratic neutrality. The former promises impersonal justice while the latter promises disinterested service. Framed by professional codes and values, academics were called upon to define a professional ethos serving universalistic values and the public interest.

Managerialism has dissolved this compromise through a restructuration of higher education in terms of cost control and neo-Taylorist management leading to the introduction of competition, a focus on decentralisation and autonomy, the systematic search for quality via evaluation and a greater awareness for the provision of services. Different steps have been associated with this restructuration: reworking budgets in terms of accounts, measuring costs and performance by indicators, considering relationships between actors from the principal–agent model or in accordance with a nexus of performance contracts, opening up competition and public–private partnerships, de-concentrating services and reducing their size.

The market is not the only reference for managerialism and the restructuring of public services. Management is considered as a means of recovering a discipline and mastering costs to increase productivity and generate 'added value'. This managerial ideology proliferated during the 1980s–1990s, while new 'theories' emerged with regard to excellence, participative management and the organisation of learning, quality and total management. Discourses on management have been diversified and have justified strategic improvement plans for effectiveness and quality in higher education. Some of them consider change as natural by adopting evolutionist perspectives claiming a necessary and ineluctable adaptation. Others announced a series of dangers and threats coming from the international environments of universities for which it is necessary to find alliances and allies. Some theorists insist on the role of management for its capacity to mobilise people in an international process of transformation of the academic organisation. The latter justified a necessity for greater flexibility or 're-engineering' favourable to the new mode of knowledge production and sharing.

The Managerial Discourse on Professionalism

The discourse of professionalism has been taken over, rebuilt and reused as an instrument of managerial control, as Julia Evetts explained (2003, 2009). Professionalism is not only the translation of a professional ethic or the mastery of an expertise; it is also the expression of norms externally applied to working situations. This professionalism may correspond to a control of the profession itself, but for the majority of employees, it is the result of injunctions of the organisation they work for (rules, norms, orders, hierarchy, etc.). The 'new professionalism' is similar to a disciplinary mechanism in that it works in contexts to inculcate 'appropriate' identities, conduct and practices among workers (Evetts 2011). Thus, professional autonomy is inscribed into a network of constraints governing conduct at a distance. In universities, two different forms of professionalism have been juxtaposed: an 'organisational' professionalism which is progressively replacing an 'occupational' professionalism.

The 'occupational' professionalism is a discourse historically built among academics, and it includes a certain form of collegial authority. It implies relationships of trust between them and the students. It is based on autonomy and judgement between peers. It depends on a common training and recruitment system, a long-term socialisation and the development of a professional identity and culture. Controls are operationalised by academics themselves and guided by ethical codes defined and regulated by professional networks or associations. By contrast, the ideal type of organisational professionalism emphasises a discourse of quality control which is being increasingly used by managers within academic institutions. It includes forms of legal-rational authority and hierarchical structures in terms of responsibility and decision-making. It implies an increasing standardisation of working procedures and practices as well as managerial controls. It is based on external forms of regulation and the measurement of results, performance, targets as well as audits.

Of course, the new managerialism maintains elements of hierarchy, bureaucracy and the standardisation of professional practices which are linked to traditional forms of work at the university. But one part of the strategy is to create professionals and managers capable of identifying themselves with a new professionalism, quality and support of students. Certain academics are tempted by the ideological components of empowerment, innovation, autonomy and responsibility. In fact, this new professionalism is translated in a demand for an explicit assessment of professional skills, for more control and audits and for performance-based targets which are reinterpreted as indications of a good, accountable and competitive professional. But it is also a means of controlling academics. It can be achieved by normative values and self-motivation, the adoption of the language of quality and the satisfaction of student needs and ideologies of entrepreneurship and teamwork. It is also a discourse of individualisation and competition in which individual performance is linked to the university's success or failure. Academic work is subjected to powerful mechanisms of control, and values of professionalism are used to promote an efficient management of activities.

Progressively, managers have gained a new legitimacy instead of administrators. Compared to 'paternalist bureaucrats', they were judged more able to define organisational effectiveness and performance; they were considered as not enclosed in dusty regulations but more concerned by innovation and better focused on client and markets. They were 'pragmatic and strategic', while bureaucrats were 'dogmatic' and 'authoritative'. The transformations of coordinated actions have been extended to collective conventions within the public administration. To be competitive, it was necessary to weaken trade unions and the principles of collective negotiation, to privilege individualised work contracts and tasks aligned on performance and productivity objectives, to reduce the size of administration units and to make them more flexible, to extend part-time work and to relativise social rights and civil servants' statuses.

New Organisational Configurations and Relationships

Relationships between services and units have been transformed as well as those between the administrations themselves. New Public Management has generated a regulation of hybrid and more or less decentralised organisations, in competition with each other, in which managers had to develop competition, to control budgets, performance and profitability, and quality of services for users. Three main conceptions of the managerial thought have been claimed for justifying these new configurations (Clarke and Newman 1997): core business, ownership and audit.

The idea of 'core business' comes from the fragmentation of public services' provision into a competitive environment composed of quasi-markets. The aim has been to break with complex organisations and to focus on the diversity of demands. The reorganisation of administration has reconsidered the activity of agents in restrictive ways in giving priority to effectiveness and performance. The notion of 'ownership', according to a conception borrowed from the economic theory of property rights, aimed to better managed conflicts of property in the services' provision for users. The mission delegated to management has been to determine who holds the responsibility for the service and to arbitrate between 'conflicts of territory' between administrations and to enhance competition and diminish expenditures at the local level. This competitive localism had to overcome more general considerations about the universal service and neutral delivery. Finally, the explosion of audit, according to the expression of Michael Power (1994), has characterised a strong growth of internal and external assessment tools to make organisations accountable. Audit has been imposed to build a minimum of trust between clients and providers, between the government and its multiple agencies, but it was a strategic response to the deregulation of public services because it enabled to impose a common discipline and it generated isomorphic trends in a strongly loose-coupled system (Power 1997). Developments of audit led to reallocate resources from production of services to information and control systems, and they intensified competition between organisations and administrative units particularly by setting up performance indicators and dashboards.

Indeed, the responsibility for efficiency and effectiveness has been delegated to different organisational levels, while costs have been externalised to the private sector. With this information policy, New Public Management has been able to organise services focused on clients and to develop surveys, focus groups and other marketing techniques to improve quality. It has produced a new representation of the user from quantitative data determining preferences, expectations and satisfaction. In discrediting informal judgements from public agents, who was trying to resist to this consumerist discourse, this information has been used to develop quality insurance procedures and to extend performance criteria.

However, the academics' control of their own work remains important, while their professional associations and trade unions are seeking to maintain their relative advantage in peer regulation. By assisting governments in the implementation of new regulations, they continue to have political and moral control of their members. Indeed, academics, as a professional bureaucracy, historically gained autonomy in their working practices and they have profited from strong legitimacy and power. Furthermore, knowledge production does not easily fit within standardisation and measurement. Therefore, many academics can escape from performance controls and accountability. However, without speaking of a decline, it seems that organisational techniques have been developed to control occupational professionalism, such as the imposition of targets and indicators for academic work, and have ended up regulating research and teaching activities. The increase in forms to fill in, the development of quality indicators, the standardisation of working procedures and the spread of information-based technologies are also means of controlling academics' productivity and creativity. The strengthening of competition for access to resources has entailed changes in professional relationships and working practices. The building of trust and collegial solidarity has been transformed into supervision, assessments and external audits. In turn, this has affected the relations between academics and their institutions. When individual performance assessments are linked to the success or failure of a faculty or research unit, it threatens professional cohesion and mutual cooperation. Indeed, competition between individuals threatens teamwork and collegial support.

Paradoxes and Trials Among Academics

The growth of managerialism and new professionalism among academics has created a number of trials and paradoxes (Hood and Peters 2004). Firstly, there are trials of strength in the sense that individuals are constrained to fit their actions to standards, devices and instruments which have been imposed on them because of new institutional rules and managerial empowerment of their activities, tasks and responsibilities. Academics have no control on the introduction of quality procedures or on the definition of the criteria used to assess research by an external agency. Indeed, it is difficult for them to fight against managerial decision-making diminishing their budget and forcing them to be accountable. There are trials of justification in the sense that academics' actions take place in a space of legitimation with regard to certain conceptions of the common good and criticism directed against them. These trials, which are based on different judgement categories, emerge in interactions between people when the existing order is being challenged and when injustices are revealed. For example, a debate can occur within a faculty council about the allocation criteria for the budget allocated to the university or about the participation of students in the definition of curricula and assessments. The occurrence of a trial is conditioned by the degree of reflexivity among the engaged individuals who become more aware of changes in the social world, for example, by the fact that debates within the faculty are linked to the implementation of quality insurance at the university. It is also determined by the degree of certainty faced by the protagonists, whether the trial is instituted or not, e.g. whether it produces durable effects on the institution. For example, a change in the rules for allocating tasks and activities between academics, due to the introduction of a managerial logic, would be more disputed because of its consequences on peer regulation, while a change in national regulations about the curriculum have more uncertain effects and can be diluted in the daily management of teaching and learning.

Trials of justification are based on a categorisation of the social world and the equivalence established between heterogeneous elements gathered and placed under a similar convention of justice or common good. Trials of strength correspond to shifts which transform the social world of academia and which academics are not able to master, identify and categorise. These trials are inherent sections of managerial control and characterise:

- Transformations in the recognition of work and academic effectiveness which delegitimise professional bureaucracy's values and ideals based on collegiality, loyalty and solidarity, to raise modes of commitment focused on individual motivation and success, the building of a project and an entrepreneurial identity
- A new regime of responsibility and decision-making based on the delegation of tasks and activities, accountability and procedures focusing on the search for effectiveness and performance to the detriment of peer regulation and an attachment to hierarchy and the traditional community
- The adoption of managerial techniques and instruments presented as objective, adaptable and flexible, and justifying a dynamic of change, the search for excellence and quality and the extension of partnerships against the arbitrary power of interests or partisan strategies and selfishness
- The shift from a hierarchical organisation to a networking organisation overcoming the divide between the public and the private, associating the community of policymakers and stakeholders in decision-making, transforming the modalities of knowledge production and sharing and supporting creativity and innovation against the unproductivity of the academic enclosed in his or her ivory tower and rooted in his community

The new professionalism, giving autonomy academics but also controlling them, align their activities on managerial standards and requirements while they negotiate between different conventions. The first one refers to their tradition and practices, combining their experiences and sense of justice into a professional vision emerging from their daily interactions and practices, self-regulation and forms of political representation inherited from tradition. The second one characterises a regime of performance linked to the state and NPM agendas and expectations, seeking standardisation and the measurement of academic tasks and responsibilities from external pressure and incentives. This new regulation does not only concern the internal organisation and work of academics but has now been extended to the ways they produce knowledge in a new academic regime.

The Knowledge-Based University: A New Academic Regime?

Academics are not only professionals working in a bureaucracy converted to New Public Management principles. They are also involved in knowledge production, for example, via research they contribute to the evolutions of their discipline (Bleiklie and Henkel 2005). However, this knowledge production, in a managerial environment, is itself subjected to performance-based assessments as attested by the development of journal metrics and rankings. Moreover, the growth of the mode 2 of knowledge production, promoted in an increasing number of calls for tender and projects, has made funding completely dependent on expected results and their impact on society and the economy. Incentives for interdisciplinary research have diminished the importance of knowledge produced by a dedicated scientific community. Academics are put under pressure to extend the types and contents of knowledge outside the university and to produce 'truth-oriented knowledge' or 'utility-oriented knowledge' on what works. Some new links have been established between fundamental research, technological development and applied research; some new partnerships have been created with business and industry as well as some research clusters and transfer platforms. These new interests and alliances specify new regimes of knowledge which are no longer based on the academic tradition and the Enlightenment model.

The Entrepreneurial University: An Emerging Concept

The notion of an entrepreneurial or networking university has become popular in international organisations' reports and recommendations, as well as in textbooks written by researchers and experts promoting knowledge management (Lewis et al. 2005). It is too early to evaluate the impact of this new knowledge regime in the current work of academics and organisations in higher education institutions. It is easy to adopt a fallback position by denouncing the utopic feature of these statements, or the diversity of paths being taken by the evolutions in higher education systems, or the partial and uncertain features of certain implementations. In the following pages, we shall consider this new academic regime as an ideal type or new ideological configuration authenticating a new stage in the implementation of academic capitalism. It consecrates a new representation of the university and academic work which, if it is far from being achieved, produces a vision penetrating the discourses of international organisations as well as those of experts and policymakers. It participates more or less directly in a radical criticism of existing institutions. This normative literature, beyond its technocratic aspects, has a strong moral tonality when defining what the future academic will look like. It conveys an ideology which, while it denounces the academic tradition, legitimises rules of conduct, managerial precepts, visions of higher education as well as new aspirations for desired evolutions or changes to be implemented.

There is now a considerable international literature addressing the notion of what has been termed 'the entrepreneurial university' in reference to Burton Clark (Wasser 1990; Clark 1998; OECD 2004; Barsony 2003; Jacob et al. 2003; Etzkowitz 2004; Gibb and Hannon 2006; Kirby 2006; Lazzeroni and Piccaluga 2003; Wong et al. 2007; Mohrman et al. 2008). In 2004, Etzkowitz, another leading writer on this issue, put forward five propositions concerning the entrepreneurial university concept, namely, that such institutions focus on the capitalisation of knowledge, managing interdependence with industry and government, but are nevertheless independent of any particular sphere, are 'hybrid' in managing the tension between independence and interdependence and embody reflexivity, via a continuous renewal of internal structures.

Much of the literature on university entrepreneurship assumes an institutional focus in understanding how the organisation and performance of universities have addressed and adapted to the challenges of the shift towards an entrepreneurial regime. Rothaermel and Hess (2007) identified many studies that addressed the impact of organisational design on university entrepreneurship. These studies focused on incentive systems, university status, location, culture, administrators, research focus, technology transfer experience and the role of the university in the local economy. Other studies sought to identify and measure the impact of formal knowledge transfer programmes, cooperative research agreements with industry, research support, licensing, marketing activities, the quality of commercialisation (licences, patents), involvement in joint research ventures and the existence of incubators and science parks (Mollas-Gallart et al. 2002; Siegel et al. 2003). Collectively this literature provides a comprehensive portrait of the entrepreneurial aspects of contemporary universities and aptly illustrates the system of entrepreneurial innovation.

Over the past decade, the way in which universities disseminate knowledge has been analysed (Lee 1996; Mendoza and Berger 2005). An almost universal approach to dealing with this problem via such knowledge transfer institutions and mechanisms was the creation of science and technology parks, adjacent to, and sometimes owned by, universities; the development of the role of intermediaries such as industrial liaison offices; the opening of technology transfer and information offices (Chapple et al. 2004); the development of student and staff incubators (Ylinenpää 2001); the launching of new venture capital programmes for staff and students; the development of clearer IP policies and arrangements for the licensing and patenting of university know-how (Baldini et al. 2006); the organisation of spin-off activities; and the creation of venture and loan funds. A growing body of literature (Hughes 2003; Link and Scott 2006; Dooley and Kirk 2007; Abreu et al. 2009) argues that the key to successful knowledge transfer is having in place a process of continuous dialogue building up social networks (Nicolaou and Birley 2003) and success based on the development of strong personal (as opposed to institutional) relationships over time leading to the creation of trust (a key element in entrepreneurial activity).

In addition to the core missions of teaching and research, the newly emphasised and frequently commercially oriented activities are now framed in what is called a new Third Mission (Etzkowitz 1997; Laredo 2007; Mollas-Gallart et al. 2002). In the broadest terms, this mission is defined as everything that is not traditional teaching and research (Jongbloed et al. 2008), while elsewhere this term has been more narrowly conceived in terms of knowledge and technology transfer (Hackett and Dilts 2004). In both instances the commercial engagement of universities has become a cornerstone of national and regional innovation policies. It is in the field of knowledge transfer and engagement that the regional role of universities has been most highlighted (Boucher et al. 2003; Charles 2003, 2006; IHEP 2007; Arbo and Benneworth 2007). There is an obvious potential link between a university's contribution to innovation and its contribution to a region's development (Smith 2007). This link is reflected in the growing focus since the 1980s of European government regional policies on innovation and technology development and the exploitation of university knowledge (particularly with the support of the European Commission). Worldwide, the models of MIT (O'Shea et al. 2007), Silicon Valley and North Carolina in the USA have become iconic along with the Cambridge Phenomenon (Segal 1985) in the UK. There are, however, many other European examples, for example, Linkoping in Sweden, Turku in Finland and Twente in the Netherlands (Braun and Diensberg 2007). The 'entrepreneurial university' label is, therefore, frequently associated with the notion of the university as a regional innovation hub (Sole-Parellada et al. 2001). It appears to be widely accepted in this context that successful innovation must involve a highly interactive process of engagement among universities, industry and government.

This engagement process has been labelled the triple helix model (Benner and Sandström 2000; Shinn 2002; Leyesdorff and Meyer 2003; Zhou 2008; Etzkowitz 2008). The model portrays an interactive process of research funding through private and public partnerships focused on the development of research and learning, by all partners, from this process. This model is not solely a regional one, but has a strong regional orientation particularly when it engages with small and medium-sized firms. It assumes that entrepreneurs will work with the university and that academic staff will work in the company, that the partnership may also link with other sources of funding and that there will be clear patterns of coordination (Etzkowitz 2008). The model is also associated with the mode 2 concept of a university as discussed in chapter "An Epistemic Governance of European Education" (Gibbons et al. 1994; Nowotny et al. 2003).

Academic Entrepreneurs and Leaders

According to this vision, entrepreneurial universities have a strong bottom-up development and initiative focus, empowering individuals at all levels of the organisation and giving them freedom of action. The dominant controlling and motivating parameter is not systems but shared missions, values and culture and trust (Davies 2001; Daumard 2001). Thus, one of the universities' major challenges and opportunities is to build entrepreneurship upon the considerable freedom enjoyed by departments and individuals, traditionally embodied in the notion of a 'community of scholars' shifting towards a 'community of practice' (Todorovic et al. 2005; Wenger 1998).

According to this vision, universities can be characterised as pluralistic organisations with different departments having very different external orientations and indeed academic values. While a strong central steering group, as argued by Clark, may therefore be desirable in reinforcing the mission, the major challenge is that of placing ownership of innovation and change with academic departments, finding champions therein who, perhaps incrementally, can move innovation up the departmental agenda. By stimulating academic initiative, formal strategic planning and mission statements may be less important than the encouragement of flexible strategic thinking and the integration of action with strategy when confronting opportunity and threats (Shattock 2000). Entrepreneurial innovation also requires flexibility in organisation design to allow the growth of overlap and interdependency among different departments, projects and even individuals by adjusting flexibly to the demands of society for new knowledge combinations. This may lead to the Schumpeterian 'creative destruction' (Schumpeter 1934), as these departments are slow to adapt, or they simply fade or merge into new units.

According to this main orthodoxy, there are at least three categories of individuals who can take initiative and create the context in which the entrepreneurial university can thrive (Zaharia and Gibert 2005). The first category includes the 'catalysts', those who instigate entrepreneurship formation and renewal. They shape an environment of collaborative behaviour and challenge the *status quo* and key success factors. These individuals are acknowledged as leaders who build a context of business collaboration and who create a spirit of common purposes and ambition. The second category features the 'doers', those who build on the foundations established by the leaders. They are responsible for the university's entrepreneurial initiatives. Entrepreneurs fall between leaders and operational managers. Their major tasks involve attracting new skills and resources in the support of trust-based university–business relationships, endeavouring to achieve the continuous performance improvement needed to nurture the spirit of common purposes and aspirations, and the creation and pursuit of opportunities in phase with the new ideas the leaders have envisioned. 'Developers', the third category, are those who transform the ideas of the leaders into concrete proposals, which the entrepreneurs then convert into reality. The developers' profile is similar to that of the operational managers, as they link the resources and skills attracted by the entrepreneurs, develop initiatives for the opportunities that the entrepreneurs have opened up and align short- and long-term commitments on the basis of the entrepreneurs' performance metrics.

A key issue is the degree to which the entrepreneurial leader concept sits with the above challenge and functions and how it fits in the entrepreneurial university framework (Schein 1992; Kilgour 1992; Kuratko and Hornsby 1999; Dulewicz 2000; McInnis 2001; Vecchio 2003; Gupta et al. 2004) The result has much in common with 'transformational leadership' (Bass and Riggio 2008; Epitropaki 2001). Intellectual and visionary leadership is needed for two major reasons: firstly, to remove the ideological and 'concept of a university' barriers associated with the entrepreneurial paradigm and, secondly, to carry this through in the particular context of the nature of the university itself and its existing culture, mission and strategy. A key challenge is to create entrepreneurial role models within departments and gradually to build a culture of rewarding innovation in every department rather than a culture of defence. This will require the capacity to identify potential change agents and to build teams around them, encourage risk and protect them. Identifying potential departmental change agents will demand an ability to recognise different styles of leadership and different attitudes associated with potentially enterprising 'clever people' (Goffee and Jones 2007; Bolden et al. 2009). The overall mission would be to infuse departments with entrepreneurial values. The key instrument for

creating transformation will be finding the resources to support innovation in departments, even more so in the present climate.

Considerable attention has also been focused upon the leadership challenges
involved in the changing modes of governance of higher education, particularly in
the UK (CEL 2006, 2007, 2008; Middlehurst et al. 2009; Burgoyne et al. 2009;
Collinson and Collinson 2009). It has been argued that leadership in the departmental context is low status with relatively few rewards for heads of programmes or
chairing departmental committees (Bryman 2009). Identifying potential departmental change agents will demand an ability to recognise different styles of leadership
and different attitudes associated with potentially enterprising 'clever people'
(Goffee and Jones 2007) The overall mission would be to infuse departments with
entrepreneurial values. The key instrument for creating transformation will be finding resource to support innovation in departments, particularly so in the present
climate.

The leader in this respect will need to be the bridge between stakeholders and
departments and between bottom-up and top-down initiatives (Kweik 2008) as such
the persuader and fixer role will be dominant (Boer and Goedegebuure 2009). Some
resources may have to be found for new units and some of which may reach across
traditional discipline and departmental boundaries. Some researchers defend the
idea of an entrepreneurial leadership capacity of academics (Blackmore and
Blackwell 2006) incrementally from existing practice. The nature of the leadership
challenge is also considered, focusing upon personal, relational and institutional
development (Scott et al. 2008). In particular, the focus is upon the issue of 'leading
innovation from the bottom', creating leaders and empowering academics to take
risks and build rewards around new ways of doing things. A key component is network and relationship management and building trust-based relationships with the
local, regional, national and international environment (Bolden et al. 2008). These
researchers set out more broadly, by way of a substantial review of the literature, the
nature of the challenges to leadership of universities arising from changes in the
global environment and the implications for the entrepreneurial design of the higher
education sector (Gibb et al. 2009; Bolden et al. 2009). The focus is upon the impact
of a growing complex and uncertain environment on key areas of university activity
and the leadership challenges involved. The researchers aim to provide a strong
conceptual base for the development and delivery of the Entrepreneurial University
Leaders Programme.

An increasing awareness of the importance of social relations in the leadership
contract, the need for a leader to be given authority by their followers and a realisa-
tion that no one individual is the ideal leader in all circumstances have given rise to
a new school of leadership thought. Referred to as 'shared', 'collective' or 'distributed' leadership, this approach argues for a less formalised model of leadership
(where leadership responsibility is dissociated from the organisational hierarchy)
(Gronn 2009). It is proposed that individuals at all levels in the organisation and in
all roles (not simply those with an overt management dimension) can exert leadership influence over their colleagues and thus influence the overall direction of the
organisation. Recent years have seen burgeoning calls and directives for improved

university leadership. Like the rest of the education sector (schools and further education), the majority of research on leadership and management in higher education concludes that leadership is widely distributed or should be distributed across the academic institution.

The leader in this respect will need to act as a bridge between stakeholders and departments and between bottom-up and top-down initiatives (Kweik 2008). Some resources may have to be found for new units, some of which may reach across traditional discipline and departmental boundaries. But the key will be in building the entrepreneurial leadership capacity of academics (Blackmore and Blackwell 2006) incrementally from existing practice. The nature of the leadership challenge also has to be considered, focusing upon personal, relational and institutional development. In particular, the focus is on the issue of 'leading innovation from the bottom', creating leaders and empowering academics to take risks and innovate.

A Synthesis

At this point, it is possible to formalise the transformations of academic organisations and work during the last decades through configurations displaying the newly instituted trials by management (see below):

	Knowledge		
Bureaucratic control	Academia	Knowledge-based university	**New Public Management**
	Professional bureaucracy	New professionalism	
	Profession		

Historically, the academic profession was shaped as a corporation benefiting from recognition and privilege in the training of the elite and the advice given in public or state affairs. Created in imitation of religious orders, it progressively specialised in disciplines and at the same time research progressively overcome teaching. The state, while maintaining its control at distance, institutionalised the profession by attributing a certain monopoly in knowledge production (bureaucratic control). With the expansion of higher education, state control was strengthened, in particular, by recruitment and career management and also in the organisation of curricula. The profession was organised and structured in trade unions and professional associations. While its disciplinary expertise was recognised, it continued to profit from strong autonomy and peer regulation (the shift from the academia to professional bureaucracy). The implementation of New Public Management challenged this corporatist compromise and deconstructed traditional hierarchies to institute a flexible academic organisation individualising careers and remuneration. While collegiality has lost its power, certain academics have espoused new roles and responsibilities related to NPM, which at the same time has developed new instruments (evaluations, contracts, partnerships) and has proposed a new professional ethos (new professionalism). However, this managerialism has gone beyond the academic profession to tackle the production and management of knowledge (knowledge-based university). These new forms of relationships with business and industry, the role of ICTs in the promotion of a networking university and the recognition of leadership or entrepreneurship functions among academics have projected a new organisation form justified by the mode 2 and triple helix theories (or their followers).

Conventions at Work for a New Homo Academicus

It is time now to return to the sociology of trials formulated by Luc Boltanski and Chiapello (2005). We have seen the distinction established by the two sociologists between a trial of justification and a trial of strength in the analysis of the new spirit of capitalism and the introduction of a managerial logic in the academic organisation. The authors characterise these transformations by describing the emergence of a 'city by projects' in which people's activities are built through a succession of projects and connections in large-scale networks. Flexibility, adaptability and autonomy are qualities recognised as professional skills, while the entrepreneur and the leader have become authentic figures of a connecting and connected world. The 'city by projects' is a grammatical term instituting new relationships between people and organisational devices while at the same time being built against other types of convention defining the academic work. In the following pages, we shall characterise these conventions of the academic work as ideal types allowing the shift from a traditional world to the performative world which is sometimes described in terms of modernisation by managerial language (cf. schema). These conventions are divided into reputational effects (linked to recognition within a community or a network) and competitive effects (linked to the differentiated access to positions and resources). These ideal types describe each time the fabrication of a specific identity related to different principles of justice as Luc Boltanski and Laurent Thévenot described in their book (2006; see also chapter "The Politics of Standards and Quality").

The first figure of academic work is the mandarin as criticised by Pierre Bourdieu (cf. supra). The mandarin has been part of the academic tradition since the Middle Ages and manifested his greatness by his distinction and eloquence. He reigned over a court, in which, like the society of aristocrats described by Norbert Elias, he distributed rank, titles and positions in the knowledge production and animation of the scientific world (Elias 1983). According to this convention, academics were placed under the authority of their peers to whom they were subordinated. They are subjected to a logic of gifts and counter-gifts, of debt and recognition, of building relationships and orders of greatness. The academic had to comply with the rules and conveniences of the academic world. Respect was a principle of conduct as recommendation by a legitimised person. The mandarin system is rooted in the reproduction of the elite marked by a series of trials for distinction which can be found in social gatherings (where conversations establish the legitimacy of claimants to the estate) or in moments of more or less tacit competition and selection preceding an appointment.

The second figure of the academic work is the 'primum inter pares'. The Peer identifies with a collective group and defines his or her greatness by his or her participation in the scientific community and his or her representation of its interests. His or her mandate is attributed by his or her peers, under the form of election, but it is also recognised by the law and regulations. The Peer is invested in academic groups, selection committees, trade unions and professional associations. He or she respectively serves the functions of elected, representative and delegate, and he or she can claim a spirit of solidarity and fights to defend the interests of his or her corporation. Relationships between academics are circumscribed by membership campaigns, elections of representatives and the delegation of skills to a spokesperson. The material environment of interactions includes membership cards, lists and election and representation procedures. This convention of academic work is particularly open to discussion and debate in general assemblies or more limited groups which themselves generate of both membership and mobilisation and rejection and exclusion procedures. The community of peers is subject to trials to determine the legitimacy of representation but also access to positions and resources through assemblies, congresses, meetings and sessions in which proposals and motions are adopted, strategic orientations are chosen or representatives or spokespersons are elected or appointed.

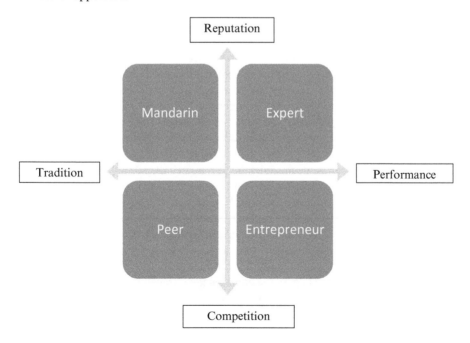

Two other conventions of work can be added to these historical figures. They are related to the transformations of higher education institutions, particularly the implementation of a new managerial and professional order in a context of internationalisation and openness spreading beyond the academic world. These conventions shifted at the same time trials were instituted against the tradition. The figure of the Entrepreneur takes into account an increasingly competitive environment while making projects the backbone of new relationships to be established between academic actors. The Entrepreneur is creative and opportunistic, but also flexible and autonomous. He is supported by creators and innovators in order to meet the challenges of competition particularly in the search for funds and responding to national and international calls for tender. To enact his projects, the Entrepreneur forges alliances and cooperation with a variety of agents including those outside of the academic field. He judges his success with regard to the performance revealed by a number of publications, the scope of his project and the size of his or her network while he is internationally mobile. The main trial is to make links, to be connected with other individuals and collective actors, in order to capitalise resources and realise new technological and scientific investments. Therefore, networking becomes a common activity along with lobbying in order to influence decision-making and bring policymaking and business closer together.

The figure of the Expert corresponds to the last convention of academic work. Like the Entrepreneur, he aims to extend his network and adopts an opportunistic conduct in the selection of projects and contracts. In establishing connections, he positions himself or herself as a mediator in the accumulation of knowledge which builds his reputation with policymakers. But he first of all defines his or her greatness with regard to his reliability, precision and relevance in the knowledge production required by a sponsor or a funder. The Expert claims his polyvalence and capacity to work in interdisciplinary contexts. He is surrounded by other experts who have also mastered a whole set of tools and methods leading to them being recognised as specialists. The Expert considers that he is capable of mastering uncertainty and risk. He thinks that it is good to invest in technical and scientific progress in order to improve the state of the economy and society. For this, he draws up recommendations, criteria and standards, seeks to build indicators and other measurements and maps the whole causal factors and their consequences. The Expert believes in measurements which he sees as an indispensable trial to establish evidence and truth. By measuring and formalising the social reality, he helps both policymakers and stakeholders to control evolutions and to schedule them. The Expert has the power to gather heterogeneous elements into a system and to propose procedures and standards to effectively implement a policy or a programme.

The four above-described figures of academic work remain ideal types. They can implement hybrid forms and compromise between several principles of justice. As we shall show in the next chapter, the experience of academics is subjected to various logics of action in accordance with a specific institutional, political and academic environment. Consequently, there are diverse agencies between persons and things in the framing of the self. The mandarin-Expert can be part of expert institutions or transnational epistemic communities by being positioned as a hierarchical authority, by having a good reputation and by developing the capacity to connect large-scale networks.

The entrepreneur can adopt an activist attitude and devolve his or her main projects to societal innovations or to the organisation of protests and resistance against managerialism. The collegial dimension and issues of representation can be found among expert groups which can also be in competition in the lobbying and influencing of policymakers. However, the four figures of academic work have to be considered in a diachronic as well as in a synchronic register because they characterise a long-term transformation of the academic institution. The shift from a mandarin system to peer regulation is the consequence of the change in the relationships between the academic profession and the state and the replacement of the order of the chair or the magister by those of occupational status. The shift in the figure of peer/representative to the contracting entrepreneur is the direct consequence of the implementation of New Public Management, the ranking regime, the increase in international mobility and the weakening of trade unionist and associative powers. The rise of expertise can be explained by the emergence of new forms of knowledge production and a regime of evidence which has been strongly internationalised and disseminated to policymakers. By shifting instituted trials, these new figures of the academic work have conquered a space of legitimacy in accordance with new principles of justification, while denouncing former conventions by a radical or corrective criticism. They have also profited from trials of strength which have led to shifts, through different forms of standardisation and instrumental equipment of academic work, and have created asymmetries in favour of the new spirit of academic capitalism.

Conclusion

By identifying new conventions of work in relation to the emergence of a new spirit of academic capitalism, we have shown that management institutionalises new trials while relativising those upon which the academic tradition was built. The gradual institutionalisation of quality standards and the new epistemic regime in knowledge production, designed at the scale of transnational networks, have confirmed the weakening of the state intervention and the mode of self-regulation of the academic profession. The denunciation of these transformations is made difficult by the fact they base their legitimacy on previous criticism of the academic community by policymakers and international organisations in charge of higher education reforms. Analyses are also partial when they reduce current evolutions to the marketisation of higher education and ignore some aspects of the state's transformation or when, on the pretext that they are analysing the diversity and hybridisation of reforms, they tend to underestimate the role of transnational actors and networks as well as the international circulation and transfer of ideas and instruments.

The shift in instituted trials generates asymmetries between those who hold managerial values and instruments and academics who endure them in their daily tasks and responsibilities. When faced with rapid changes in the academic institution, the latter seems relatively powerless to establish equivalences between, on the one hand, international agencies and networks designing the standards and tools of NPM and, on the other hand, controlling frameworks and devices implemented locally. Strikes and protests have not been successful against this empowerment, while protesters have difficulties in mobilising people on such complex and difficultly definable issues. It explains why a lot of academics prefer to adopt strategies of exit and loyalty, instead of voice, to resume the expression Albert O. Hirschman's trilogy (Hirschman 1970) because they judge these reforms to be irreversible. Some schemes of interpretation are being built and they carry a new criticism as well as a theory of exploitation calling for new forms of resistance. However, the convergence towards a new common good suggests operations of categorisation and justification which do not have much influence on the discourses of truth disseminated by international organisations and reformist policymakers. Reversing the order of criticism which has targeted the academic profession for the past few decades does not just require an additional effort of reflexivity to avoid the drift towards pamphleting, conspiracy theories or prophecy. It needs the capacity to recognise concerns, to develop them and to guide them according to a new grammar of exploitation but also of self-fulfilment.

References

Abreu, M., Grinevich, V., Hughes, A., & Kitson, M. (2009). Knowledge exchange between academics and the business. *Public and Third Sectors UK Innovation Research Centre.* http://eprints.soton.ac.uk/357117/1/AcademicSurveyReport.pdf

Arbo, P., & Benneworth, P. (2007). *Understanding the regional contribution of higher education institutions: A literature review* (OECD education working papers, Vol. 9). Paris: OECD Publishing.

Baldini, N., Grimaldi, R., & Sobrero, M. (2006). Institutional changes and the commercialization of academic knowledge: A study of Italian universities' patenting activities between 1965 and 2002. *Research Policy, 35,* 518–532.

Ball, S. J. (2008). New philanthropy, new networks and new governance in education. *Political Studies, 56*(4), 747–765.

Ball, S. J. (2012). *Global Education Inc.: New policy networks and the neo-liberal imaginary.* London: Routledge.

Barsony, J. (2003). Towards the entrepreneurial university. In *SEFI 2003 conference-global engineer: Education and training for mobility. European Society for Engineering Education.* http://www.sefi.be/wp-content/papers2003/sefi-f57.pdf

Bass, B., & Riggio, R. E. (2008). *Transformational leadership.* London: Taylor and Francis.

Bell, D. (1960). *The end of ideology* (Vol. 3). New York: Free Press.

Benner, M., & Sandström, U. (2000). Institutionalizing the triple helix: Research funding and norms in the academic system. *Research Policy, 29*(2), 291–301.

Blackmore, P., & Blackwell, R. (2006). Strategic leadership in academic development. *Studies in Higher Education, 31*(03), 373–387.

Bleiklie, I. (2005). Organizing higher education in a knowledge society. *Higher Education, 49*(1–2), 31–59.

Bleiklie, I., & Henkel, M. (2005). *Governing knowledge* (Vol. 9). London: Springer.

Bleiklie, I., & Lange, S. (2010). Competition and leadership as drivers in German and Norwegian university reforms. *Higher Education Policy, 23*(2), 173–193.

Bleiklie, I., & Michelsen, S. (2013). Comparing HE policies in Europe. *Higher Education, 65*(1), 113–133.

Bleiklie, I., Enders, J., Lepori, B., & Musselin, C. (2011). New public management, network governance and the university as a changing professional organization. *The Ashgate Research Companion to New Public Management, 16*, 161–176.

Boer, H. de., & Goedegebuure, L. (2009). The changing nature of the academic deanship. *Leadership, 5*(3), 347–364.

Bolden, R., Petrov, G., & Gosling, J. (2008). Tensions in higher education leadership: Towards a multi-level model of leadership practice. *Higher Education Quarterly, 62*(4), 19.

Bolden, R., Petrov, G., & Gosling, J. (2009). Distributed leadership in higher education: Rhetoric and reality. *Educational Management Administration Leadership, 37*(2), 257–277.

Boltanski, L., & Chiapello, E. (2005). *The new spirit of capitalism.* London: Verso.

Boltanski, L., & Thévenot, L. (2006). *On justification: Economies of worth.* Princeton: Princeton University Press.

Boucher, G., Conway, C., & Van der Meer, E. (2003). Tiers of engagement by universities in their region's development. *Regional Studies, 37*, 887–897.

Bourdieu, P. (1988). *Homo academicus.* Stanford: Stanford University Press.

Braun, G., & Diensberg, C. (Eds.), (2007). *Cultivating entrepreneurial regions-cases and studies from the network project' baltic entrepreneurship partners' (BEPART).* Rostock: Univ.-Bibliothek, Schriftentausch.

Bryman, A. (2009). *Effective leadership in higher education.* London: Leadership Foundation for Higher Education.

Burgoyne, J., Mackness, J., & Williams, S. (2009). *Literature review: Baseline study of leadership development in higher education.* Lancaster: Lancaster University.

CEL. (2006). *World-class leadership for global excellence.* CEL http://www.centreforexcellence.org.uk

CEL. (2007). *Leadership kills for governance.* 2008–2009, programme and support guide. CEL http://www.centreforexcellence.org.uk

CEL. (2008). *Research on diversity and governance in the FE sector recommendations and action plan.* CEL http://www.centreforexcellence.org.uk.

Chapple, W., Lockett, A., Siegel, D., & Wright, M. (2004) *Assessing the relative performance of UK university technology transfer offices: Parametric and non-parametric evidence.* Department of economics, rensselaer polytechnic institute. Working papers in economics, No 0423. Source: http://www.rpi.edu/dept/economics/www/workingpapers

Charles, D. (2003). Universities and territorial development: Reshaping the regional role of UK universities. *Local Economy, 18*(1), 7–20.

Charles, D. (2006). Universities as key knowledge infrastructures in regional innovation systems. *Innovation, 19*(1), 117–130.

Chitty, C. (1989). *Towards a new education system: The victory of the new right?* London: Psychology Press.

Clark, B. R. (1983). The contradictions of change in academic systems [1]. *Higher Education, 12*(1), 101–116.

Clark, B. R. (1998). *Creating entrepreneurial universities: Organizational pathways of transformation. Issues in higher education.* New York: Elsevier Science.

Clark, B. R. (2004). *Sustaining change in universities: Continuities in case studies and concepts.* Maidenhead: Open University Press.

Clarke, J., & Newman, J. (1997). *The managerial state.* London: Sage.

Clarke, J., Gewirtz, S., & McLaughlin, E. (Eds.). (2000). *New managerialism, new welfare?* London: Sage.

Collinson, D., & Collinson, M. (2009). 'Blended Leadership': Employee perspectives on effective leadership in the UK further education sector. *Leadership, 5*(3), 365–380.

Communication from the European Commission. (2003). *The role of the universities in the Europe of knowledge* (pp. 58). Brussels: COM (2003).

Communication from the Commission. (2005). *Mobilising the brainpower of Europe: Enabling universities to make their full contribution to the Lisbon strategy.* Brussels: European Commission.

Daumard, P. (2001). Enterprise culture and university culture. *Higher Education Management, 13*(2), 67–75 OECD.

Davies, J. L. (2001). The emergence of entrepreneurial cultures in European Universities. *Higher Education Management, 13*(2), 25–45 OECD.

Deem, R. (1998). "New managerialism" and higher education: The management of performances and cultures in universities in the United Kingdom. *International Studies in Sociology of Education, 8*(1), 47–70.

Deem, R. (2001). Globalisation, new managerialism, academic capitalism and entrepreneurialism in universities: Is the local dimension still important? *Comparative Education, 37*(1), 7–20.

Deem, R., & Brehony, K. J. (2005). Management as ideology: The case of 'new managerialism' in higher education. *Oxford Review of Education, 31*(2), 217–235.

Deem, R., Hillyard, S., & Reed, M. (2007). *Knowledge, higher education, and the new managerialism: The changing management of UK universities.* Oxford: Oxford University Press.

Dooley, L., & Kirk, D. (2007). University-industry collaboration: Grafting the entrepreneurial paradigm onto academic structures. *European Journal of Innovation Management, 10*(3), 316–332.

Dulewicz, V. (2000). Emotional intelligence. The key to successful corporate leadership. *Journal of General Management, 25*, 1–15.

Dunleavy, P., & Hood, C. (1994). From old public administration to new public management. *Public Money and Management, 14*(3), 9–16.

Elias, N. (1983). *The court society* (E. Jephcott, Trans.). New York: Pantheon Books, 8, 55.

Epitropaki, O. (2001). *What is transformational leadership.* Sheffield: Institute of Work Psychology.

Etzkowitz, H. (1997). The entrepreneurial university and the emergence of democratic corporatism. In H. Etzkowitz & L. Leydesdorff (Eds.), *Universities and the global knowledge economy: A triple helix of university-industry-government relations* (pp. 141–152). London: Cassell.

Etzkowitz, H. (2004). The evolution of the entrepreneurial university. *International Journal of Technology and Globalisation, 1*(1), 64–77.

Etzkowitz, H. (2008). *The triple helix. University– industry – Government, innovation in action.* London: Routledge.

European Commission. (2006). *Delivering on the modernisation agenda for universities: Education, research and innovation.* Communication from the commission to the council and the European Parliament, COM (2006) 208 Final.

European Union. (2010). *The EU contribution to the European higher education area.* Luxembourg: Publications Office of the European Union.

Evetts, J. (2003). The sociological analysis of professionalism occupational change in the modern world. *International Sociology, 18*(2), 395–415.

Evetts, J. (2009). New professionalism and new public management: Changes, continuities and consequences. *Comparative Sociology, 8*(2), 247–266.

Evetts, J. (2011). A new professionalism? Challenges and opportunities. *Current Sociology, 59*(4), 406–422.

Ferlie, E., Musselin, C., & Andresani, G. (2008). The steering of higher education systems: A public management perspective. *Higher Education, 56*(3), 325–348.

Gibb, A., & Hannon, P. (2006). Towards the entrepreneurial university. *International Journal of Entrepreneurship Education, 4*(1), 73–110.

Gibb, A., Haskins, G., & Robertson, I. (2009). Leading the entrepreneurial university. *The paper published in cooperation with NCGE & Oxford University's Said Business School.*

Gibbons, M., Limoges, C., Nowotny, H., Schwartzman, S., Scott, P., & Trow, M. (1994). *The new production of knowledge, the dynamics of science and research in contemporary societies.* London: Sage.

Goffee, R., & Jones, G. (2007). Leading clever people. *Harvard Business Review*, Reprint R0703D.

Gonzales, L. D., & Núñez, A. M. (2014). Ranking regimes and the production of knowledge in academia: (Re) shaping faculty work? *Education Policy Analysis Archives, 22*, 31.

Gronn, P. (2009). Leadership configurations. *Leadership, 5*(3), 381–394.

Gupta, V., MacMillan, I. C., & Surie, G. (2004). Entrepreneurial leader leadership; developing and measuring a cross-cultural construct. *Journal of Business Venture, 19*, 241–260.

Hackett, S. M., & Dilts, D. M. (2004). A systematic review of business incubation research. *The Journal of Technology Transfer, 29*(1), 55–82.

Hirschman, A. (1970). *Exit, voice and loyalty: Responses to decline in firms, organizations, and states.* Cambridge, MA: Harvard University Press.

Hirschman, A. O. (1991). *The rhetoric of reaction. Perversity. Futility, jeopardy.* Cambridge, MA: Harvard University Press.

Hood, C. (1991). A public management for all seasons. *Public Administration, 69*(1), 3–19.

Hood, C. C., & Margetts, H. Z. (2007). *The tools of government in the digital age.* Basingstoke: Palgrave Macmillan.

Hood, C., & Peters, G. (2004). The middle aging of new public management: Into the age of paradox? *Journal of Public Administration Research and Theory, 14*(3), 267–282.

Hughes, A. (2003). *Knowledge transfer, entrepreneurship and economic growth: Some reflections and implications for policy in the Netherlands.* ESRC Centre for Business Research, University of Cambridge.

IHEP. (2007). *Regional universities and civil society development. A symposium and study tour.* Washington, DC: IHEP.

Jacob, M., Lundqvist, M., & Hellsmark, H. (2003). Entrepreneurial transformations in the Swedish University system: The case of Chalmers University of technology. *Research Policy, 32*(2003), 1555–1568.

Jongbloed, B., Enders, J., & Salerno, C. (2008). Higher education and its communities: Interconnections, interdependencies and a research agenda. *Higher Education, 56*(3), 303–324.

Kauppinen, I. (2012). Towards transnational academic capitalism. *Higher Education, 64*(4), 543–556.

Kilgour, F. G. (1992, Winter). Entrepreneurial leadership. *Library Trends, 40*(3), 457–744.

Kirby, D. A. (2006). Creating entrepreneurial universities in the UK: Applying entrepreneurship theory to practice. *The Journal of Technology Transfer, 31*(5), 599–603.

Kuratko, D. F., & Hornsby, J. S. (1999). Corporate entrepreneurial leadership for the 21st century. *Journal of Leadership and Organisational Studies, 5*(2), 27–39.

Kweik, M. (2008). Academic entrepreneurship vs. changing governance and institutional management, structures at European Universities. *Policy Futures in Education, 6*(6), 757–770.

Laredo, P. (2007). Revisiting the third mission of universities: Toward a renewed categorization of university activities? *Higher Education Policy, 20*(4), 441–456.

Lazzeroni, M., & Piccaluga, A. (2003). Towards the entrepreneurial university. *Local Economy, 18*(1), 38–48.

Lee, Y. S. (1996). Technology transfer and the research university: A search for the boundaries of university-industry collaboration. *Research Policy, 25*(1996), 843–863.

Lewis, T., Marginson, S., & Snyder, I. (2005). The network university? Technology, culture and organisational complexity in contemporary higher education. *Higher Education Quarterly, 59*(1), 56–75.

Leydesdorff, L., & Meyer, M. (2003). The triple helix of university-industry-government relations. *Scientometrics, 58*(2), 191–203.

Link, A. N., & Scott, J. T. (2006). US university research parks. *Journal of Productivity Analysis, 25*(1–2), 43–55.

Marginson, S. (2006). Dynamics of national and global competition in higher education. *Higher Education, 52*(1), 1–39.

Marginson, S., & Considine, M. (2000). *The enterprise universities: Power, governance and reinvention in Australia.* Cambridge: Cambridge University Press.

Marginson, S., & Rhoades, G. (2002). Beyond national states, markets, and systems of higher education: A glonacal agency heuristic. *Higher Education, 43*(3), 281–309.

McInnis, C. (2001). Promoting academic expertise and authority in an entrepreneurial culture. *Higher Education Management, 13*(2), 45–57. OECD.

McLaughlin, K., Osborne, S. P., & Ferlie, E. (2002). *New public management: Current trends and future prospects.* London: Psychology Press.

Mendoza, P., & Berger, J. B. (2005). Patenting productivity and intellectual property policies at research I universities: An exploratory comparative study. *Education Policy Analysis Archives, 13*(4). http://files.eric.ed.gov/fulltext/EJ846515.pdf

Middlehurst, R., Goreham, H., & Woodfield, S. (2009). Why research leadership in higher education? Exploring contributions from the UK's leadership foundation for higher education. *Leadership, 5*(3), 311–329.

Mohrman, K., Ma, W., & Baker, D. (2008). The research university in transition: The emerging global model. *Higher Education Policy, 21*(1), 5–27.

Mollas-Gallart, J., Salter, A., Patel, P., Scott, A., & Duran, X. (2002). Measuring third stream activities: Final report to the Russell Group of Universities. Brighton: SPRU. Available at http://www2.lse.ac.uk/economicHistory/Research/CCPN/pdf/russell_report_thirdStream.Pdf

Musselin, C. (2013). Redefinition of the relationships between academics and their university. *Higher Education, 65*(1), 25–37.

Newble, D., & Cannon, R. (2013). *Handbook for teachers in universities and colleges.* London: Routledge.

Nicolaou, N., & Birley, S. (2003). Social networks in organizational emergence: The university spinout phenomenon. *Management Science, 49*(12), 1702–1725.

Nowotny, H., Scott, P., & Gibbons, M. (2003). Mode 2 revisited: The new production of knowledge. *Minerva, 41*, 179–194.

O'Shea, R. P., Allen, T. J., Morse, K. P., O'Gorman, C., & Roche, F. (2007). Delineating the anatomy of an entrepreneurial university: The Massachusetts Institute of Technology experience. *R&d Management, 37*(1), 1–16.

OECD. (2004, August). The internationalisation of higher education. *Policy Brief.* Cambridge, MA: OECD Publishing.

Paradeise, C., Reale, E., Bleiklie, I., & Ferlie, E. (Eds.). (2009). *University governance.* The Netherlands: Springer.

Pollitt, C., & Bouckaert, G. (2004). *Public management reform: A comparative analysis.* Oxford: Oxford University Press.

Power, M. (1994). *The audit explosion.* London: Demos.

Power, M. (1997). *The audit society: Rituals of verification.* Oxford: Oxford University Press.

Rhoades, G. (1998). *Managed professionals: Unionized faculty and restructuring academic labor.* Albany: SUNY Press.

Rothaermel, F. T., & Hess, A. M. (2007). Building dynamic capabilities: Innovation driven by individual-, firm-, and network-level effects. *Organization Science, 18*(6), 898–921.

Schein, E. H. (1992). *Organisational culture and leadership.* San Francisco: Jossey Bass Publishers.

Schumpeter, J. A. (1934). *The theory of economic development: An inquiry into profits, capital, credit, interest, and the business cycle* (Vol. 55). New Brunswick: Transaction Publishers.

Scott, G., Coates, H., & Anderson, M. (2008). *Academic leadership capabilities for Australian higher education*. Sydney: Australian Learning and Teaching Centre.

Segal, N. S. (1985). The Cambridge phenomenon. *Regional Studies, 19*(6), 563–570.

Shattock, M. (2000). Strategic management in European universities in an age of increasing institutional self-reliance. *Tertiary Education Management, 6*, 93–104.

Shattock, M. (2010). *Managing successful universities*. Maidenhead: McGraw-Hill Education.

Shinn, T. (2002). The triple helix and new production of knowledge: Prepackaged thinking on science and technology. *Social Studies of Sciences, 32*, 599.

Shore, C., & Wright, S. (1999). Audit culture and anthropology: Neoliberalism in British higher education. *Journal of the Royal Anthropological Institute, 5*(4), 557–575.

Siegel, D. S., Waldman, D., & Link, A. (2003). Assessing the impact of organizational practices on the relative productivity of university technology transfer offices: An exploratory study. *Research Policy, 32*(1), 27–48.

Slaughter, S., & Cantwell, B. (2011). Transatlantic moves to the market: The United States and the European Union. *Higher Education, 63*(5), 583–606.

Slaughter, S., & Leslie, L. L. (1997). *Academic capitalism. Politics, policies and the Entrepreneurial University*. London: John Hopkins University Press.

Slaughter, S., & Rhoades, G. (2004). *Academic capitalism and the new economy: Markets, state, and higher education*. Baltimore: Johns Hopkins University Press.

Smith, H. L. (2007). Universities, innovation, and territorial development: A review of the evidence. *Environment and Planning C, 25*(1), 98.

Solé-Parellada, F., Coll-Bertran, J., & Navarro-Hernández, T. (2001). University design and development. *Higher Education in Europe, 26*(3), 341–350.

Soley, L. C. (1995). *Leasing the ivory tower: The corporate takeover of academia*. Boston: South End Press.

Strathern, M. (2000). *Audit cultures: Anthropological studies in accountability, ethics, and the academy*. London: Psychology Press.

Todorovic, W. Z., McNaughton, R. B., & Guild, P. D. (2005). Making university departments more entrepreneurial: The perspective from within. *The International Journal of Entrepreneurship and Innovation, 6*(2), 115–122.

Van Vught, F. A. (1989). Creating innovations in higher education. *European Journal of Education, 24*(3), 249–270.

Van Vught, F. A., & Westerheijden, D. F. (1994). Towards a general model of quality assessment in higher education. *Higher Education, 28*(3), 355–371.

Vecchio, R. P. (2003). Entrepreneurship and leadership: Common trends and common threads. *Human Resources Management Review, 13*(2003), 303–327.

Wasser, H. (1990). Changes in the European university: From traditional to entrepreneurial. *Higher Education Quarterly, 44*(2), 110–122.

Weber, M. (2002). *The protestant ethic and the spirit of capitalism: And other writings*. London: Penguin Books.

Wenger, E. (1998). *Communities of practice: Learning, meaning and identity*. Cambridge: Cambridge University Press.

Wong, P. K., Ho, Y. P., & Singh, A. (2007). Towards an "entrepreneurial university" model to support knowledge-based economic development: The case of the National University of Singapore. *World Development, 35*(6), 941–958.

Ylinenpää, H. (2001). Science parks, clusters and regional development. Luleå University of Technology; Department of Business Administration and Social Sciences, Division of Industrial Organization & Small Business Academy. Luleå University of Technology: AR 2001: 48. Paper presented at 31st European small business seminar in Dublin, 12–14 September.

Zaharia, S. E., & Gibert, E. (2005). The entrepreneurial university in the knowledge society. *Higher Education in Europe, 30*(1), 31–40.

Zhou, C. (2008). Emergence of the entrepreneurial university in evolution of the triple helix. *Journal of Technology and Management of China, 3*(1), 109–126.

The Making of a New Homo Academicus?

Introduction

The new spirit of academic capitalism, as implemented by New Public Management, has not just created shifts in organisational and regulative devices for academics activities. It institutionalises trials which have significantly modified academics' conventions at work and professionalism. New figures have emerged, such as the Entrepreneur and the Expert, while a new epistemic regime has been implemented in knowledge production. These transformations have been made possible because they are agreed and legitimised by a part of the scientific community and because the former model, based on tradition and collegial authority, has faced widespread criticism.

Indeed, criticism is an essential driver of social transformation in that it delegitimises an instituted order to make a proposal which, if it generates adhesion or truly convinces, forces change or in extreme cases deletes or destroys existing frames. This criticism is not only a sociological capacity. Social actors, as individuals or groups, use their critical skills in daily circumstances. Criticism is more or less shared, but it requires a reflexive judgement and collectively a capacity of empowerment to change the state of the world.

In the previous chapter, we showed that the academic profession is subjected to criticism, and it has contributed in advancing the new spirit of capitalism and managerial devices. In this chapter, we would like to consider how managerialism is welcomed by academics by the questioning of possibilities it creates within the academic community. In order to do so, we shall seek to provide a comprehensive picture of the challenges faced by academics in their tasks and responsibilities controlled by the management. We need to focus on the principles of justice used by academics to qualify their experience and work situations from which they guide their action towards the common good. In revealing the type of trials instituted by these new managerial devices and the potentialities for criticism they raise, we shall

© Springer International Publishing Switzerland 2016
R. Normand, *The Changing Epistemic Governance of European Education*,
Educational Governance Research 3, DOI 10.1007/978-3-319-31776-2_7

put into perspective the creation of a new agency and the emergence of new subjectivities in the accommodation of the European academic with his environment.

Before we do so, we have to explain the difficulties encountered by academics in voicing and rendering acceptable the criticism addressed against the new spirit of capitalism by their representatives on behalf of the academic profession. They are linked to a weakening of the academic world's defences because of the higher education reforms being enacted in Europe which have considerably transformed working conditions. These difficulties can also be explained by policymakers and managers' capacity to institutionalise discourses of truth which have potentially disarmed criticism. Finally, the academic profession has subjected itself to segmentation and diffraction processes which have considerably altered its collective identity and capacity to unite diverse interests.

The Weakening of the Academic World's Defences

Higher education reforms in Europe and throughout the world have considerably weakened the academic world's defences by exposing it to the new spirit of capitalism. Under managerialism, sources of identity shaped in the 1960s–1970s have been undermined by the transformations of higher education institutions' internal organisation and academic statuses (Enders and Musselin 2008). A gradual deconstruction of the academic world occurred through a series of change often justified by the need to adapt higher education and research systems to internationalisation and to make them more innovative so that they become economically competitive. These consequences, in terms of restructuring the academic world, have been broadly analysed by the research literature. We shall just examine the current state of knowledge which is useful for our analysis before providing a sociological account of the shifts and trails instituted by managerialism and its effects on the profession itself.

In order to characterise the weakening of the academic world's defences, it is necessary to understand the transformations of academic work over a long period, several decades, when assuming that the diffusion of the new global spirit of capitalism takes time and has been the result of successive shifts dealing evidently with institutional and cultural traditions in different countries and regional areas (Robertson 2010a, b; Sum and Jessop 2013). As Bob Jessop demonstrates, imaginary economies are materially constituted and reproduced at different spatiotemporal scales, and they are extended in economic organisations, networks and clusters structuring new macroeconomic regimes. These regimes, by semiotic effects but also by social learning and power relationships, create interdependencies by articulating organised interests, visions and projects which manipulate knowledge and powers to stabilise borders, temporalities and tendencies progressively imposed despite some contradictory, interstitial, residual and marginal elements temporarily escaping from them. In doing so, they institute new technologies of governance on behalf of a hegemonic conception of knowledge-based economy.

Susan Robertson confirms the 'regulatory regionalism' of the knowledge-based Europe, but it has to be nuanced to take into account the extra-regional (neighbour economies, more distant strategic domestic economies, former colonial relationships and networks, new interregional entities) which is enrolled, mobilised and transformed through the deployment of governance tools in the European Higher Education Area. Within this assemblage, the 'extra-regional' in the European higher education political project seems guided by a combination of forces and projects. While Europe extends its political project, particularly through the Bologna process, it has other geostrategic requirements while it attracts neighbour domestic actors which want to import some technologies of governance.

In Europe as elsewhere, strong trends can be identified and they primarily affect young generations (Musselin 2013). The first trend is the end of lifetime employment. Academic positions as tenure are slowly disappearing, while young academics join the profession after short-term contracts and probationary periods. Even in previously protected systems such as France, Italy or Spain, due to Napoleonic tradition of public administration, young PhDs accessing an academic career go through a phase of uncertainty and precariousness. This has led to an increase in the number of 'precarious intellectuals' with a PhD but waiting to be recruited in a higher education institution. Short-term contracts and part-time jobs have also increased during the past few decades. In addition, neo-recruited people have to meet objectives in developing research projects, obtaining contracts and funds, while recruitment is linked to accountability requirements. Using Doeringer and Piore's analyses (1971), we can say that the academic labour market in European countries is a dual one, composed of an internal market protecting academics in a corporatist–statist system and an external market in which young postgraduates are in a position of competition with diminished opportunities for their inclusion.

This dualism of the labour market has been observed within the profession by more experienced academics. With the New Public Management, the academic profession has faced segmentation and differentiation. While some academics have taken advantage to increase their number of publications, to obtain contracts and sources of funding, others are relatively powerless because they remain at a distance or they have resisted these evolutions, or their academic discipline does not fit the stratagem of profitability and performance, or they are not involved in networks to increase their social capital. The dual feature of the profession has being strengthened by the individualisation of salaries or advantages bestowed to the most performative and renowned academics. The divide increases between those developing their research activities and those relegated to teaching tasks.

Some academics try to maintain control of their activities and the managerial criteria for their work by defending the academic community's power within professional organisations and trade unions. Others are subjected to managerial standards and frameworks focusing on flexibility, competition or accountability. An important part of a chancellors' strategy is to create professionals or managers capable of implementing New Public Management (Hyde et al. 2013). The discourse of quality, service to students, innovation and responsibility is translated by external assessments of academic activities and professional skills, while internal assessments are developed at the same time. As has been shown by the UK, assessment is a means of controlling professionals and intensifying their workload. Research Assessment Exercises (RAE) are a system of assessments inciting departments and research teams to carry out organisational restructuring and to modify their recruitment strategies according to performance-based objectives (Shattock 2015). In comparing performance with quality standards, they impose a narrow definition in the validation of knowledge and the use of funding budgets while strengthening managerial control. Academic work is considered as an added value for universities. But managerial empowerment is also effective in the field of human resource management, particularly the selection and recruitment procedures of academics which are no longer regulated by peers. Management controls job profiles, labels chairs of excellence to attract the best applicants and modifies the composition of recruitment juries by mobilising external partners.

These managerial technologies, by imposing objectives to the academic work, have ended up directing academic activities and the allocation of tasks and responsibilities (Kwiek 2012). Filling in forms are not just dedicated to bureaucratic tasks and managing students. Performance indicators, sometimes linked to salaries or budget increases for research units, are more defined by the university than by the profession. The standardisation of work, particularly through the digital technologies, is also a means of controlling academics' productivity and creativity. The relation between academics and policymaking is established through supervision, assessment and auditing. While the assessment of each academic's performance is linked to his or her organisation's success or failure, it threatens professional cohesion and mutual cooperation, as well as pitting people into competition which each other, thus undermining collegiality with the community of peers. Relationships between academics and students have also been converted into services in which satisfaction surveys, quality measurements and performance-based budgets have replaced trust and interindividual links.

As shown once again in the UK, trade unions were incapable of resisting New Public Management's empowerment (Radice 2013). Their recruitment and capacities have been weakened because of the precariousness affecting more and more academics who have no choice but to accept short-term contracts and private funding. Focused on defending pay and service, the UK trade unionism has had to come to terms with the diversification of situations and work flexibility, thus undermining its capacity to establish equivalences in terms of the degradation of working conditions, and it has struggled to mobilise people to a common cause. Furthermore, it has been attacked by the media and most political parties which have accused them of conservatism and corporatism. Some academics have even used quality management to shift responsibility and accountability on to other colleagues while junior members and women have suffered from these new forms of exploitation between peers (Worthington and Hodgson 2005).

From these examples, we can understand that the academic profession's capacity to control its activities and recruitment procedures has diminished over the past few years. The collegial organisation has been restructured into a managerial one, one which discards modes of attachment to a scientific community and peer regulation.

However, while the new managerialism has been restructuring the academic profession, some academics have taken advantage of it, as we shall see later. Some restructuring policies have led to new professional segments and strategies to own new skills and get more responsibilities within an academic organisation. Therefore, a weakening of the corporatist–statist model has been observed for several years, but these evolutions have generated other figures and spaces of compromise with the new spirit of academic capitalism. Academic borders are being challenged, while competition between academics has been transformed to take into account this new institutional environment. Before considering in detail internal changes in the academic condition, we have to analyse the discourses of truth held by the institution itself while it maintains a 'reformist common sense' to legitimise an interpretation of current mutations and the disappearance of the collegiate model.

The Academic Institution's New Discourses of Truth

Academic institutions' discourses of truth borrow their semantic references from the NPM rhetoric. However, their persuasive force comes from their capacity to formulate a coherent and stable vision of the academic world's new state in an exposure relayed by reports, official papers, conferences and authorised spokesmen' statements. The institution and its representatives have, via the chain of delegation and authorisation required by reforms, the necessary legitimacy to express what is thinkable, to only give a possible viewpoint regarding the new academic world, and in doing so to provide the norm of truth. However, these discourses are not sufficient to frame possibilities of action. That is why they are mediated by organisational arrangements and juridical rules which coordinate academic activities and control academics by limiting possibilities of dispute and criticism. It relays, as we have seen, a denunciation against the traditional conception of academic work and the weakening of its defences with regard to the coming world.

Discourses of truth, themselves, are subjected to an internal coherence while they represent institutional actors. The use of words by the academic institution is not neutral and they have to be perceived as legitimate. At the same time, discourse of truth includes normative and prescriptive features and they aim to make targeted people to adopt a certain behaviour. They have also to meet some challenges: they have to appear as transparent, to not easily raise debates or polemics, to be relatively unified and homogeneous to appear reliable and to be understood by a large audience, particularly the media. Discourses of truth formulate statements which aim to make the institutional language coherent by smoothing out asperities and presenting an impersonal character, timeless and decontextualised events and modesty and deference from the spokesman. Discourses of truth are built as authoritative arguments which normalise a certain representation of the world.

The first one occurs when creativity, which is a fundamental aspect of academic work in its theoretical and conceptual dimensions, is celebrated (Kleiman 2008). Historically, the creative and inspired gesture has been considered as the essence of the intellectual or scientist creating ideas that challenge traditional legacy and the scientific community. The author's perspicacity and his or her inventiveness and sometimes genius character are identified for the common good preserved by intellectual property rights. However, this praise of creation underestimates human and material investment, as well as networking, underlying a conceptual and theoretical shift while the credit is given to a single person. The awarding of the Nobel Prize or other scientific rewards is an example of this personalisation while it maintains legends that academics themselves have ended up believing. From this traditional basis, a rhetoric of innovation and creativity has been progressively affirmed, while the inspired gesture has been driven towards people outside the scientific community in terms of social and economic utility but also societal fame. Creativity and innovation, or the capacity to provide a prospective or a futurist vision of progress, are considered as academic work's intrinsic qualities for consecration. It is perceptible in the shift from the academic tradition to a new era in which creative originality is more and more channelled towards an innovative dynamic dealing with performance and profitability. At the same time, in 'truth-oriented' research, illumination, the imaginary, discrepancy as well as pamphlets, utopia or prophecy are considered as risky investments, unstable content or subversive proposals.

Traditionally, the academic institution's discourse of truth was couched in moral authority delegated to academics and celebrated in the recognition of chairs and ex cathedra speeches from which science could claim its universality. Authority was instituted according to a hierarchical order regulating peers, while signs of worth were recognised in academic titles like gowns and other formal clothes worn for diverse ceremonies such as thesis defences or the award of an honorary doctorate. While these rituals of confirmation have not entirely disappeared, and remain very vibrant in certain disciplines, this authoritative form of academic power has been reduced by the New Public Management to its most folkish aspects. The chain of dependency has shifted to chancellors and managers. Authority no longer comes from the magisterium but from hierarchic top-down power uncoupled with reproductive logics within a same community. In addition to status or a diploma, it depends on the academics' leadership qualities and empowerment capacities, i.e. being capable of giving a strategic vision and leading change (Bolden et al. 2009). The leader, like the entrepreneur, is assigned as being the academic who has exceptional qualities, charisma within the meaning of Max Weber, but they are no longer based on grace, brilliance or virtuosity because other values are being promoted: opportunism, empowerment, risk taking, vision, etc.

A part of the humanist tradition in humanities and social sciences was built against *doxa*, this common sense based on prejudices, beliefs and prenotions which impeded access to the knowledge of understanding the psychological and social reality of human beings. Critique and epistemology have relayed this movement. The crisis of universalism in opposition to particularisms, but also the revival of the religious spirit, has blurred the definitions of 'truth', and the academic institution has had to deal with the world of opinion and its extension through the development of the media and the Internet galaxy. Generalised access to information, and intertwined opinions, values and knowledge, has diminished the importance of the enlightened and academic intellectual in the public debate, while academics close to the media and communication networks have been able to diffuse messages at the edge of ideological manipulation and cultural propaganda. Storytelling has become the weapon of specialised academics who have close links with think tanks and policymaking spheres.

The university itself has been accused in books, the subject of biased reports and simplistic statements to support or criticise reforms. The mediatisation of debates on tuition fees, the brain drain, dropout rates and the Bologna process have paradoxically supported the increasingly shared idea of important challenges that require radical changes. The profusion of opinions has also led the academic institution to increase its claims for truth and a new epistemic order. The weight of data and modelling in the treatment of complex situations and problems has been strengthened. An apodictic norm has been sought to renew with the modernised positivist tradition in the development of advanced technologies like the meta-management of data which is now possible via new digital architectures (Hazemi et al. 2012). The discourse on 'big data' today proposes a description of the world based on figures and indicators which have by themselves a persuasive force enhanced by evidence-based methodologies. The call for the production of evidence, to bring clear and relevant answers from science to society in which the density of information increases the weight of *doxa*, reduces possibilities for an alternative science treating facts differently.

Once discourses of truth are institutionalised, they also transform legitimate modes of political representation within higher education. While the election mode between peers remains a principle of regulation in the academic world, the power of policymakers and managers in the appointment of academics for different positions and responsibilities is increasing. The representation of interests has been extended, beyond professors and students, to stakeholders who participate in research activities, partially fund them or have a right of scrutiny to look at their use (Amaral and Magalhaes 2002). This diversification of interests can also be observed through the powerful upswing of civil rights movements (feminist, gay, ethnic, racial, disability, senior) who claim the right to be different in the delivery of diplomas or in the training provided by universities. The consequence is that the voice of academics is being undermined in a general discourse justifying the recognition of differences and calling for the political expression and representation of diversity and the fight against discrimination. These discourses, coupled with those seeking to conciliate effectiveness and equity, have surreptitiously introduced the idea that it is necessary to better assess academic work, to allocate resources in relation to accountability, to increase the tuition fees of middle-class students and to improve the quality of provision. In doing so, they transfer political representation from the academic community to policymakers and stakeholders at local or national levels.

Finally, a last discourse of truth faced by academics is subverting the tradition of autonomy based on a separation between the sphere of knowledge production/transmission and the sphere of policy and market. Until now, academia had fostered the illusion that it is neutral and impartial with regard to statist and private interests, arguing for research without partisan stakes and based on a universalistic commitment. The academic institution has diverted this conception of autonomy to enforce the representation of a responsible and opportunist academic, interested not only in his or her reputation in the academic world but also in profits and performance. This maintains the idea of a skilled academic, capable of finding contracts and funds to ensure the development of his or her research. This discourse has developed the opportunistic dimension of academic work while until now has been limited to career strategies and games of power in national groups or professional networks. It legitimises a large space of conquest because of the internationalisation of academic activities. It is no longer at the community scale but at the global scale that success and increasing capital are recognised. Academic qualities are also valorised in the capacity to publish, as an index of productivity, and this has generated a schizophrenic compulsion to be published in the best journals, at least those assessed in international rankings. The celebration of the 'publishing researcher' also depends on activities such as technological and scientometrics watch which maintain the idea of an objective measurement of research qualities.

New Spaces at the Boundaries of Academia

Andrew Abbott (1988) studied the competition between professions and the way they seek to defend or extend their territory. Professions, in competition with each other, aspire for growth by taking over spheres of work in which they transform into 'jurisdiction' to gain legitimacy with public authorities. What occurs in a profession has consequences for a neighbouring profession. Jurisdiction is strengthened by the implementation of a set of resources and devices: associations, exams and journals, while submitting its professional claims to different 'audiences' (the state, the general public, colleagues in the workplace, etc.).

Other processes are related to disputes and negotiations in jurisdictions and more within organisations than in labour markets. Professional groups try to control tasks and the division of labour according to their interests, and they use their authority and legitimacy to maintain their domination. For example, in management, competition is increasing between professionals (accounting, engineering, human resources) to colonise key positions, to occupy certain roles and to take decisions within large organisations. These organisations are arenas for inter-professional competition and a means of serving traditional objectives such as social mobility, advancement in terms of status, financial rewards, quality of service, etc.

Finally, professional configurations have spokespersons who make public discourses and deal with local definitions to advocate other conceptions of the profession or to defend its inherited and traditional constituents. These configurations belong to a broad societal context which impacts them: the demographic evolution, which effects newcomers and people leaving the profession (the increase in education or the number of migrants affects flows), and the technological evolution, with the development of digital technologies, are challenging the definitions of work and employment, political changes impacting professions on a legal and regulatory basis and the transfer of management techniques from the private sector to the public sector. The academic profession has not escaped this trend.

As Chris Shore and Laura Mclauchlan (2012) have shown in New Zealand, the Third Mission assigned to academics, e.g. activities of knowledge transfer, establishing links between universities and industry and the commercialisation of research and teaching activities, in addition to services to the community, has not only redefined power relationships in favour of the management which controls budgets and human resources but also contributed to transforming internal relationships in the academic profession by creating new divisions and hierarchies and strong tensions within universities. The new heroes of university storytelling increasingly appear to embody the qualities of the Schumpeterian ideal-typical entrepreneur and individualistic operators who display a strong sense of agency, who take management into their own hands and who take it upon themselves to put the wealth of untapped research in universities to use.

Hybridisations and Borders

The response of academics to the transformations of their environment can also be analysed as a gradual shift of the boundaries between science and business and a renegotiation of their positions and modes of commitment in different knowledge regimes (Lam 2010). Between tradition and modernity, most of them adopt hybrid strategies within intermediary spaces which characterise new forms of professionalisation. Alice Lam distinguishes two hybrid positions besides the traditional academic and the entrepreneur. Her sample consisted of academic scientists from five major research universities in the UK, covering the following main disciplines: biological sciences, medicine, physical sciences, computer sciences and engineering. In her classification, Type I 'Traditionalists' (17 % of the survey sample) are characterised by a strong belief that academia and industry should be distinct, and they search for success primarily in the academic arena. Although they may develop some links with industry (e.g. collaborative research, student sponsorships), they seek to acquire financial and other resources to support academic research. Type I scientists do not pursue commercial modes of engagement and tend to be suspicious of those who do so. In contrast, Type IV 'Entrepreneurial' see the boundary between academia and industry as highly permeable, and they believe in the fundamental importance of science–business collaboration for knowledge application and commercial exploitation.

Between the two polar types, nearly three quarters of the scientists surveyed exhibited a 'hybrid' orientation. 'Traditional hybrids' share the old school commitment that the boundary between academia and industry should be distinct, while at the same time recognising the need to engage in science–business collaboration for scientific advancement. Type III 'Entrepreneurial hybrids' comprises the largest category of those surveyed (39 %). They are scientists sharing the new school belief in the importance and benefits of science–business collaboration, while maintaining an old school commitment to the core scientific values. Besides obtaining funding for research, they are motivated by a range of other knowledge, reputational and network-building factors in their pursuit of industrial links. These scientists are also hybrids in that they combine a new school entrepreneurial orientation with an old school commitment to the core values and norms of academic science. For these scientists, the boundary between university and industry is permeable and provides an open space within which knowledge production and application can be effectively combined. They emphasised an interactive relationship between basic and applied research and appeared to be comfortable and confident in crossing the science–business boundary.

In another vein, Celia Whitchurch has shown how a third space, at the border of academic and nonacademic work, has been progressively built (Whitchurch 2006, 2008, 2009). It is not defined by a particular discipline, but it gives space to cross-functional activities not only between professional and academic staff but also with people working in consultancy, business and the community. These people can be in charge of partnerships, the management of knowledge centres, the contracting and superversion of contracts, student placements, organisation and media services, and links with industry and regional agencies. The identity of these professional administrators and managers is generally defined by their belonging to different areas as knowledge production and institutional management according to specific budgetary rules and frameworks. But the emergence of an 'Inside Out University' has forced them to overcome institutional boundaries when leading and working on transversal projects, for example, the supervision and care of students, the management of human resources and the development of partnerships with business and the community.

As Cecilia Whitchurch notes, these cross-boundary professionals, distinct from bounded professionals enclosed in their roles and structures, are able to hold together multiple identity components, see boundaries as opportunities rather than as constraints, and are pragmatic about relinquishing elements of these components if necessary, taking advantage of any opportunities that arise to invest in alternative spaces, knowledge and relationships. Other unbounded professionals disregard organisational structures and boundaries or their positioning in relation to these. Less mindful of fixed points of reference, they have a flexible and open-ended approach to their activity, working in extended networks and acting as nodal points. The mobility of cross-boundary and unbounded professionals is facilitated by the exchange of institutional intelligence and professional practice through extended professional networks, which are likely to become an increasingly significant feature of professional life. Both categories have 'strong' and 'weak' ties within their institutions (Granovetter 1973). 'Strong ties' are apparent in one-to-one relationships with line managers or other key individuals. Cross-boundary professionals also have networks of 'weak ties' external to their institutions, inside and outside the higher education sector. In the case of unbounded professionals, 'weak' ties tend to be to networks outside, rather than inside, the sector.

The digitisation of the academic profession has also had an impact on its work and networking as demonstrated by Decuypere and Simons (2014). Daily academic work displays interactions between human and non-human beings, as new technologies which have relational qualities in allocating tasks and responsibilities within different networks and clusters of variable sizes. Different boundary actors associate different regions and in this way stabilise academic work; they can switch quickly and efficiently from one region to another adjacent one and hence from activities related to convening to retrieving, from communicating to planning, etc. As such, boundary actors do not possess one unequivocal function but, on the contrary, install a certain efficiency and flexibility that makes it possible to conduct a manifoldness of different activities in the course of one single day. Despite their heterogeneity, actors, through different socio-material assemblages, maintain a *relationality* in emergent mechanisms which cannot be assimilated to functional and institutional definitions.

This new connectionist order has been well described in the actor–network theory. Some criticism has been addressed to the social theory of networks (Ball 2012): it would be interested only by the visible aspect of relationships between actors, it would underestimate state powers, the distribution of powers would not be easily assessable and relationships would be instable, in perpetual transformation, and hardly identifiable. We have demonstrated in our own work that these obstacles could be overcome if a specific methodology is adopted to disclose invisible links between experts and policymakers and to complete network analysis by the study of relationships between science and policy from a historical and genealogical perspective (Normand 2010). In defining a connectionist order, we are not interested by the social imaginary it produces but by the manner it becomes a reality in managerial theories and organisations with the development of horizontal communications and digital technologies. The concept of network has raised an increasing interest among social scientists to explain relationships between human beings. But the structural or institutionalist approaches tend to overestimate the weight of hierarchical dependencies. Against the dominant explanation of social classes or determined structures, network analysis demonstrates complex relationships between individuals and the importance of face-to-face and at-a-distance connections. The idea of communication between human beings, in open spaces, with borders or fixed points, but with different modalities of flows, transfer, exchanges of information and knowledge, has enabled social sciences to characterise main societal transformations (Castells 2000). However, network analysis has to avoid two potential drifts: a naturalisation of the social world which would analyse the interplay between actors and social processes in taking into account only the numbers and shapes of the network, in discarding other forms of coordination by hierarchy or the market, etc., and a positivist reduction which would seize, under the empowerment of technology, human relationships through properties revealed by statistical calculations.

A Connectionist Academic World

The connectionist order is at the centre of the theory of the new spirit of capitalism developed by Luc Boltanski and Eve Chiapello (2005) and presented in the previous chapters. Principles of justice inspiring the management at the university level are based on identification to a reticular world which is potentially not limited in its global extension. It incites academics and other professionals to forge links and to be connected, on the basis of hindrance-free circulation and mobility, in which the development of activity and projects becomes the key issue of any legitimate enterprise. In a connectionist world related to the academic profession, academics have no other ambition than being connected with each other, developing relationships, knowing how to communicate at a distance and being trustful. It requires qualities praised by the management (flexibility, adaptability, polyvalence, etc.) as well as a certain capacity for taking risks and confronting uncertainty.

The connectionist order also brings new academic roles to the fore, particularly entrepreneurship and expertise that we built as ideal types in the previous chapter. The first role characterises the *network maker* able to build one or several networks within a given community and activity and to seek broad associations of people. This activity is close to a kind of political mobilisation in a professional association or a trade union. The number of members or associates ensures the greatness of the network but also that of its leader who has a legitimate authority and influential power. The community can include academics, experts, political entrepreneurs or a mix of several categories. The role and position of a *network broker* has been mainly developed with the coming of mode 2 in knowledge production. He or she is positioned as an intermediary between several networks (as researchers, policymakers, stakeholders, practitioners) and provides links and means of facilitating meetings and exchanges of ideas and data. The broker benefits from his or her dominant position in several networks to connect them to activities of knowledge production, dissemination and use. The network spokesperson is an academic with sufficient legitimacy and recognition to act on behalf of the network and to voice its agenda. It consists of representing interests, but it does not need many acquaintances and much proximity because the activities are mainly done at a distance. One aspect underlying this representational work is the possibility of acting as a *gatekeeper* by controlling access to the network and its activities, particularly in terms of communication and publication. Finally, a last role is the *connector* who creates links between people in immanent and opportunistic ways, without a set plan in difference to the broker. However, in connecting persons, he or she ensures an empowerment of their activities while anticipating a form of recognition which guarantees midterm reciprocity. Of course, some of these roles already existed in the academic world, but the extension of a networking world has strengthened them and they now predominate the traditional roles based on affinity relationships in proximity and hierarchical positions, local and communitarian rootedness, reputations built face to face or a collusion of interests invested in the defence of professionalism.

Another feature of the connectionist academic world is its openness to mobility (Kim 2010; Kim and Locke 2010; Larner 2015). In a global and networking space, relationships between academics define differentiated and asymmetric positions, between those who have the capacity to be included in extended networks and those who continue to operate in national or local spaces with weaker links. The supremacy of the former, attested by their international recognition and capacity to circulate from one country to another, acts as a counterbalance to the impoverishment of the others not only in terms of social but economic capital due to a rarefaction of resources (particularly contracts and funds) at lower scales. Mobility, or the capacity to move autonomously, to create new links, generates a process in which a section of the scientific community is excluded. This shift is the corollary of empowering asymmetries on international networks, with some academics benefiting from connections, while others are assigned to immobile positions and face casualisation in their working conditions under pressure from the management. Therefore, this differential of mobility is the source of deeper inequalities between academics, but it also generates new trials for the most mobile people in that sense connections are transitory because they last the length of a project, and they have to be renewed under permanent pressure to link and build new networks.

Principles of Justification and Potentialities for Criticism

As we have seen, the conversion of academic work to the new spirit of capitalism has revealed a set of exogenous and endogenous transformations in and outside the academic institution. The weakening of the academic world's defences has facilitated the penetration of NPM principles. The creation of new intermediary spaces and hybrid roles has challenged the traditional division of labour between teaching and research (Watermeyer 2015). New discourses of truth have been instituted to give coherence and stability to a new order by diminishing the profession's power and autonomy, while new professional configurations have emerged. We would now like to draw a parallel between the modes of restructuring/rebuilding of the academic profession and a certain number of new trials to which it has been subjected for several years. In the previous chapter, we already made a distinction between 'trials of strength' and 'trials of justification' by using the terminology of Luc Boltanski and Eve Chiapello. We shall not return to the 'trials of strength' which are the result of shifts made by the management transforming the conceptions of academic work because we already described them in great detail. In chapter "The Politics of Standards and Quality", we rapidly evoked the principles of justification by which human beings justify their actions and denounce those of others during moments of dispute and criticism. We would like to use this theoretical framework to describe the action of academics subjected to the new spirit of academic capitalism and its imperatives.

Indeed, academics use principles of justice linked to different perceptions of the common good, but these also reflect the various trials that academics identify and encounter in their working experience. In such challenging situations, academics typically react by justifying their own actions and criticising others. As responses to problematic situations, the justification and denunciation process generate disagreement and controversy, but they rarely lead to conflict; people make compromises and learn to live with each other in order to maintain a working and workable collegiality. Boltanski and Thévenot's social theory offers an explanation of why and how these compromises prevail and why and how some principles of justice uphold the common good. In the following pages, I will illustrate some of the arguments typically put forward by academics in a range of challenging situations.

An academic may, for example, be inspired when he or she is involved in creative thought and writing (I). This orientation is important in France, where the philosophical tradition plays an important role, particularly in the social sciences. The model of the philosopher – the creator of ideas – is particularly valued in the public sphere through *cafés philosophiques*, where the layperson can access and participate in philosophical discussions and debate; the French intellectual is a symbolic constituent of this historical tradition. The academic must also respect her or his peers (D) and be appreciated and celebrated if he or she wants to build an academic reputation that is recognised by the general public, in a nonacademic arena and by the media (O). Such peer regulation characterises the academic establishment as it is described by Pierre Bourdieu in his study of academics' areas of power and the establishment's nobility. When it comes to formulating and promulgating opinion, there is more ambivalence; the promotion and advancement of reason represents a departure from common sense (*doxa*). In the human and social sciences, it requires the objectification of the social world, in particular the application of quantitative tools and a positivist approach (Ind). Paradoxically, by aspiring to influence public opinion, some academics have found themselves in the media spotlight. The public intellectual, representing the juncture of – and compromise between – the world of inspiration and the world of opinion (I compr. O), is sometimes considered a vehicle for disseminating critical thought to nonacademics, for the purpose of enlightening and emancipating them.

In her or his day-to-day activities, an academic also has to demonstrate effectiveness (Ind) and awareness of the need to respond to market forces (M), for example, by meeting editorial deadlines and by considering how her or his latest book will be promoted and marketed. Despite most academics' disregard for performativity, marketisation-focused thinking is facilitated by metrics, accountability mechanisms and rankings. Academics would argue that cost-effectiveness and managerial performativity do not sit easily with what they see as their purpose of serving the public interest (C). In some countries, like in France, academics are civil servants, paid by the state, and accordingly their role is to defend public services and the public interest against the intrusion of marketisation – a perspective that is widely shared by the influential trade unions.

But, as he or she goes about his or her daily business, the academic has to make compromises and act according to principles that are not always shared by colleagues. In the interests of academic creativity, he or she may, for example, resist – or complain about – the effects that performativity and marketisation have imposed on her or his publications (I/M). He or she may battle against collegial interference that threatens to undermine the effectiveness of his or her research unit by developing new research projects (D/I). He or she may be criticised by others as a selfish, uncooperative person seeking self-aggrandisement and reluctant to engage in academic citizenship (O/D). These tensions remain part and parcel of academic life, but compromise can secure a relative peace and harmony and a sense of civility; academic authorship, for example, may facilitate situations that represent compromise. Far from being an independent activity, authorship represents the application of different 'rules' of behaviour and interactions that reflect fairness, such as when a senior academic co-authors with a junior colleague (D) to help establish the latter and raise his or her profile (O) or the belonging to a community (of practice) (C). Academic authorship has the potential to create reputations (O) within an academic peer group (D) and also within a research community and within a wider society (C); it represents inspiration (I) on the part of a researcher formulating new concepts or/and methodologies, while also including him or her in a competitive environment (M) for reasons of creativity (I) and ranking (Ind).

The sense of justice among academics includes a variety of argumentative repertories linked to situations they experience daily within the institutions in which they work. They project different positions in front of the management and this generates tensions between them. It is at least possible to characterise two groups (Winter 2009): the *academic manager* who has generally the right to lead his or her colleagues and to subject them to the standards of efficiency and productivity required by the academic organisation and who accepts some managerial principles and the *managed academic* who seeks to preserve his or her professional autonomy and to challenge the managerial orthodoxy by expressing alternative choices and visions. As a middle or line manager, the academic manager takes on a variety of managerial roles within the university, ranging from course leader to head of department and dean. He or she generally uses managerial language while he or she tries to empower colleagues and to associate them in the decision-making process. In contrast, the managed academic has less influence on the academic institution, and he or she emphasises his or her professional identity by being given specialised teaching roles and creating discipline expertise. Using Luc Boltanski and Laurent Thévenot's concepts, in terms of justification, we could say that the academic manager forges a compromise between the domestic, industrial and connectionist worlds, while the managed academic establishes equivalences between the inspired, domestic and civic worlds. As the research literature on academics shows, only a few of them accept to justify their action with regard to the market world and which is largely subject to numerous denunciations.

Consequently, faced with managerial empowerment and academic institutions' discourses of truth, academics are able to mobilise different registers of justification and denunciation to enact their capacities of critical judgement. They can develop a simple reflexivity when they note transformations in the work organisation which test them and challenge their habits and/or traditions. They can deploy a complex reflexivity or meta-criticism when they are capable of linking changes in the normal, daily life of an academic to more global events and facts on which they have no direct influence. But bringing the new spirit of academic capitalism to light requires significant work on their behalf in order to seize power relationships and have asymmetrical positions or to implement modes of circulation of ideas, tools and standards at a global level. The main difficulty faced by meta-criticism is the identification of culprits or the people responsible for this new academic order particularly when it is the product of multiple games of influence among European and international actors. It is also difficult to deconstruct normative discourses, enclosed in their own logical and semantic coherence as can be observed in the reading of official reports, and to advocate universalistic values and a common good which is agreed by all. It requires a capacity of generalisation to go beyond individualistic and local situations and a collective mobilisation to voice and protest against injustice.

Trials and Criticism of Managerialism

The academic who criticises managerialism has reflexive skills while he presents himself as the spokesperson of a more or less large inherited or future community which seeks to challenge the established order and its discourses of truth. This reflexive dimension constitutes the experience and perception of a gap between the true reality of existing devices and the expectation of a fairer world. This challenge to a coherent world has been revealed through a series of trials from which criticism emerges. These trials have caused a certain number of shifts in academic work as Jenny Ozga wrote when talking about the researcher–entrepreneur (Ozga 1998). The use of contracts as mechanisms of steering and issuing short-term contracts has consequences on the characters of academics. Indeed, independent assessment, replacing assessment between peers, has forced research teams to solve previously defined problems. The management of research takes a fundamental place as well as performance indicators and accountability which in turn strengthen control. But this entrepreneurial mode has also seduced certain academics who take pleasure in being chosen and to be closer to power, or who are satisfied by just-in-time and flexible work, or who simply like to work under pressure.

Furthermore, academics are not only involved in multi-task activities and technical problem-solving. They also face moral dilemmas in accordance with their choices and the time management of their daily activities (Calvert et al. 2011). Some of them feel a deep tension between what they feel they ought to do, what they feel obligated to do and what they feel it is possible to do. It is therefore possible to make a distinction between 'oughtness', which has its roots in personal values, beliefs and feelings, and 'obligation' which is related to the expectations of others and legitimate demands. The tension between 'oughtness' and 'obligation' is magnified by what is 'possible', which is to some extent related to individual experience, skills and capability. Based on these considerations, it is possible to distinguish two types of trials as indicated by Luc Boltanski (2011): 'trials of reality' and 'existential trials'. Trials of reality test the claims of general validity from discourses of truth and the academic institution by showing the differential that exists between prescription and reality or in showing the contradictions between different forms of normative expressions. Existential trials take into account experiences of humiliation, suffering and injustice. They are not easily sharable because it is difficult for academics, contrary to trials of reality, to fit their personal experiences and feelings within a coherent framework of juridical or moral justification. These experiences are often perceived as contempt or denial, of lonely lives being lived in isolation and privacy. They incite academics to withdraw into their shells rather than voicing their resistance.

However, trials of reality and existential trials serve to arm criticism by revealing contradictions in the managerial organisation. Trials of reality challenge instituted trials in the conventions of the academic work while giving birth to a corrective or reformist criticism: conditions of the trial have to be changed as well as institutional rules to ensure a fairer world. Consequently, the academic institution can respond in three different ways: it can show that the criticism is biased by providing convincing evidence and legitimate arguments, it can adapt the trial to silencing denunciations, or it can circumvent criticism by achieving a certain number of shifts which make it obsolete. Furthermore, existential trials are one of the motives from which a radical criticism can emerge as well as a move towards the recognition of new rights. But it is only possible if the dominated, excluded or exploited people are able to see the connections between their individual situations and to build a collective interest body to explicit their claims. However, this type of criticism is confronted by the fact that the academic institution can legitimise certain modes of political representation or postpone the consideration of claims to weaken collective mobilisation.

We shall now give a few examples of the trials faced by the academic profession by analysing the potentialities for reformist or radical criticism. We put aside de facto the criticism addressed against the establish order or the academic tradition because we have presented arguments in the previous chapter. We have also shown that this first-order criticism has justified shifts in academic work due to the new spirit of academic capitalism and managerialism. We shall therefore focus on arguments which feed second-order reformist and radical criticism against the academic institution by analysing some trials found in our review of research literature dedicated to academics' narratives and identities and in our own interviews conducted with European academics.

A first trial of reality is related to *performativity* (Ind) as described by Stephen Ball (2003). The performances of individuals in the academic organisation serve to measure productivity and to demonstrate quality. Accountability instruments put professionals in a position of insecurity with the fear of doing worse than others and having to permanently improve themselves. They also guide choices by creating a tension between what they feel they must do and what performativity forces them to do. There is therefore a flow of changing demands, expectations and indicators which make academics accountable by creating a climate of stress and schizophrenia. They are split between 'economies of performance' in the way they are assessed and 'ecologies of practices' in the way their practices are based on beliefs and habits they develop in their work. However, as it has been demonstrated in *Research*

Assessment Exercises, academics' behaviour is ambivalent. Some of them consider that assessment is an opportunity to secure and improve their status, in particular due to the positive impact on research and publications, while others judge it as a threat to their identity and that assessment criteria are not adjusted (Harris 2005). But anyway RAE forces them to attend meetings with their colleagues and heads of research to develop a common strategy for the next cycle of assessments. Both activity and profile of the team are analysed in graphs, benchmarks, rankings and impact factors from the Social Science Citation Index (SSCI) (Watson 2011). It is completed in the UK by the TRAC (Transparent Approach to Costing) tool, a standard methodology used to provide 'reliable' and 'relevant' data about the use of public funds by researchers. It generates a trial of *traceability* (Ind) in which the academic has to be accountable in detail with regard to his or her work in order to meet quality standards.

The trials of *competition* (M) characterise the exposure of academics to comparison with other higher education institutions, particularly those included in international rankings, which incite the latter to concentrate their resources and to focus on their areas of excellence. Some targets are assigned to academics to align each performance with strategic objectives or they are convoked for appraisal interviews to present their knowledge and skills with regard to those identified within the team. At the same time, in this race, academics are invited to adopt opportunistic behaviour, while *opportunism* (M) can be considered a trial of reality and adaptability to the market in order to acquire new funds and contracts or to develop partnerships. The capacity to take decisions improves the academic's career, particularly 'heroes' who have proved their success in terms of corporate directions or who have given an entrepreneurial overtone to their experience. The trial of *reputation* (O), marked by financial, material or symbolic rewards, depends on the cognitive and emotional commitment of academics in this managerial momentum, on their capacity to learn the language of corporate storytelling and on showing that they are able to permanently search for new solutions {trial of *creativity* (I)}. This reputation also depends on their ability to use digital technologies, particularly the blogs and websites they build, or to develop connections on social networks or media such as LinkedIn, ResearchGate or Twitter, to assert their skills and activities and to develop their links (Mewburn and Thomson 2013).

In addition to these situations directly introduced by new managerial devices, some trials of reality are due to the restructuring of the academic community's features under managerial empowerment. Academics are subjected to a trial of *segmentation*. A *segmentation of work* (I) which, on behalf of effectiveness, diversifies activities and tasks to serve the community and consultancy and forces academics to multiple commitments to meet short-term managerial objectives. It is also a *segmentation of interests* (C) which has unified the academic profession which now has to deal with the interests of multiple stakeholders who or which are competing to give a meaning, to impose a dominant discourse or to reinforce ideologies by sometimes using strategic manipulations to introduce new practices among academic staff.

Other trials concern the ontology and identity of academics and they are not very visible and public. It explains why specific inquiry methodologies are used by researchers, such as auto-ethnography or narratives, to bring them to light (Watson 2006, 2007, 2009; Trahar 2011). It is the *denial of recognition* for academics dedicated entirely to their students and teaching and who cannot share their experiences with their colleagues playing the game of management, thus giving them a feeling of being *isolated*. This *isolation* is increased by requirements of flexibility, or an extensive use of emails, which limit the opportunities for encounters, while academics no longer have any time to exchange about their working practices and are increasingly facing mobility constraints. It is the loss of *responsibility and autonomy* generated by the dominant discourse of managerialism and accountability with academics feeling *guilty* on behalf of transparency. Some of them consider they have been *cheated* and *betrayed* by the new expected roles far removed from their conception of the academic work. They face *uncertainty* and they feel *useless* and *marginalised*. Isolation can also be a form of *passive resistance* to escape from managerial surveillance and to remain *invisible* from the hierarchical authority.

Based on these trials, academics' criticism exploits the inherent contradictions of the management by pointing out the incoherence of regulative principles or by showing how trials or reality arranged in different contexts at work reveal divergence and antinomy with their conception of the common good. This criticism is fed by denunciations and accusations against the managerial regime and questions its sense of normality. At the same time, it discloses the incompleteness of the institutional reality as well as its contingency, and it invites reform of this type of organisation (reformist criticism) or, more radically, to make it disappear (radical criticism). On the one hand, 'reformist' academics criticise the imperfection of the metrology used to evaluate their activities by explaining that measurements include biases or that they have fashioned an imperfect account of the diversity of tasks and responsibilities achieved by them. But, at the same time, they paved the way for the sophistication of measurement tools and their extension into the sphere of academic work. Radical criticism, on the other hand, challenges these instruments and calls for their disappearance on behalf of the loss of academic power in assessment and the necessary restoration of autonomy. Routines, standardisation and competition generated by these managerial devices can be denounced for the loss of responsibility, autonomy and identity felt by academics (reformist criticism which can be transformed into radical criticism if it is embodied by the whole profession). It can be accused of increasing inequalities of funding and of extending marketisation and privatisation into the academic work (radical criticism). In the first case, the management attempts to attenuate trials by inviting academics to adhere to interdisciplinary regulations and communities of practices in order to strengthen the dialogue and to share experiences. Managers can also claim a polyvalence of activities and a share of responsibilities by coupling the new organisation with professional development activities. The feeling of loss of responsibility and autonomy can be counterbalanced by increasing leadership in teaching and research. In the case of radical criticism, academics would demand that public funding is restored back to previous levels or increased, that the influence of stakeholders be limited, that professional identity and academic legitimacy be maintained and that MOOCs be restricted and framed so that they do not threaten the profession.

These examples of trials and criticism show that managerial prescriptions can be the subject of different arguments and actions depending on the interpretation given by academics and the definition of their work conditions. The management shapes devices that can display various arrangements and commitments with regard to the definition of the common good and principles of justice claimed within the academic community. Criticism faces uncertainty because of the perpetual changes and shifts introduced by the management, and it meets challenges to establish equivalences and similarities while these transformations are more often locally understood, according to specific spatial and temporal contexts, but also legitimised by the academic institution's discourses of truth. It therefore becomes difficult to qualify these contradictions, while on the one hand, criticism is too idealistic and barely audible, while tradition is rejected and the 'crisis of ideologies' is claimed everywhere, and on the other hand, in a multipolar world, criticism is barely capable of identifying the powers which take decisions and are shaping the new representations of reality, and yet it is not able to link situations and claims to enable an alternative voice to become better recognised. Therefore, the question addressed to criticism is, as we shall see in the conclusion, how to find new positions of exteriority and to differentiate itself from the current discourses of expertise to give a greater visibility to the actors' practices, experiences and narratives.

Agencies of the Self and Academic Subjectivities

As Jon Nixon (2015) wrote, during the last years, the academic agency in Europe has faced austerity measures which have increased its professional insecurity and institutional fragmentation by strongly impacting on academic identity. Regulations, financial incentives, rewards and quality standards are forces operating on institutions; they shape the manner academic identities are defined, between harmonisation and hierarchy, collaboration and competition, conformity and difference. The adoption of New Public Management and the strengthening of market-oriented policies, as the development of rankings, accountability and audit, challenge the shaping of academic identity. It is a process of mediation between individual agency and contingent circumstances in which individuals seek to exercise their agency in terms of self-organisation, life-project and process of self-constitution. Consistency is no longer the definition feature of identity. The latter is a bricolage, an assemblage and a pragmatic accommodation to contingent events and moral disorders. If academic identities are also formed in a professional world, because they are accountable to the public, they also have a private world of intimacy, and it is this rich mix or relationality that constitutes academic identity. So academic practices cannot be divorced from the plurality of identities that make up the self and whatever it means to be a whole person engaged in academic work. Academic practices are also oriented towards common goods and virtuous dispositions that have to be taken into account: truthfulness, accuracy, sincerity, respect, authenticity, courage and compassion (Nixon 2004, 2008).

In discussing the 'grammar' of the common good that reflects the various decisions made by academics in their day-to-day work, and the inner (cognitive) resources that they draw upon, I have revealed something of the reflexive and voluntary practices that underpin the rules that the academic community imposes on itself and something of the ways in which it deals with managerialism. The conception of reflexivity we discussed in the previous pages, by focusing on the trials and critical capacities of actors, can be related to Margaret Archer's work on agency (Archer 2000, 2003). At the same time, we have completed this reflection with some ideas expressed at the end of chapter "The Politics of Standards and Quality" regarding standardisation. In her dialogue with philosophy, while distancing herself from Anthony Giddens' model of structure/agency, Margaret Archer demonstrates that the shaping and differentiation of the self appear not only through language and reflexive deliberation but also through a corporal engagement in the world. The reflexivity of social actors is built in a personal project from which they are committed and it takes the form of an internal conversation. The activation of a causal power depends on existing projects that human beings internally forge and on an introspection which is only accessible from a first-person perspective. So, there is an intrinsic deliberation which contributes to modifying the self and an extrinsic deliberation which can mediate and transform society.

We have demonstrated that this reflexivity can be revealed by different trials required for the emergence of criticism. However, Margaret Archer insists on the internal conversation from which the agent, every day, has an idea, clarifies his or her beliefs and inclinations, diagnoses situations and deliberates about concerns and projects likely to impact his or her future existence. This internal deliberation ends when different parts of the self reach a consensus on the course of action which best expresses the authentic identity of the subject but also what is feasible under certain circumstances. Therefore, internal conversation includes subjective projects and objective circumstances in a *modus vivendi* which can be worked out and considered as the link between structure and agency. Applied to the analysis of academic work, Margaret Archer's theoretical model is helpful in accounting the complexity of academics' personal projects not only because of the multiplicity of spaces and situations in which they develop their activities but because of a reflexivity built from their commitments in different imaginary spaces and epistemic conceptions at the university which relativise the place of disciplines (Clegg 2008). However, beyond the resilience of class, gender and family, and the affective dimension of the academic self it reveals, focusing on the sociological questioning of the internal conversation relativises the impact of performative work and managerialism on the framing of identities and the relationships between academics.

In fact, Margaret Archer, in her work, tends to ignore George Herbert Mead's approach (1934) because she finds it hyper-socialised and externalised. However, the American sociologist also has a conception of internal reflexivity which links the 'I' and the 'Us', or the self and society. This theory is at the root of symbolic interactionism which is useful, as demonstrated by Erwin Goffman (1967), in showing that actions and interactions are supported by an intrapersonal as well as an intersubjective regime. This latter dimension is fundamental for criticism which, if it remains enclosed in a internal deliberation, can lead to different attitudes of passivity, resistance, circumvention and trickery but needs the other to access generality, to make comparisons and to establish equivalences which collectively determine the course of action and guide denunciations. As Paul Ricoeur (1995) wrote, the narration of the self, through narratives, in which actors make them coherent to each other and frame their personal identity, is also a way of considering oneself as another and to call for testimony and responsibility, two important moral figures in the shaping of the self and social commitment. By taking into account the temporal dimension of the self, Paul Ricoeur observed that the singularity of action is embedded within the past and the future. History and narrative combine to assign identities to individuals or groups that reflect life's changes and cohesiveness. While 'sameness' injects a degree of permanence into time, the temporal unicity of narratives takes account of and reflects the individual's identity, the unity of his or her life history, his or her singularity and uniqueness in relation to encounters with unforeseen problems and events. It is through their personal stories that identities are forged out of the merging of individuals' uniqueness, the immutability of their characters that have been shaped by their habits and their 'sameness': individuals' enduring immutability.

Furthermore, as Tom Popkewitz and Catarina Silva Martins explain, after Foucault, reason was historically seen as an original intellectual force to formulate the order to the world and in that process bring about the fulfilment of progress (Popkewitz and Martins 2013). The power conferred by knowledge was epitomised by the image of the cosmopolitan individual whose life was ordered by reason and rationality (science). Political and liberal theories have also contributed to define human agency in terms of the pursuit of progress and 'happiness'. The new links of individuality with collective norms of belonging and responsibility have led to a particular way of thinking and acting than can be considered as the 'homeless mind'. Secular, abstract and distant relation orders and classifies interpersonal and personal life and, by governing conduct, embodies a new concept of the secular 'self'. The 'homeless mind' is a recent notion in the making of the European as a particular type of historical person. Furthermore, distance abstractions of the knowledge society or economy provide the category of the lifelong learner revising the cosmopolitanism of the Enlightenment and thus making possible the 'homeless mind'. The new social sciences technologies, particularly through numbers and standards, as well as claims for objectivity, have forged the academic as a certain type of human being, with the risk of relativising the intellectual and critical reflexivity inherited from the tradition, by fabricating a 'mindless mind'.

As we have seen throughout this book, with Foucault we can postulate a historical series of regimes of power/knowledge, all of which are incommensurable with one another, and each of which sustains a different type of subjectivity (Foucault 1982; Foucault and Senellart 2010). The Enlightenment idea of a universal reason actually represents one historically specific form of reason, and it is currently being replaced by the knowledge-based economy. And the liberal view of freedom actually represents a normalising force implicating academics in a process of standardisation. Knowledge of the self, informed through having to deal with a succession of trials, plays a part in defining the truth in relation to what the academic as a moral subject is capable of. Therefore, in order to understand the subjectivities of the academic self in these contexts, it is important to keep in mind the governing mechanisms and regimes of truth that dictate the direction and nature of academic activity by imposing collective standards over which individuals have no control. It invites us to pay attention to how practices, discourses and material relations in science constitute particular kinds of subjectivities and the reworking of these subjectivities towards different possibilities of thought and action (Bazzul 2012). Viewing science as a site for biopolitical engagement and reworking, subjectivities can help to confront oppressions linked with scientific practices and pressing social problems. Since power works as a relation, biopolitical engagement consists not of overthrowing biopower but working within various networks and institutions to produce alternative subjectivities and forms of life and the possibility for criticism.

However, in this analysis of agency, there is a lack of reference to objects as mediators of interactions and the relations of the individual within the society. As has been shown by the Sociology of Sciences and Technology, and particularly in Bruno Latour's work (1996), objects participate in the definition of situations, and they sometimes guide the actions of human beings. As mediators, they work as a delegation by creating social relationships or actions instead of people. Based on examples from daily life, Latour wrote that the function of closing a door is delegated to a mechanical groom, the lost morality of a driver is delegated to the security belt in cars, and a hotel keyboard reminds clients that he or she has to leave his or her keys at the hotel. This process of delegation defines scripts, but at the same time, it opens up a space of negotiation on uses between human and non-human beings. By reintroducing the place of objects in the study of social relationships, the Sociology of Sciences and Technology demonstrates the framing and reduction of complexity made by artefacts. Cognitive capacities of human beings are not only enacted through intra- or intersubjective relationships but also through an adjustment to a physical and material environment as confirmed by cognitive sciences (Hutchins 1995). The actor–network theory offers possibilities of a different understanding of academic work as embedded in relationships between human and non-human beings; over time managerial devices have extended into restructuring tasks and responsibilities (Fenwick and Edwards 2010; Alcadipani and Hassard 2010). It thus demonstrates that the heterogeneity of academic practices consists of a variety of distributed and localised roles in a network of social relationships, while academic reality emerges through an assemblage of practices and objects, as measurement tools, standards and digital technologies giving consistence to different individual and collective projects (Decuypere and Simons 2014).

Consequently, the idea of the project as a basis for the conception of human agency can be questioned. As Laurent Thévenot showed in his sociology of engagements and when he expanded his work with Luc Boltanski in the *Economies of Worth* (2006), government by objectives arranges a liberal construction of the person prepared to invest and exercise responsibilities with complete autonomy as specified by the NPM standards (Thévenot 2001, 2007, 2009). This liberal grammar stipulates that the academic is able to make choices and to reveal his or her preferences according to a range of options provided by the instrumental devices and functionalities of accountability and evidence-based research. This assumption about the capacity of a 'regular planned action' reduces the possibilities for other modes of commitment serving the common good and openness to associated principles of justice. Furthermore, it undermines the importance of attachments and familiar commitment by maintaining the academic in a known entourage and a familiar use of the academic world which generates trusts and self-accomplishment. This reduction of commitments related to a common sociality creates oppressive mechanisms and strengthens the discipline of standardisation and other forms of objectification.

Laurent Thévenot also proposed linking the transformation of agency to a change in forms of authority thus ending the hierarchy and subordination on which traditional modes of government were based on. He explained that metamorphoses of authority are related to the contemporaneous deployment of assessments and their tools and methods in order to coordinate persons and things differently. By extension, in academic work, we can say that the authority based on the domestic principle of justification, and an equal and collective solidarity related to civic worth, has been denounced in order to promote the figure of the academic to whom a 'liberal' authority has been delegated and which was announced as being a liberation or liberalisation from statist and paternalist power. The new spirit of academic capitalism is not only devolved to a human agency dealing with opportunistic interests and strategies related to market worth, it also delegates authority to assessment devices and standards, e.g. things or objects, by claiming that the individual is at the initiative of the project. Everyone is therefore invited to achieve the objectives and to carry out a plan and to become his own entrepreneur but within an epistemic regime fixed by assessment and its different functionalities. This explains why expertise grasps it with so much accuracy.

Conclusion

By identifying academics' reflexivity and potentialities for criticism in relation and against the new spirit of academic capitalism and its managerial devices, we have highlighted the gradual construction of a liberal and instrumental agency which has made the individual project a structuring constituent of the academic community. Progressively, the figure of the entrepreneur has been sketched against the form of authority embodied by the state and the collegial tradition. The European academic is ascribed with qualities and attributes at the borders of the market-based, industrial and connectionist worlds, according to work conventions which legitimise other principles of justice. It has entailed new trails faced by individuals in their work situation (trials of reality) or challenging their subjectivities (existential trials). If some forms of individual resistance remain, besides leaving the profession, most academics have accommodated themselves to this new political and epistemic order without necessarily fully committed themselves. Possibilities of collective protest and resistance are limited due the weakening of the academic world's defences but also by the discourses of truth maintained by the academic institution and its policymakers.

Simultaneously, a liberal agency has benefited from the restructuring of the academic institution beyond its walls. Market globalisation coupled with the development of rankings has institutionalised new asymmetries between mobile and immobile academics, ranked or downgraded ones, English speakers and non-English-speaking natives, 'world-class' researchers and 'precarious intellectuals'. Expertise and new modes of knowledge production outside the academic space have gained legitimacy, while the belonging and identification to a same discipline has been gradually eroded. Every day, this global and increasing differential undermines the collective identity of the profession and its attachment to the public interest and universal knowledge. The academic epistemic authority has also been challenged and its capacity to bring sufficient levels of evidence to justify scientific statements with the risk, as proven by numerous examples, of politics and the market extending their domination of science, of creating a confusion between knowledge, opinions and beliefs and weakening a little more the foundations of the democratic debate.

References

Abbott, A. (1988). *The system of professions*. Chicago: University of Chicago Press.
Alcadipani, R., & Hassard, J. (2010). Actor-network theory, organizations and critique: Towards a politics of organizing. *Organization, 17*(4), 419–435.
Amaral, A., & Magalhaes, A. (2002). The emergent role of external stakeholders in European higher education governance. In *Governing higher education: National perspectives on institutional governance* (pp. 1–21). Dordrecht: Springer.
Archer, M. S. (2000). *Being human: The problem of agency*. Cambridge: Cambridge University Press.
Archer, M. S. (2003). *Structure, agency and the internal conversation*. Cambridge: Cambridge University Press.
Ball, S. J. (2003). The teacher's soul and the terrors of performativity. *Journal of Education Policy, 18*(2), 215–228.
Ball, S. J. (2012). *Global education inc: New policy networks and the neo-liberal imaginary*. London: Routledge.
Bazzul, J. (2012). Neoliberal ideology, global capitalism, and science education: Engaging the question of subjectivity. *Cultural Studies of Science Education, 7*(4), 1001–1020.
Bolden, R., Petrov, G., & Gosling, J. (2009). Distributed leadership in higher education rhetoric and reality. *Educational Management Administration & Leadership, 37*(2), 257–277.
Boltanski, L. (2011). *On critique: A sociology of emancipation* (G. Elliott, Trans.). Cambridge: Polity.
Boltanski, L., & Chiapello, È. (2005). *The new spirit of capitalism*. (G. Elliott, Tans.). London: Verso.

Boltanski, L., & Thévenot, L. (2006). *On justification: Economies of worth*. Princeton: Princeton University Press.

Calvert, M., Lewis, T., & Spindler, J. (2011). Negotiating professional identities in higher education: Dilemmas and priorities of academic staff. *Research in Education, 86*(1), 25–38.

Castells, M. (2000). *The information age: Economy, society and culture. Vol. 1, The rise of the network society* (The rise of the network society, Vol. 1). Oxford: Blackwell.

Churchman, D. (2002). Voices of the academy: Academics' responses to the corporatizing of academia. *Critical Perspectives on Accounting, 13*(5), 643–656.

Churchman, D. (2006). Institutional commitments, individual compromises: Identity-related responses to compromise in an Australian university. *Journal of Higher Education Policy and Management, 28*(1), 3–15.

Churchman, D., & King, S. (2009). Academic practice in transition: Hidden stories of academic identities. *Teaching in Higher Education, 14*(5), 507–516.

Clegg, S. (2008). Academic identities under threat? *British Educational Research Journal, 34*(3), 329–345.

Decuypere, M., & Simons, M. (2014). On the composition of academic work in digital times. *European Educational Research Journal, 13*(1), 89–106.

Doeringer, P., & Piore, M. J. (1971). *Internal labor markets and manpower adjustment*. New York: DC Heath and Company.

Enders, J., & Musselin, C. (2008). Back to the future? The academic professions in the 21st century. *Higher education to, 2030*, 125–150.

Fenwick, T., & Edwards, R. (2010). *Actor-network theory in education*. London: Routledge.

Foucault, M. (1982). The subject and power. In H. L. Dreyfus & P. Rabinow (Eds.), *Michel Foucault: Beyond structuralism and hermeneutics* (pp. 208–226). Chicago: University of Chicago Press.

Foucault, M., & Senellart, M. (2010). *The birth of biopolitics: Lectures at the Collège de France, 1978–1979*. New York: Picador.

Goffman, E. (1967). *Interaction ritual: Essays on face-to-face behavior*. Garden City: Anchor/Doubleday.

Granovetter, M. S. (1973). The strength of weak ties. *The American Journal of Sociology, 78*(6), 1360–1380.

Harris, S. (2005). Rethinking academic identities in neo-liberal times. *Teaching in Higher Education, 10*(4), 421–433.

Hazemi, R., Hailes, S., & Wilbur, S. (Eds.). (2012). *The digital university: Reinventing the academy*. Berlin: Springer.

Hutchins, E. (1995). *Cognition in the wild*. Cambridge, MA: MIT Press.

Hyde, A., Clarke, M., & Drennan, J. (2013). The changing role of academics and the rise of managerialism. In *The academic profession in Europe: New tasks and new challenges* (pp. 39–52). Dordrecht: Springer.

Kim, T. (2010). Transnational academic mobility, knowledge, and identity capital. *Discourse: Studies in the Cultural Politics of Education, 31*(5), 577–591.

Kim, T., & Locke, W. (2010). *Transnational academic mobility and the academic profession*. London: Centre for Higher Education Research and Information, The Open University.

Kleiman, P. (2008). Towards transformation: Conceptions of creativity in higher education. *Innovations in Education and Teaching International, 45*(3), 209–217.

Kwiek, M. (2012). The growing complexity of the academic enterprise in Europe: A panoramic view. *European Journal of Higher Education, 2*(2–3), 112–131.

Lam, A. (2010). From 'ivory tower traditionalists' to 'entrepreneurial scientists'? Academic scientists in fuzzy university–industry boundaries. *Social Studies of Science, 40*(2), 307–340.

Larner, W. (2015). Globalising knowledge networks: Universities, diaspora strategies, and academic intermediaries. *Geoforum, 59*, 197–205.

Latour, B. (1996). On interobjectivity. *Mind, Culture, and Activity, 3*(4), 228–245.

Martin, B. R. (2011). The research excellence framework and the 'impact agenda': Are we creating a Frankenstein monster? *Research Evaluation, 20*(3), 247–254.

Mead, G. H. (1934). In C. W. Morris (Ed.), *Mind, self, and society*. Chicago: University of Chicago Press.

Mewburn, I., & Thomson, P. (2013). Why do academics blog? An analysis of audiences, purposes and challenges. *Studies in Higher Education, 38*(8), 1105–1119.

Musselin, C. (2013). Redefinition of the relationships between academics and their university. *Higher Education, 65*(1), 25–37.

Nixon, J. (2004). Education for the good society: The integrity of academic practice. *London Review of Education, 2*(3), 245–252.

Nixon, J. (2008). *Towards the virtuous university: The moral bases of academic practice*. London: Routledge.

Nixon, J. (2015). In L. Evans & J. Nixon (Eds.), *Identities in higher education: The changing European landscape*. London: Bloomsbury.

Normand, R. (2010). Expertise, networks and indicators: The construction of the European strategy in education. *European Educational Research Journal, 9*(3), 407–421.

Ozga, J. (1998). The entrepreneurial researcher: Re-formations of identity in the research marketplace. *International Studies in Sociology of Education, 8*(2), 143–153.

Popkewitz, T. S., & Martins, C. S. (2013). "Now We Are European!" How does it get that way? *Sisyphus-Journal of Education, 1*(1), 36–64.

Radice, H. (2013). How we got here: UK higher education under neoliberalism. *ACME: An International E-Journal for Critical Geographies, 12*(2), 407–418.

Ricoeur, P. (1995). *Oneself as another*. Chicago: University of Chicago Press.

Robertson, S. L. (2010a). Corporatisation, competitiveness, commercialisation: New logics in the globalising of UK higher education. *Globalisation, Societies and Education, 8*(2), 191–203.

Robertson, S. L. (2010b). The EU, 'regulatory state regionalism' and new modes of higher education governance. *Globalisation, Societies and Education, 8*(1), 23–37.

Shattock, M. (2015). The impact of the UK research assessment exercise. *International Higher Education, 56*, 18–20.

Shore, C., & Mclauchlan, L. (2012). 'Third mission' activities, commercialisation and academic entrepreneurs. *Social Anthropology, 20*(3), 267–286.

Sum, N. L., & Jessop, B. (2013). Competitiveness, the knowledge-based economy and higher education. *Journal of the Knowledge Economy, 4*(1), 24–44.

Thévenot, L. (2001). Pragmatic regimes governing the engagement with the world. In K. Knorr-Cetina, T. Schatzki, & E. V. Savigny (Eds.), *The practice turn in contemporary theory* (pp. 56–73). London: Routledge.

Thévenot, L. (2007). The plurality of cognitive formats and engagements moving between the familiar and the public. *European Journal of Social Theory, 10*(3), 409–423.

Thévenot, L. (2009). Postscript to the special issue: Governing life by standards a view from engagements. *Social Studies of Science, 39*(5), 793–813.

Thévenot, L. (2011). Power and oppression from the perspective of the sociology of engagements: A comparison with Bourdieu's and Dewey's critical approaches to practical activities. *Irish Journal of Sociology, 19*(1), 35–67.

Trahar, S. (2011). Changing landscapes, shifting identities in higher education: Narratives of academics in the UK. *Research in Education, 86*(1), 46–60.

Watermeyer, R. (2015). Lost in the 'Third Space': The impact of public engagement in higher education on academic identity, research practice and career progression. *European Journal of Higher Education, 5*(3), 331–347.

Watson, C. (2006). Narratives of practice and the construction of identity in teaching. *Teachers and Teaching: Theory and Practice, 12*(5), 509–526.

Watson, C. (2007). Small stories, positioning analysis, and the doing of professional identities in learning to teach. *Narrative Inquiry, 17*(2), 371–389.

Watson, C. (2009). 'Teachers are meant to be orthodox': Narrative and counter narrative in the discursive construction of 'identity' in teaching. *International Journal of Qualitative Studies in Education, 22*(4), 469–483.

Watson, C. (2011). Accountability, transparency, redundancy: Academic identities in an era of 'excellence'. *British Educational Research Journal, 37*(6), 955–971.

Whitchurch, C. (2006). Who do they think they are? The changing identities of professional administrators and managers in UK higher education. *Journal of Higher Education Policy and Management., 28*(2), 159–171.

Whitchurch, C. (2008). Beyond administration and management: Reconstructing the identities of professional staff in UK higher education. *Journal of Higher Education Policy and Management, 30*(4), 375–386.

Whitchurch, C. (2009). The rise of the blended professional in higher education: A comparison between the United Kingdom, Australia and the United States. *Higher Education, 58*(3), 407–418.

Winter, R. (2009). Academic manager or managed academic? Academic identity schisms in higher education. *Journal of Higher Education Policy and Management, 31*(2), 121–131.

Worthington, F., & Hodgson, J. (2005). Academic labour and the politics of quality in higher education: A critical evaluation of the conditions of possibility of resistance. *Critical Quarterly, 47*(1-2), 96–110.

Young, D. J., & Meneley, A. (2005). *Autoethnographies: The anthropology of academic practices.* Peterborough: Broadview Press.

Conclusion

By conceptualising epistemic politics in education, we have looked at the way in which different actors and networks interlink, how ideas and instruments circulate at the international scale and how certain reforms have been implemented to transform the relationship between science and policy. We have shown the work of expertise, the emergence of evidence-based technologies and the new configurations of academic work. We have emphasised the deployment of normative and critical discourses regarding the new possibilities of knowledge production, dissemination and use. Even if we have not considered intellectual polemics and scientific controversies, or the shape of public problems, we have addressed criticism towards the empowerment of a technocratic and positivist vision of the academic world and the progressive affirmation of the expert's authority.

This authority is supported by the idea of perpetual changes and managerial devices through which they have to be enacted. In presenting a modelled vision of social reality, while anticipating and translating it into instruments for policy, expertise has been deployed in irreversible and often invisible forms which do not leave much place for criticism. Once the latter is raised, with protest movements and diverse accusations (debate, controversy, polemic), it faces a constraint of relevance and acceptability. It has to be subjected to trials and discourses maintained by experts themselves, by using the same categories of judgement and representation, as was shown by the discussions around the PISA survey. The criticism embodied in change and reformist proposals becomes a quarrel of experts leaving lay people outside of the loop.

Positivist epistemology and rationalist technic forge decision-making, as proven by the success of experimental economics, making us think that these methods are the only ones which provide a 'solid' knowledge of educative facts. Its defenders claim that they can solve problems and eliminate sources of criticism and conflicts related to reforms. The vision of education is then framed in a technical and abstract formulation, in which data plays an important role, by being able to split with the 'common sense' of lay people and to bring an 'enlightened' and 'neutral' vision far from ideological stances on education. The effective problem-solving strategies are

© Springer International Publishing Switzerland 2016   227
R. Normand, *The Changing Epistemic Governance of European Education*,
Educational Governance Research 3, DOI 10.1007/978-3-319-31776-2_8

expressed in mathematical formula and quasi-experimental methods aiming to orientate decision-making and policymaking. This scientific rationalisation, based on technical criteria, tends to ignore the social and cultural dimensions of education as the values and principles of justice guiding the action of individuals. The rational person is the one subjected to technical and managerial knowledge arising from expert methodologies. The authority of the expert overcomes the democratic exchange of opinions. The consensus conference, as the organisation of 'great debates', is the artefact of this type of encounter between expert knowledge and lay knowledge. Even if they assume a convergence of interests between the protagonists, instituted trials are considered as non-revisable, and the discussion is deliberately situated outside the arena of controversy and conflict. The claim for 'neutral' and 'objective' sciences and technical solutions aims to circumscribe the range of arguments to just a few recommendations without really questioning the conditions of policy implementation in a sociopolitical context.

In this confrontation providing input to the public debate regarding the stakes of educative reforms, criticism is no longer based on different representations of the public interest (e.g. between trade unions and government) but on the opposition between a realism claimed by expertise and a relativism attributed to other proposals, particularly those coming from critical social sciences and protesting movements. This opposition is epistemological, while the description of reality is monopolised by experts and extensively so by evidence-based technologies. This regulatory objectivity delegitimises other actors and institutions, while at the same time it is implementing a new political experimentalism which benefits supranational organisations more than the state. Thus, expertise distributes power among networks and groups of actors with a weak level of explicit coordination with regard to the national context, and it makes criticism difficult, if not improbable, without a worldwide coalition of interests but also regarding the challenges to be met in establishing equivalences between different devices and instruments at the international scale.

Considering the production of this 'discourse of truth' in delocalised and international experts' meetings or in consensus conferences, we have seen that predefined objects and places circumscribe registers of action and discourse held in accordance with codified rituals and institutionalised hierarchies which do not leave much place to uncertainty, contingency and criticism. Voice is delegated to an expert authority which, through its own attendance and a subtle framing of devices, limits the divergence of interpretations and builds the 'norm of truth'. The establishment of an 'official truth' is facilitated by ritual and ceremonial forms through which indisputable assumptions are advocated, because they are based on 'irrefutable evidence' and undisputed claims because the data is not accessible to lay people or because they would require a counterdemonstration that the short time dedicated to the discussion does not allow. Through its coherence and saturation, the 'discourse of truth' succeeds in setting up a common representation of a problem and produces a confirmed and stabilised norm during the course of the same meeting. In doing so, these proposals have the capacity to restrict the field of criticism and lead to the pos-

sibility of gaining control of a discourse which has its own semantical and herme-
neutical coherence.

However, criticism has not disappeared and it has reinvested the field of education policies as well as contesting reforms. During the past few decades, there have
been increasing accusations against the damaging effects of testing and accountability on the teaching profession, while a certain number of trials have been identified: stress, burnout, demotivation and leaving the profession. The gap between the
professed theories of evidence-based education and the reality of teaching practices
has also been denounced, while the PISA survey and its effects have come up
against an increasing number of contradictors. Therefore, there is a significant tension between the epistemic governance sustained by international expert networks
and policymakers, on the one hand, and the practitioners' real day-to-day life in
schools and classrooms, on the other. Criticism, particularly from trade unions,
brings dolorous experiences to the public attention, such as the contempt and lack
of recognition of teachers, by challenging discourses of truth which, under reformist
proposals, are enclosed in a rhetorical circularity detached from existential trials.

This criticism would be enhanced if it could claim a democratisation of expertise
in educative problem-solving, as called for by John Dewey in the 1920s. The role of
experts would not only offer technical solutions but would facilitate the public
debate and educators' learning. Working as interpreters, these experts would participate in a deliberative inquiry process before the organisation of a space of discussion and deliberation with people being symmetrically informed. The challenge
would be to establish connections with empirical data, normative assumptions
structuring the representations of the world and interpretative judgements from pluralistic theories and methodologies and to take into account specific circumstances
and contexts in which policies are implemented. Even if scientific and technical
aspects play a role in the framing of a policy and its evaluation, the arguments used
by actors are also fundamental in solving a public problem. Therefore, processes of
judgement are extended to experts and inquiries by non-expert stakeholders engaged
in the educational world, and evaluation comes from the confrontation of arguments
and practical reasons more than from demonstration and technical verification.
Consequently, these interpretations are used to link decision-making to political
options with regard to implementing contexts.

As the Sociology of Science and Techniques (SST) has shown, it is possible to
assume that controversies are the enrichment of democracy and that the emergence
of new actors, with their own justifications and problem definitions, has given more
meaning to the situation. This process can lead to collective learning which is not
limited to what the experts bring to the table and what political representatives
decide. The examination of 'hybrid forums' in different sectors of society demonstrates that there are some possibilities to challenge this Big Divide and to create
compromises and learning between multiple actors exploring problems together,
subjecting them to discussion through crossed-linked exchanges between specialists and lay people (Callon et al. 2009). The Big Divide corresponds to the relative
isolation of experts who have to produce robust certified knowledge and to adopt a
position. These experts work autonomously to implement methods and protocols

allowing them to obtain conclusions which are considered to be 'reliable'. Experts have the monopoly in knowledge production and keep lay people on the margins. Once the Big Divide was established between specialists and lay people, and uncertainty removed, all that remained was to organise the debate in accordance with the delegation from ordinary citizens to elected or representative people. It confers another monopoly to representatives which is the exclusive power of the voice due to the mandate it has been delegated. But the rise of political uncertainties, and the debates, controversies and polemics they create, has led to the occurrence of unexpected groups breaking the silence and bringing their voice to the forefront.

Therefore, the hybrid forum is a device of elucidation between experts and lay people. Each hybrid forum is a new worksite in which new organisational forms and procedures are invented to facilitate exchanges and cooperation between experts and lay people, but also to make visible and audible ordinary groups without representation. It means extending the process of inquiry to lay people and not opposing lay knowledge to expert knowledge. Non-specialists can participate in the collective inquiry, in the emerging debates and in decision-making. Experts and policymakers have to recognise the relevance of data and knowledge brought to the table by lay people. The aim is not to accumulate information and knowledge in order to enlighten decision-making but to create a back and forth collective exploration of the social reality. It is the strength of a dialogic process helping to build a common world.

However, the development of a hybrid form and participative inquiry has raised the issue of using tacit knowledge and modes or learning. As Michael Polanyi (1966) has shown, all knowledge has a tacit dimension which is directly available for the inquiry and the explicit forms of knowledge related to positivist epistemology. This tacit knowledge is based on experiences and perceptions which are difficult to objectivise but are essential for the life of a professional community of experts or practitioners. It is also important to support a participative inquiry and a deliberative process in which lay people and professionals are involved.

We have seen how policy learning is effective in the forging relationships between policymakers and experts. It is the same for teachers involved in cognitive activities regarding their knowledge and practices. Recent conceptions of professional development have shown the importance of reflexivity with regard to tacit knowledge and practices in the transformation of teaching and learning, something which is largely ignored by the theories of evidence-based teaching.

Professional learning and its agency need to allow actors to participate in a deliberative process and a collective inquiry. It requires a device in which practitioners are capable of judging their experiences and their ways of acting, and contributing to different and new perspectives and orientations, without being reduced to coercive pressure and gathering evidence to demonstrate their performance. These practitioners have to make their voice be heard beside that of experts and policymakers, not in a technocratic approach reducing the diversity of their experiences but in the creation of institutional and intellectual conditions in which a critical transformation is reflected and enacted when opening up some possibilities of emancipation.

The professional learning community as proposed by the research literature can be a solution to the implementation of policy inquiry and deliberation (Hord 2004).

It characterises a collective group of learners learning through shared beliefs and analyses, interacting between members, with strong interdependence and concern and one which respects differences and possesses a demanding solidarity and inter-personal ethics. The development of a professional learning community requires the creation of a culture in which teachers have to reflect on their practices and to collectively use information and data to improve teaching and learning. The sharing of common values and visions is quite important along with collective responsibility. A professional community is shaped by a 'reflexive dialogue', conversations about educative issues and problem-solving, which require a de-privatisation of practices, the frequent examination of practices based on mutual observations and case studies, a common pedagogical planning, the search for new knowledge, the conversion of tacit knowledge into shared knowledge during interactions and the application of new ideas for solving problems and taking charge of students' needs.

Unfortunately, too often, accountability policies have reduced professional learning communities to a narrow vision based on the use of data instead of creating a context open to cooperation and a new professional culture (Hargreaves and Shirley 2009). On the contrary it would be necessary to let these professional learning communities master their capacities of deliberation and transformation themselves, by recognising their voice in the formulation of public problems in education and by praising their ethical commitments and imaginary power beyond a technical and instrumental rationality which disqualifies their narrative and interpretative modalities. It would also be a means of sharing experiences which, through different narratives, can develop a new corrective or radical criticism against the new spirit of capitalism in education and challenge the certainties established by the new political experimentalism. The history of the English comprehensive school, bringing together professionals against the scientific psychology's 'discourses of truth', is a reminder that these shifts are possible (Fenwick 2013).

But criticism cannot only be left to professionals. It requires a complex external stance that only social and educational sciences are able to take in order to not become enclosed in engineering supporting expertise and reformist proposals. In this book, we have sought to draw a general picture of the new epistemic order in education by raising doubts and questioning the evidence of policymaking, a role which belongs to a reflexive and critical sociology. However, this picture is partial and requires wider investigations of the configurations and networks we have described and analysed.

The actor–network theory provides grids of analysis to design connections at the international scale and socio-material assemblages which, from mediation to mediation, produce power relationships and asymmetries for the benefit of supranational organisations and the world of expertise. By giving the possibility of seeing the vast range of human and non-human beings involved in these networks, it reveals forms of existence hidden to lay people by proposing a critical decentring which goes beyond the classical perspective of structure and agency. In rehabilitating scale effects, it also offers a research programme to think about the numerous circulations between the local and the global as well as the principles of a political epistemology far removed from engineering sciences and positivism, thus reducing disputed issues to matters of facts. The ANT proposes, as Bruno Latour wrote, to describe and analyse associations and long chains of actors which, via shifts, transformations, translations and delegations, participate in giving order to the scientific and political worlds and establishing connections between local sites and global infrastructures or centres of calculation (Latour 2005).

If we take PISA as an example, the survey's findings are the result of a series of international actors who have transformed the first international surveys from an association between professionals to a vast consortium including multiple organisations and expert-linking centres which produce instruments of measurement worldwide. Once the global is localised, it is necessary to redistribute the local, e.g. to understand the way in which some mediators, including non-human actors such as material technologies and instruments, structure social interactions in time and space as well situations. The latter depends on the interference of heterogeneous entities which build local sites and convey different formats, the models and frameworks which allow human beings to interpret the situation in which they are positioned but also to be inscribed in different forms of attachment to their environment. If we pursue with the example, it is easy to study the way in which the PISA results, through accountability policies, produce circulations of assessment tools which, from ministries to schools, have configured new relationships between teachers and students. The third movement proposed by Latour is to connect sites, e.g. to locate the types of connectors and mediators which shape social relationships or thinking categories among actors, often through normalisation, metrology or standards, and affirm a stabilised definition of some scientific and technical statements. We have shown in this book how quality standards were designed at the European scale to contribute to this type of circulation and normalisation.

Criticism, as Michel Foucault wrote, can also be conceived as an act of distrust or a challenge addressed to the art of governing which some people try to transform, reduce or flee (Foucault 1997). During the fifteenth century, some intellectuals sought to challenge the truths established by the church and the law which they considered to be unfair with regard to the common good they were claiming. And today, when sciences of government subject individuals and social practices through mechanisms of power, like management, and force them to adhere to the new 'discourses of truth' of the positivist epistemology, resistance and insubordination can appear as arms of fight. As Foucault explained, during the Enlightenment, the critical stance focused on the issue of legitimacy of knowledge and its limits. He proposed to reverse this perspective and to consider epistemology through the relationship between knowledge and politics, as we have tried to do in this book. Instead of searching for what is false or true, well founded or not, real or illusionary, scientific or ideological and legitimate or abusive, critical thought has to establish connections between mechanisms of coercion and elements of knowledge particularly when the latter becomes the justification for rational, calculative and technical efficiency. This leads to discussions on the system of acceptability, or the role of contingency and arbitrary, which allow positivism to be extended and asserted.

However, as Foucault put it, this search also requires a 'critical ontology of our-selves' and of the area of possibilities offered to us in order to escape from disci-pline and domination. The aim is not to delete power relationships, which exist in all societies, but to oppose some of its forms by showing the singularity and contin-gency of practices.

We have proved it in describing the new trials faced by academics in their daily professional activities. We have shown that New Public Management has institu-tionalised discourses and devices transforming the university's missions and distrib-uted tasks within faculties and research units. While academics have been used to professional bureaucracy and collegial–corporatist solidarity between peers, the new spirit of academic capitalism has progressively undermined the foundations of the scientific community in giving more place to flexibility, contracts and account-ability. Third Mission, expertise and entrepreneurship have been praised by chan-cellors and policymakers as a mean to support innovation and creativity for economic competitiveness. But not only the academic work organisation and peer relation-ships have been modified. This transformation also has impacted on modalities of knowledge production and assessment. In a climate of competition and perfor-mance, but also of relative uncertainty with the emergence of new educative and social problems, academics have to produce robust, utilitarian and interdisciplinary knowledge to respond to short-term requirements. Standards, best practices, guide-lines and protocols have been invented by evidence-based research and policy to frame the production of new scientific knowledge, while this trend has been sup-ported by international organisations like the OECD and European Commission. In the introduction of this book, we have shown that this move towards positivism and experimentalism was not new.

Charles Wright Mills, in his book *The Sociological Imagination* (1959), was already concerned that some sociologists by adopting the methodology of natural sciences, by aligning themselves behind bureaucrats or remaining in a disordered anarchy, were preventing the development of historical, biographical and comparat-ist analyses or the study of instituted powers. He regretted that sociology was becoming an expertise and a science of government, by fetishising the normative order in an abscond functionalism (like Talcott Parsons) or by wanting to measure everything (like Paul Lazarsfeld). The confinement in technique and bureaucracy was impending sociologists thinking about institutional structures and power. On the contrary, Mills proposed a research policy insisting on the role of the sociologist as a craftsman and an intellectual capable of maintaining his or her independence in order to access the truth. He opposed the figures of the philosopher, consultant or expert with those of the sociologist who proposes to maintain an adequate definition of reality and to deconstruct arbitrary forms of authority. Mills also defended the idea of distinguishing between the 'personal trials of context' and the 'collective challenges of the social structure'. He explained that trials affect the self and the social context in which the individual has a personal experience and a reflexive activity. But these trials are overcome by the weight of institutions and collective entities which give him or her his or her social and historical meaning.

By being inspired by these analytical categories in our study of academic work, we have tried to characterise the agency of *Homo Academicus* facing new norms of academic capitalism. The last part of the book focused on academic narratives, experiences and practices in European knowledge-based policies. It shows how each individual negotiates with the elements of policy he or she has to implement and which modifies his or her relation to the environment and to others. By embodying norms but also in opening up a space of possibilities, the academic transforms his or her own self into alternative figures of resistance and acceptance of new regulations. The new *Homo Academicus* is shaped as a subject through the assemblage of human and non-human actors, relational capacities in connecting different networks, including governing technologies in his or her daily practice. His or her behaviour is shaped by a system of practices and interactions subjected to the requirements of governmentality, but also by narratives distant from managerial standards and accountability aiming to structure academic activities.

This agency of the self would have required more biographical analysis and empirical work than was possible to provide in this book. It could have been enriched by a historical and comparatist perspective studying the shifts in the moral and political philosophies that have shaped *Homo Academicus* from his or her diverse inscriptions in the scientific, intellectual and political spaces during the last decades, without reducing them to a series of statistical tables artificially claiming an international comparison.

If the erudite and people from society have been brought closer in the same posture, the figure of the scholar, which lost its religious dimension after being converted to the figure of the organic and/or committed intellectual, has lost his or her credentials while the public space has been conquered by doxa-sophists and rhetoricians reinterpreting the tradition or claiming a new modernity. Between relativism and positivism, the sociology of education has since tried to maintain its position and to find its own way, while at the same time it has been a victim of the crisis in disciplines and the weakening of social criticism. In these conditions, can it maintain its sociological imagination? In order to do so, it probably has to accept to make the world more visible (and readable) via new interpretative schemes and to renew with a promise of emancipation from power relationships and discourses of truth.

References

Callon, M., Lascoumes, P., & Barthe, Y. (2009). *Acting in an uncertain world. An essay on technical democracy*. Cambridge, MA: MIT Press.

Fenwick, I. G. K. (2013). *The comprehensive school 1944–1970: The politics of secondary school reorganization* (Vol. 6). Abigdon: Routledge.

Foucault, M. (1997). What is critique? In S. Lotringer & L. Hochroth (Eds.), *The politics of truth*. New York: Semiotext(e).

Hargreaves, A. P., & Shirley, D. L. (Eds.). (2009). *The fourth way: The inspiring future for educational change*. Thousand Oaks: Corwin Press.

Hord, S. M. (Ed.). (2004). *Learning together, leading together: Changing schools through professional learning communities*. New York: Teachers College Press.

Latour, B. (2005). *Reassembling the social-an introduction to actor-network-theory*. Oxford: Oxford University Press.

Mills, C. W. (1959). *The sociological imagination*. Oxford: Oxford University Press.

Polanyi, M. (1966). *The tacit dimension*. London: Routledge & Kegan Paul Ltd.

CPI Antony Rowe
Chippenham, UK
2018-03-14 21:34